Advance praise for
Be the Awesome Man

"Dennis Gazarek has provided a road map to maturity with specific and measurable goals. A must-read for the young man in your life."
—**Doug Manning**, educator

"*Be the Awesome Man* is a great resource for young men wanting to make a change and difference in their lives. Dennis provides great advice, supported by real-life examples and practical tools to start any young man on his awesome journey."
—**Kerry Johnson**, EdD, Ontario Tech University

"Gazarek offers a mother lode of valuable advice to help young men strive for self-excellence . . . a practical, solid guide for any young man looking to improve himself as he matures."
—*Bookz, Cookz, & Nookz*

"Dennis Gazarek has done an awesome job. Using his experience and knowledge, he gets into the minds of young men and provides them with an insight to explore, estimate and establish themselves to fight the battles, not only for themselves but to inspire others."
—**Vaqar Raees**, president of Friends Indeed Canada

"A compelling read—*Be the Awesome Man* diagnoses the problem, then provides inspiring yet practical advice for men who wish to change their life's trajectory from mediocre to awesome! Highly recommended."
—**Daniel Whittal**, lawyer and martial arts instructor

"With a society currently lacking in empathy, inclusiveness, and direction, *Be the Awesome Man* is the right book at the right time. Sprinkled with relatable examples, this book is a guide for young men to make the right choices and become the leaders and overall good people the world so desperately needs."
—**Barry Finlay**, best-selling and award-winning author of *Kilimanjaro and Beyond* and the Marcie Kane thriller collection

"*Be the Awesome Man* by Dennis Gazarek is a valuable blueprint for self-actualization that every man should have. The book provides readers with a step-by-step guide on how to become the best version of themselves. Through the use of real-life examples from his life, and the lives of others, Gazarek is able to draw in readers from various backgrounds. His clear and direct language enables readers to easily understand the strategies mentioned; and his practical tips inspires the reader into action to begin their journey of transformation. Regardless of what stage you are at in your life, every man, young or old, will find great value in reading *Be the Awesome Man*. Parents, teachers, coaches, and mentors, this book is also for you. If you have a role in shaping boys into young men, this book will assist you in helping them become awesome. Get it for yourself. Buy it for a friend. You will not be disappointed."
—**Jeannine Henry**, youth minister, St. Francis de Sales Parish, Toronto

BE THE AWESOME MAN

A Young Man's Guide to Achieving Discipline, Success, and Happiness

Dennis Gazarek

Fresno, California

Published by Quill Driver Books
An imprint of Linden Publishing
2006 South Mary Street, Fresno, California 93721
(559) 233-6633 / (800) 345-4447
QuillDriverBooks.com

Quill Driver Books and Colophon are trademarks of
Linden Publishing, Inc.

Cover design by Tanja Prokop, www.bookcoverworld.com
Book design by Andrea Reider

ISBN 978-1-61035-337-3

135798642

Printed in the United States of America
on acid-free paper.

Library of Congress Cataloging-in-Publication Data on file.

I dedicate this book to the young men of the world who are fighting against the currents of today's culture and seeking to better themselves— our future Awesome Men.

Contents

Introduction

Have you ever felt you could be so much more than you are now? Are there men you admire and wish to emulate, but have no idea how to go about doing so? Do you sometimes feel that your friends, your environment, and even you yourself are holding you back from being the sort of man you know you could become? Are you dissatisfied with your life as it now is and aspire for so much more? Do you yearn for a life lived with purpose and filled with achievement, happiness, joy, and contentment?

If so, then good! Your dissatisfaction means you are ready and motivated to change who you are and how you live your life. You are ready to do the hard work of growing into the man you are destined to be.

Be the Awesome Man is a tool designed for a single purpose—to help you become what I call the Awesome Man. It is written for the individual who wants to make a positive impact on the world, for the young man who has searched within himself and sees that he has a purpose in life, even if that purpose is not yet entirely clear.

Young men have historically played an eminent role in shaping and molding the world. A few have done so by war and conquest, like Alexander the Great, but most have done so by stepping up and shouldering the responsibility that was required of them by their families and communities. They hunted game, captained ships, ran the family business, tended to the ill, built great houses of worship, married and became great husbands, and in other ways too numerous to mention became the rock-solid foundation that society depended on. But every one of these men knew it was the little things that made a difference. Even actions at the smallest levels, such as cleaning out the barn or helping in the family grocery shop, led to transformative results in the world. I define these men as Awesome Men, and in the pages that follow, I will introduce you to some of them. You will see in many ways they are just like you.

Be the Awesome Man provides you with a guide, a road map so to speak, for your journey to awesomeness. And while I hope the book helps you step into a better future, your success in reaching your goals will depend on you and your determination. It will be hard work, because challenging yourself to develop as a man can be uncomfortable at times. But I am on this journey with you and I know you have what it takes.

This is an exciting time for you, and the possibilities are endless. By recognizing the true purpose in your life, and in making a difference in yourself, your family, and your community, the world will benefit. Every little forward step you make to better yourself will reward both you and those you love.

Much like one lighted candle can banish darkness, each positive action you make will illuminate the world.

Young Men Are in Crisis

While there are many Awesome Men around us—some whom we know personally, others public figures—something has changed in our society. The path to manhood is now strewn with obstacles. The way forward is no longer clear for young men.

Some of you may be familiar with Ryan Lochte, the disgraced US Olympic swimmer who falsified a police report at the Rio Olympics in 2016. For those not acquainted with the story, Lochte and some male friends went partying in Rio one night after his events were completed. Afterward they stopped at a gas station and, in some sort of pseudo-macho display, vandalized the restroom. The gas station's security staff approached them and told Lochte and his friends that they had to pay for the damage or the police would be called. The security staff allegedly pulled their weapons to reinforce the seriousness of the matter. Lochte and his friends made restitution and the matter was settled.

The next day Lochte told his mother that he had been robbed at gunpoint. This was an outright lie. Obviously, thirty-two-year-old Lochte did not want to be honest with his mother or assume responsibility for his actions. His mother relayed the robbery story to Fox Sports, which reached out to the Rio police. Lochte, still in Rio, was contacted by the police and filed a report that he had been robbed at gunpoint. After further investigation, the Rio police discovered the truth, resulting in a huge embarrassment for Lochte and the United States.

What was going on in Ryan Lochte's mind? Why would a young man who had the benefit of a free education at the University of Florida, who had won numerous Olympic, international, and national swimming medals, and who was likely financially set for life:

a. vandalize a restroom,

b. lie to his mother about what happened, and

c. lie to the police investigating the alleged robbery?

Lying to avoid responsibility is something we are used to dealing with in children, but sadly we are seeing this immature behavior in young men as well. Because of their failure to face the truth, accept responsibility for their actions, expend effort to achieve something meaningful, and exhibit care for others, our society is overall much worse off than it could be. And as much as our society is suffering, these young men are suffering even more by not reaching their full potential.

For many different reasons young men are staying in their childhood roles much longer than ever before. This is detailed in several scholarly books such as *Guyland: The Perilous World Where Boys Become Men*, by Michael Kimmel; *The Case Against Adolescence: Rediscovering the Adult in Every Teen*, by Robert Epstein; and *Man Disconnected: How Technology Has Sabotaged What It Means to Be Male*, by Philip Zimbardo and Nikita D. Coulombe. For ease of description I call this phase "super-adolescence." Even though the super-adolescent male has the external appearance of an adult, his behaviors and actions are those of a boy in many ways. As a result of this delayed transition to adulthood, we have full-grown men behaving as man-children, seeking fun as if they were children and rejecting the responsibilities and benefits of adulthood.

It's fair to observe that since time immemorial, adults have complained about the youth of their day. The common refrain for generations has been something along the lines of "The youth are lazy, unmotivated, underachieving, and unprepared to take on the responsibility of the future. We couldn't get away with that when we were young. Today's youth are too coddled." You might think that my premise is just the same old complaint and that today's young males are going to be just fine.

But there is *real* cause for concern. What is different today is that there is statistical evidence that young men are not achieving standards and benchmarks set by men of previous generations. One specific area, for example, is in postsecondary education. The National Center for Education Statistics (NCES) produces statistics annually that show the percentage of males and females enrolled in postsecondary institutions in the United States. Recent trends show that males are not pursuing postsecondary education anywhere near historical levels.

Historically, more men attended post–secondary schools than women, but in the last few decades there has been a dramatic change. In the US, the ratio of males to females in the ten to fifteen year old age group is 1.04, or for every 100 females there were 104 males. We would therefore expect that men would attend post-secondary educational institutions in numbers equal to or slightly greater than women. If we apply this 1.04 ratio to 2018 post-secondary enrollment figures, for the 9.4 million females enrolled in postsecondary education that year there should have been about 9.7 million males enrolled. Yet the actual number was 7.2 million, a statistical shortfall of over 2.5 million men. Where are they and why are they not attending school? They all cannot be entrepreneurs or tradesmen or in the military.

The point I am making, even if you disagree with my numbers and methodology, is that a great number of males in our society are not achieving at the level they could be. The number might not total 2.5 million, but even if it is only 100,000 that is still way too many.

Just last year I attended the funeral of a friend's son, who at twenty-eight took his own life. The pain that radiated through the family and friends because of the self-inflicted death was palpable. Suicide is just too common and too many fathers and mothers are burying their children these days. Ask any high school or college administrator how many young people have died in their schools and you will be shocked. The suicide rate of white males ages fifteen to forty-four went up 27% between 1999 and 2017.* This is a huge increase, considering the great strides we have made in psychiatric medicine in those years.

Suicide is just one of the areas where males are showing signs of greater personal angst. The second obvious area where young men are suffering greatly is the loss of life through illicit drugs. The overdose death rate went up over 310% between 1999 and 2017.† We have too many young men dying unnecessarily in our country. Suicide and drug use, in simplistic terms, are signs of a very unhappy person, someone who has lost hope and belief in their value.

I do not believe there is one simple explanation or solution to the woes of today's males. But I do know we can utilize a great number of tested and proven tools and strategies to help these men change the course of their lives and reach their full potential. My goal in writing this book is to help young men leave childhood behind and become Awesome Men. To achieve that goal, each man will have to leave the irresponsibility of childhood and take on the challenges of adulthood to truly achieve happiness and fulfillment in his life.

Who Is the Awesome Man?

If you are a young man who does not live his life with purpose and who has not truly experienced happiness, joy, and contentment, or if you are anxious about transitioning to the responsibilities of adulthood, I believe that this book can be a great help to you. By reading and adopting the suggestions in this book, you will significantly increase your level of personal satisfaction and look toward a bright future. *You* can be the Awesome Man!

But who exactly is he? I define the epitome of male adulthood as the Awesome Man. He is a man who has left behind the behaviors of a child, which are focused on fun, and has taken on the responsibility of adulthood, utilizing all his natural talents and gifts to lead a healthy, productive,

---

* Centers for Disease Control and Prevention, National Center for Health Statistics, "Suicide Mortality in the United States, 1999–2017," http://www.cdc.gov/nchs/data/databriefs/db330_tables-508.pdf#page=2.
† Ibid. Overdose drug deaths were 11,258 in 1999 and 46,552 in 2017, an increase of 35,294 deaths annually (313%).

and meaningful life. Only by being an Awesome Man will you find happiness and fulfillment. To be an Awesome Man, you have to

- accept responsibility for your thoughts and your actions,

- exercise your most important assets: personal character and integrity,

- treat everybody with respect and dignity always,

- make decisions that are great choices in the long term,

- be open to others and their opinions, for only with understanding and knowledge will you make great choices,

- set goals and objectives that are worthy of you,

- give of yourself to others, because the more you do for others, the more you do for yourself,

- work very hard and expend much effort to reach your goals and objectives,

- be very aware of the how the media, culture, fashion, consumerism, and the pursuit of fun and pleasure can influence you and lead you away from true happiness.

Growth and change are hard, slow processes, but they are *always* worth the effort.

I wrote *Be the Awesome Man* for two closely connected groups of people. The first group is, of course, young men themselves who are ready to take on the challenges and assume the responsibilities of full adulthood, and reap the happiness they so richly deserve. The second group is the parents, teachers, coaches, counselors, mentors, youth leaders, and all other individuals who care about young males. I refer to these people as caretakers.

How to Use This Book

This book is divided into three parts, which ideally should be read in order.

Part One: Your Awesome Destiny

This motivational, inspiring section describes who the Awesome Man is. The world always is in need of Awesome Men, males who are willing to make a positive contribution to the people and community around them and thus to the world. I honestly believe that each man through his character, integrity, and respect can make a meaningful impact in society. Through selflessness, self-discipline, and effort, each man in unique and special ways can become awesome and therefore achieve personal happiness in life. The world needs you to be this sort of man.

Many books on similar topics spend a great deal of time discussing the causes of the problems that young men are facing today, ranging from the media and culture, modern music, lack of structured religion, hypocritical religion, bad public education, inadequate parenting, poverty, excessive wealth, and a myriad other factors. One fact that I am constantly aware of and amazed by is the thousands of young Awesome Men among us who overcame the so-called disadvantages and challenges of modern life to achieve and produce wonderful benefits for themselves and others. In part one, I will discuss why and how every young man can become an Awesome Man.

Part Two: Principles and Concepts

In part two we will delve into a number of topics that are relevant to men struggling to achieve full maturity and become Awesome Men. The very important key to understanding what is contained in the chapters of this book is to keep an open mind. Too often we reject ideas and concepts even before we have read or truly understood them. If you truly believe as I do that humans have a tremendous capacity to grow, learn, and develop, then you have an attitude that positions you to get the greatest benefit from the material in this book.

The first word most young children learn is "No." As we become elementary school students, we tell ourselves, "I can't," "It's too hard," "I don't know how," or "I don't want to." Now is the time to rid your mind of all that negativity and be open.

Part Three: Be the Awesome Man Instructional and Motivational Guide

In the final section of the book we put it all together for you by connecting the themes and concepts from the first two parts of the book to create an actual program you can use to take those critical first steps to becoming an Awesome Man. Here you will find concrete tools and strategies to achieve the important goals in your life.

A Final Word

I believe if you read this book and follow its guidance, you will soon find yourself well on your way to becoming an Awesome Man. You will make better decisions, gain self-confidence and self-respect, and enjoy a richer and more fulfilling life. Happiness, joy, and contentment are priceless. It does not matter how many billions you may acquire in your lifetime, how many mansions you may own, I assure you, you are not guaranteed a fulfilling and happy life. What's most encouraging is that these blessings are available to you and everybody you come into contact with, regardless of your material circumstances, so long as you dedicate yourself to being the best man you can be.

It may take effort for you to finish reading this book, but nothing can be achieved without effort. That's one of the messages of this book—perhaps the single most important one. The first steps on your journey to awesomeness can be challenging. But they will also deliver results. You will soon see that as you grow and become a quality individual, a person of character and integrity, and one who treats everybody with respect and dignity, your opportunities for satisfaction and happiness are limitless. And society as a whole benefits too.

I have confidence in you. I know you have the talents and abilities to be the best that you can be. I wish you much success on your journey to becoming the Awesome Man.

Part One:

Your Awesome Destiny

1

The World Needs *You* to Be an Awesome Man

The key to accepting responsibility for your life is to accept the fact that your choices, every one of them, are leading you inexorably to either success or failure, however you define those terms.

—Neal Boortz, author and radio host

My Solemn Commitment to You

Dear Reader, if you are a young male, I want to speak to you seriously and most sincerely for the next few paragraphs. You are important to me, and you are important to your friends and family. As this book will show, you are important to the world.

Think for a minute about your overall current life situation. Are you satisfied and fulfilled? Are you on the right path to reach the important long-term goals in your life? Do you even have long-term goals?

Or do you feel trapped in your current situation? Do you spend most of your time looking to have fun, yet feel empty and at times frustrated? Do you sometimes feel like you don't control your own life and are being pushed around by outside forces and people? Do you often feel pressured by others to do things you do not want to do but "have" to do or you will be punished?

If you answered yes to any of these last questions and feel like you are stuck in a rut, jammed, or just going through the motions, I have great news for you. I *know* you have the power and ability to change your life to one in which you have great goals—goals that you can and will achieve. And I know you are fully capable of living live a life of meaning and fulfillment, if you put in the effort. This book will give the tools you need to become the man you aspire to be. And my solemn commitment to you is to help you along the way.

Your new great goals will likely not be fame, riches, or popularity; they will be much more important and significant. They will be the great and important things you can accomplish for yourself, your family, and society. You have all the tools within you to live a truly fulfilling life. You can achieve the happiness, joy, and contentment you deserve. All you have to know and believe are two simple things: First, that you have the strength to make great and responsible decisions and, second, that you are capable of making the serious, dedicated effort needed to reach your goals. Have confidence in yourself. I do. I know that with desire and effort you can become an Awesome Man!

Who Is the Awesome Man?

An Awesome Man is fully engaged with life because he is relentlessly focused on making the next right decision. He understands that in life, *every* choice is important and has an impact—big or small—on his happiness and on the happiness of those around him. He spends his time wisely, and he uses all the natural gifts and talents he has to make his own life better and the world a better place for others.

He is virtuous, disciplined, caring, and always mindful of the consequences of his actions. He does not exploit, hate, or ridicule; instead he teaches, guides, mentors, helps, and cares for others. He is a builder and creator who earns respect through his actions and his deeds. Whether he is wealthy or poor, he is rich in confidence, love, and admiration, while remaining humble, circumspect, and sensitive.

The Awesome Man is aware that having "fun" is not an appropriate objective for an adult. He instead vigorously pursues worthy goals that he knows will bring happiness and that far exceed any momentary or transitory fun. Having fun is a valid goal for children, but the Awesome Man understands that when he leaves childhood his goals become more worthy of his adult stature. Like any healthy human, he still enjoys play, but the Awesome Man has replaced the continual pursuit of fun with happiness, joy, and meaning as the objectives of his life.

He knows what things in life are addictive and destructive and is very prudent with alcohol, pharmaceuticals, pornography, gambling, sexuality, gluttony, and other obsessions. He recognizes his weaknesses and is ever alert. He knows the price of personal freedom is constant vigilance.

The Awesome Man recognizes that it is better to be an actor in life than to be a spectator. Regardless of his background, family, or faith, he knows his behavior is what signifies his true value. It is his character and actions that truly make him who he is.

> **The Awesome Man recognizes that it is better to be an actor in life than to be a spectator.**

The Awesome Man is human, and makes his share of mistakes. But he learns from his errors and those of others, and when he stumbles, he gets up, overcomes his setbacks, and becomes stronger in character with each step forward. He understands that all that matters is making the *next* decision the right decision.

Each man is unique in special ways, and through selflessness, self-discipline, and effort, each man can become amazing and achieve true happiness in life for himself, and provide happiness for those around him. As I mentioned in the introduction, the world always is in need of Awesome Men, men who are willing to make a positive contribution to the people and community around them and thus to the world. Each male, through his character, integrity, and respect, can make an indisputable impact in society.

That is what you want to be—an Awesome Man who is the best that he can be in all aspects of his life, who makes the right choices, who maintains high standards for himself, and who cares for others. Importantly, there is no designated age limit for when you can become this man. Once you are aware that you are ready to move on from being a child and to take on the roles, responsibilities, and rewards of adulthood, you are ready to begin the process of becoming an Awesome Man.

The world needs you. Are you ready to join the brotherhood of Awesome Men?

Who Are the Awesome Men in Your Life?

In some communities there are many Awesome Men to inspire and motivate us. In other communities, there are sadly not as many. Social science has shown that the more Awesome Men there are in any given community, the more successful and happy you and the whole community will be. Regardless of what community you are in, it is important for you to identify and recognize those Awesome Men around you, the men who are actively striving to be the best men they can be through their actions, efforts, behavior, and commitment.

Who are the Awesome Men in your life? They could be your father, uncles, or brothers. Or they could be teachers, mentors, and coaches. What is it about them that makes them stand out? How have they made an impact on you? What things about them would you like to emulate?

Do you think that if there were more Awesome Men in your community, the whole community would be better off? If you do not know any Awesome Men, how can you make connections with some? Did you know that networking with Awesome Men is a great way to become an Awesome Man yourself? Let me introduce you to the idea of a mentor, who can be defined as an experienced and trusted adviser. I will deal with mentors in later chapters, but for now keep in mind that having someone who is trustworthy and experienced to provide you with advice and guidance is a valuable resource.

What Are the Key Characteristics of the Awesome Man?

The Awesome Man accepts responsibility for his life and everything in it.

He knows and accepts that if he wants to get anywhere in life, he has to take responsibility for his actions. Even though he always tries to do the right thing and make the right choices, he sometimes still makes mistakes and errors in judgment. But he takes responsibility when he makes a mistake and always pushes forward. He knows that shirking responsibility is immature and self-defeating. No happiness can be gained if he cannot take charge of his life.

The Awesome Man takes his education and career training seriously, putting all his effort into it. He is financially self-sufficient, knows how to handle money, pays his debts promptly, and takes pride in earning his way through life. If he lives at home, he contributes financially and emotionally to his family's well-being. If he is a father, he is active, financially and emotionally, in his children's lives.

The Awesome Man understands and accepts that he is part of the greater world and that the rest of society needs him to be actively involved in maintaining its standards and health. He happily accepts this responsibility and takes effective steps to better the world through volunteering, charity work, and mentoring others.

The Awesome Man does not blame others, luck, society, his parents, economics, culture, the media, his race, creed, color, or religion for any of his shortfalls or failures. He takes personal responsibility for his failings and looks to better himself. He is proud to take full responsibility for his life.

The Awesome Man is self-disciplined and challenges himself with meaningful goals.

The Awesome Man always does the hard work before the fun stuff. He says yes to challenges and opportunities to better himself, such as exercising, eating right, studying and learning, practicing his trade or craft, and saving money. He maintains control and never lets the pursuit of fun become his goal. He knows his limits and stops well before he endangers himself and others in meaningless activities. He obeys the laws, whether they be criminal, civil, natural, or ethical. He respects the lawgivers and those in authority and takes an active part in our democratic processes.

The Awesome Man recognizes the importance of having and achieving challenging and motivating objectives, and he acquires the tools and skills for effective goal setting and accomplishment (see part three for more on this subject). Not having meaningful goals is similar to setting out on a journey without a map or even a destination in mind; it guarantees you will wander aimlessly, will be often lost, and will likely end up in a place you do not want to be in.

When asked "Where are you going in life?", the Awesome Man never replies, "I don't know." He starts each day with purpose and works toward his goals. He has a plan for his life, and everything he does brings him closer to that destination.

The Awesome Man effectively deals with conflict and challenging situations.

He knows that whining, complaining, moaning, grumbling, and so on never solve any problems or result in productive solutions. He knows that effective coping skills, such as understanding others' points of view and having an open mind on the big picture in life, is a positive way to move through the roadblocks that life throws at him.

Through study, learning, and personal experience, the Awesome Man has acquired the skills and tools to deal with conflict, difficulties, and challenges. He always attempts to see situations in context and with patience and empathy for others' views. He knows that keeping his composure is an outward sign of his awesomeness.

Of course, venting can be a healthy way to relieve tension, and it is good to release emotions in an appropriate and safe environment. This venting should be done in a suitable and protected way. The Awesome Man is especially aware that social messaging is an extremely poor form of expressing hurtful or cruel opinions and feelings, regardless if done anonymously or not.

There are a great many things in life over which the Awesome Man has no power, so he accepts those things with patience and serenity. But when it comes to the things over which he does have power, he applies himself to make things better for everyone.

The Awesome Man is resilient.

Resilience is an important and powerful trait that helps buffer us from psychological, emotional, and physical trauma. Resilience goes by other names, such as strength of character, toughness, hardiness, adaptability, buoyancy, flexibility, and the ability to bounce back. It is the process of adapting well in the face of adversity and stress, allowing one to quickly move beyond temporary setbacks and take appropriate action. Luckily, resilience involves behaviors, thoughts, and actions that can be learned and developed by anyone, and it is a trait that the Awesome Man develops and benefits mightily from. Where others crumble in the face of adversity, the Awesome Man perseveres and, in time, triumphs.

Let me share with you certain truths about resiliency that have helped me deal with the many challenges I have faced:

- **Try to avoid seeing crises as insurmountable problems.** Nothing I am dealing with right now has not been faced and overcome by many people before me.

- **Accept change.** I often do not like it, but things do not always go my way. Things do not always work out the way I want, and I have to accept that things change.

- **Maintain a big picture view.** By no means am I the master of the universe, but I am a part of it, and my actions do affect it. By paying attention to how even my small behaviors and attitudes impact the world around me, I come to better understand and accept the adversities I may face and learn how to overcome them.

It takes resiliency to overcome failures, disappointments, illness, or loss. Most of us are familiar with the lives of Abraham Lincoln, John Kennedy, or other presidents who overcame adversity and trauma and went on to lead meaningful lives. But resilience is a quality shared by all Awesome Men, whether or not they become famous or wealthy or even presidents.

Resilience in the Face of Catastrophe

When he was 16 years old, Dean Ragone of Haddonfield, N.J., dove into a swimming pool and broke his neck. Initially paralyzed, over time Ragone regained the use of his arms but has mostly been confined to a wheelchair. It was particularly difficult in the 1970s when Ragone had his accident because, as he puts it, "Maybe 10% of buildings were accessible back then and medical technology was nowhere near what it is today." Young and athletic, suddenly Ragone had a decision to make. "I could get on with my life and make something of myself," he says. "Or I could take the other path and go into a nursing home at the age of 16 and be supported for the rest of my life." Ragone chose the former.

Now in his 50s he says that despite his early setback he has met or exceeded his goals and feels blessed to have lived the life he's lived so far. As he gets older, he feels perhaps more prepared to deal with some of the difficult challenges that lie ahead of him because he knows he can. "Everyone has choices in life," he says. "It's how you want to live." As the president and CEO of AllRisk, Inc., experts in property damage restoration, Ragone says his clients face terrible challenges as they confront rebuilding after devastating fires or other catastrophes. His advice in the face of adversity, "In life there are a lot of obstacles. It's all about how you approach them and how you overcome them. The only real obstacles you have are the ones inside your head."*

The Awesome Man is aware of his good reputation and image and works to improve and maintain them.

For the rest of your life every person you meet, every person with whom you interact, will be left with an impression of you. The Awesome Man is concerned that the impression he makes is positive and constructive. He cares what everyone thinks about him and always behaves in socially acceptable ways that bring honor to him, his family, and his community. He is courteous, kind, and thoughtful toward others. Unlike many of his peers, he is not concerned with superficiality, petty behaviors, fashion statements, shallowness, attention seeking, or trivial pursuits. His personal popularity is of no consequence to him, because he is outwardly directed and interested only in meaningful connections and relationships with others and the world.

The Awesome Man avoids any behaviors that will bring embarrassment to him or anybody else. He does not behave as the class clown, the goofball, the dummy, the stoner, the freakin' idiot, or any of those other so-called roles some males strive for. Contrary to some Hollywood portrayals, he cares what people think, and he gives a damn about the important things in life. His actions confirm his caring attitude.

---

* "Exploring Resilience in Everyday Life," by Michele Harris, Tribune, Erickson Living, April 19, 2020.

The Awesome Man never acts macho or fakes bravado.

He never intimidates, bullies, acts tough, or dominates others to show his manliness. His real strength is internal, and it shows through his character, competence, actions, and resilience. Women and men appreciate this about him, regardless of his physical presence. The Awesome Man knows that "alpha male" posturing and behavior is appropriate only for jackals, baboons, and other animals. Rather than trying to be somebody else, he is at peace with himself and accepts who he is. He is always respectful and dignified.

The Awesome Man respects himself and others.

The Awesome Man treats himself and others the right way. He does not allow his body or mind to become corrupted or polluted, and he cares for and protects others around him in the same way. He has high standards for all things and maintains them even when those standards may be unpopular, out of fashion, or "politically incorrect."

He goes about his life in a neat, clean, and correct manner, and he pays careful attention to his dress, appearance, speech, and actions. He never uses the anonymity of technology to be anything but considerate and civil when dealing with others, even complete strangers. Whether in reality or cyberspace, he does not engage in bullying of any type, be it flaming, denigration, exclusion, outing, trickery, impersonation, harassment, or stalking.

He treats all women with the highest consideration, never allowing them to be at risk physically, emotionally, or mentally as the result of his actions or behaviors in any way.

The Awesome Man carries himself well. He is humble, pleasant, and enjoyable to be around. He has self-control and observes personal limits. He can say no to frivolous and immature suggestions and requests. He lives his life by principles, rules, and respect, as he has found that this approach to living brings him both meaningful achievements and great contentment.

The Awesome Man has high standards.

The Awesome has high standards, and being "good enough" is not one of them. He has a clear-cut understanding of what is acceptable and right. He is very clear about moral, civil, and ethical standards. He has a defined standard of conduct for himself and others, in terms of dress, speech, activities, and comportment. He sets the bar high for himself and becomes the standard of quality for others. He never justifies illegal, immoral, corrupt, or dishonest activities with excuses, pretexts, or false rationalizations. He holds himself to account in all behaviors and actions.

The Awesome Man has a high level of integrity, both personally and when interacting with the world. His standards far exceed what is legal and expected by society. He will not sell his principles for a few (or a lot of) dollars; he knows that making "good business sense" never justifies ethically indefensible actions. When he crosses his boundaries, he immediately admits his error and makes appropriate amends.

The Awesome Man recognizes manipulation where it exists and rejects it.

I define manipulation as artful, unfair, or insidious means used by companies, organizations, or individuals for their own advantage (usually financial or commercial). Think about it: In our capitalist world, many misguided people see their only goal in life is to sell you something. They will point out to you in their messaging that without their product or service, you will be foolish, uncool, unlikable, unhealthy, lacking in confidence, at risk, smelly, impotent, classless, repulsive, unsafe, reckless, dull, unhip, a big loser. These forces attempt to influence you to shop at the "right" stores, buy the "right" products, and consume the "right" foods— their message is that if you want to have fun, be socially accepted, and show the world you are really successful, it will cost you.

On a more personal level, never forget that those who are trying to sell or encourage you to use alcohol, weed, meth, coke, or any other mind-altering drugs are not doing it to make you a better person. They want your money, nothing more, and could not care less about any adverse consequences you suffer from their products. Because when you are stoned, you make bad decisions, usually very bad ones, and they know that.

The key point about manipulation is to be very cautious about believing and accepting the promises of others, especially if the persuasion involves you buying something, suspending your beliefs, or weakening your integrity. And the inverse applies as well: The Awesome Man *never* seeks to manipulate or take advantage of others in an unfair manner.

A Deeper Look: The First Steps on Your Journey

Do you have trouble believing the characteristics of the Awesome Man could be applicable to you? Does the type of man described in this chapter not ring true or seem believable to you, especially when you look at the conduct of certain of your male friends and family members, not to mention today's celebrities? Everywhere you look, you see other guys having fun, chilling out, taking it easy, and not taking life too seriously. They are mainly taking care of Number 1. Many seem to have "side hustles" and scams either to beat "the system" or "the man" or to just get by. Their justifications often sound like "Whatever I need to do," "Don't be a fool, man," "I got needs to fill," and "If I don't get caught, what does it matter?" They claim to know what is wrong with almost everything, yet they have no idea how they can better their own lives, let alone make the world a better place. In their minds, it is always someone else who is screwing up society.

A few of your peers may display these negative characteristics while claiming to be rebels, radicals, or revolutionaries. In reality, they are just absolving themselves of the responsibility and actions required to do better, sort of like the Dude from the movie *The Big Lebowski*. Of course that movie is a work of fiction, and what we're talking about is real life, which carries with it very real consequences.

If the people you relate to don't exhibit great character traits, then it's natural that you might think such traits are irrelevant or impractical for you. But that is precisely why I believe it is extremely important for you to have positive role models—particularly men who were at one time in situations similar to what you are in right now—and to learn how they developed into Awesome Men.

First, you have to identify good and decent men of character in your family and community and in the society at large. They can be both historical figures and men who are making a positive difference in society today. It may take some effort on your part to learn about them in books, magazines, and newspapers, or on the web. But identifying great role models is an important step to your becoming an Awesome Man.

Once you have identified one or more role models and chosen to adapt their positive characteristics and attitudes to your own life, start with small measurable steps or goals of your own. If your room is a disaster and has been for years and your parents are always bugging you about it, try this. First accept there are many benefits to keeping a neat and organized room. I am a bit of a slob myself, but even I know that putting my soiled clothes in the laundry basket each day will make a positive impact on my personal health and hygiene.

Having a small, achievable goal such as this is a great step forward. It is not too hard, but it will have a positive impact on you and your parents or roommates. And once you get started, you'll see for yourself the many beneficial results of your efforts. By experiencing that small initial success, you will understand the benefits to yourself of responsibility, self-control, reputation, and the like, and you will see that it is in your own self-interest to acquire and foster these characteristics. Soon enough momentum will kick in, and you will add additional goals and start noticeably transforming your life for the better. The key takeaway is this: When you take action, things in your life inevitably improve.

So what's stopping you? Take action now!

Awesome Man Profile: Judge Greg Mathis

Gregory Ellis "Greg" Mathis was born April 5, 1960, in Detroit, Michigan. His father was a member of a notorious street gang that Mathis also joined as a teenager, and he soon became a criminal. Some years later, his mother, Alice, who had separated from Mathis's father, visited Mathis when he was imprisoned to tell him she was diagnosed with cancer. Mathis was released to care for his mother and started working at McDonald's as part of his probation order. He was admitted to Eastern Michigan University and eventually became a judge after graduating with a Juris Doctorate from the University of Detroit. He went from being an imprisoned gang member with no regard for his future to someone who took massive responsibility for his situation, cared for his ill mother, turned his life around, and became a positive member of society. He is now the star of his own television series, *Judge Mathis*.

What can we learn from Mathis's experience? In his early life, Mathis allowed himself to be swept up by his environment of street gangs and the exploitation of others. It was familiar and comfortable, and it was what was expected. He let his fears and weaknesses control his life. He followed the easy path and made few good choices. Fortunately, the mentoring and counseling he received while in jail and after, combined with the opportunity to be released on probation to care for his mother, set him on the path to making great choices. He took care of his mother, worked hard, earned grades in high school good enough to be accepted at university . . . and the rest is history. His path was not easy, and it took a great deal of effort and fortitude for him to leave behind the dysfunctional world of his youth. He took responsibility—which meant the rejection of his past choices and lifestyle and the loss of so-called friends—because he had a deep desire to be a positive influence in the world, to become an Awesome Man.

15

2

When to Start
Being an Awesome Man

The secret of getting ahead is getting started. The secret of getting started is breaking your complex overwhelming tasks into small manageable tasks, and starting on the first one.

—Mark Twain

No Minimum Age to Becoming an Awesome Man

Young men have been doing awesome things throughout human history, proving time and again that age does not have to be a restriction on achievement or a limit on maturity. For example, did you know that former president George H. W. Bush was the youngest American pilot in World War II? Can you guess how old he was? Just nineteen, believe it or not.

In September 1944, on his fifty-eighth combat mission—a bombing run over the Bonin Islands six hundred miles south of Japan—the Grumman Avenger torpedo bomber Bush was flying was hit by anti-aircraft fire. The plane was critically damaged and caught fire, but he managed to complete his run, strafing the targeted Japanese radio installation before heading back out to sea to bail out, as his damaged plane could not possibly make it back to his carrier. Bush parachuted safely into the water dangerously close to shore. The Japanese sent a boat to capture him, but a fellow Avenger pilot, Lieutenant Doug West, strafed the boat and stopped it. Circling fighter planes transmitted Bush's plight and position to the US submarine *Finback*, which soon surfaced nearby and picked him up from his lifeboat.

Bush was awarded the Distinguished Flying Cross for his efforts during that trying time, one of four air medals he received during his career as a US Navy pilot.

George Bush's achievements as a young man are not rare in the annals of armed conflict, as militaries have usually been more interested in skill and leadership than age. The Royal Navy had once set the minimum age for an officer at twenty but never really kept close track of officers' ages—the navy was more interested in competency. Historical figures such as Thomas Truxton, Galusha Pennypacker, and Horatio Nelson, hero of the Battle of Trafalgar, all received major commands prior to the age of twenty-one.

Even in modern times, young men have shown outstanding competency and maturity in the military. One example is David A. Christian, who served in the Vietnam War. Christian enlisted in the US Army in 1966 at age seventeen. After being rapidly promoted through the enlisted ranks to sergeant, he was admitted to Officer Candidate School and commissioned at eighteen years old, making him the youngest commissioned officer of the twentieth century. Christian was awarded the Distinguished Service Cross for extraordinary heroism and two Silver Stars (America's third-highest medal for valor) for his actions on October 29, 1968. He was leading a nine-man troop to outflank an enemy position and came upon a group of adversaries that outnumbered his team by more than three to one. Within moments Christian's team was pinned down, with three of his men wounded. Christian attacked the enemy bunker himself and destroyed it with grenades. He was wounded several times yet refused to be evacuated until all his men were safely retrieved. In January 1969, he was promoted to captain at age twenty.

Most achievement begins with just "doing it." You cannot become an Awesome Man by waiting for things to happen.

It goes without saying that many young men have achieved amazing things in arenas of life outside the military. Below is a list of such men. Notice as well that they *took action* and *exerted effort* to reach their goals. Nothing came easy for them, and their paths forward often required new learning and listening to guidance. Most achievement begins with just "doing it." You cannot become an Awesome Man by waiting for things to happen. You must seek out your opportunities in life and *make* things happen. Significantly, it's important to note that these males had mentors or coaches who greatly influenced them.

At age sixteen:

- Patrick Taylor left his home in Beaumont, Texas, with only a suitcase full of clothes, 35 cents in his pocket, and the desire to attend college. Based on his good high school grades, he received a scholarship to Louisiana State University, where he earned a petroleum engineering degree and became one of the richest men in Louisiana. He then used his wealth to create scholarships for students in financial need, having helped many thousands over the years achieve their academic dreams.

At age seventeen:

- Artificial heart developer Robert Jarvik was interested in both medicine and mechanics from a young age. He watched his surgeon father perform surgeries, and before he graduated from high school he had already earned a patent for an automatic stapler for surgical procedures.

At age eighteen:

- Prolific science and science fiction writer Isaac Asimov sold his first short story to *Astounding Science Fiction* magazine. This was after a number of rejections and a conscious effort to improve his writing while being mentored by the magazine's editor, John W. Campbell. Asimov went on to write and edit over five hundred books during his lengthy career.

At age nineteen:

- Tired of watching friends fall prey to drugs and crime, Matty Rich fought back by writing the story "Straight Out of Brooklyn" when he was seventeen. At nineteen, Matty produced the story as a feature film financed with credit cards and donations. The film was a commercial success and earned much critical acclaim.

At age twenty:

- Bill Gates left Harvard and cofounded Microsoft. His first real work with computers began at age fifteen, when he was retained by a fledgling computer company to debug its source code on various programs. Gates is now a billionaire and one of the world's greatest philanthropists and benefactors.

At age twenty-two:

- Muhammad Ali grew up in the South (Louisville, Kentucky) during a period of severe racial segregation and did poorly in school due to his dyslexia. These two factors combined to create great frustration in the young boy. A police officer, who had come in contact with Ali when he was twelve, encouraged him to take up boxing. In 1964, Ali became the heavyweight champion of the world at the age of twenty-two. Four years prior, he had won an Olympic gold medal.

Do these examples of young men achieving great things inspire you? Did you notice how the Awesome Men described above did not wait to begin their journey to manhood? They didn't waste years on frivolous activities or "chilling out" before becoming men.

You may wonder when you should begin your own journey to becoming an Awesome Man. Is it too early? Is it too late? The answer is it is neither too early nor too late. The time to begin the process is *right now*.

Now is the time.

I want you to use the examples above as motivation for what is possible for you, but you do not need to follow in those men's footsteps. Remember, it is not necessary to win an Olympic medal or invent an amazing new technology to make a huge difference in people's lives. Much as lighting one candle can begin to banish darkness, even the smallest positive action on your part will have a reverberating impact on the world.

Make sure your dreams and aspirations take shape in reality. It's fine to dream big, but the reality is that you will achieve your goals by taking small steps forward, one after another, as many as are necessary until you get to where you want to be. It is a *process*, and yes, you will certainly relish the occasionally big jump ahead—but keep in mind that the great bulk of your progress toward becoming an Awesome Man will be achieved by the steady application of time, effort, and patience. Each day, you will move a little bit forward. There may well be times during your journey when you feel like giving up, when you feel overwhelmed by the challenges you face. When this happens, stop, take a deep breath, and regroup. Take the time to analyze your situation. Break your obstacles down into small components and take on these smaller components with quiet determination. When you think about your problems this way, you'll realize things aren't that bad, and you will gain confidence in your ability to succeed.

The men in the examples above certainly faced their fair share of severe disappointments and setbacks. They has family problems, financial challenges, and education issues. One had his airplane shot down (certainly not the thing any pilot aspires to!). Others saw experiments fizzle or ideas flop or had carefully crafted strategies unravel before their eyes, forcing them to adapt—yet despite these setbacks, progress was made with each step forward.

They could have used these difficult challenges as excuses not to achieve, which would have been to the world's detriment—but they didn't. They were resilient and pushed through the obstacles on their way. You, too, will face obstacles. Be ready for them, be strong, and you will win your way through.

And, finally, let us not forget the importance of the men who mentored and encouraged Isaac Asimov and others. They were absolutely crucial to the world and were Awesome Men in their own right. Not many people know of Louisville police officer Joe Elsby Martin, but if it were not for him mentoring young men, there would not have been the Muhammad Ali we all know. You can speed up your own progress to becoming an Awesome Man by seeking out mentors who

It's fine to dream big, but the reality is that you will achieve your goals by taking small steps forward, one after another

will help you work to achieve your goals. And then, as you grow, you in turn can play the role of mentor for other young men. You can become a positive influence in their lives.

Another great strategy is to model the behavior of quality individuals. You do not even have to be in contact with the person you wish to model. Effective modeling will involve action on your part. First, you pay attention. To model (or emulate) the good qualities of someone, you have to be aware of what specific things that person does that lead to his good results. Second, put into practice what you have observed. It's as simple as that. And the great thing about modeling is its availability to you anytime, anywhere. Watch the actions of others, note their positive behaviors, and do the same things.

Guyland: The Road to Distraction

Merriam-Webster Collegiate Dictionary defines *adolescence* as

- "the state or process of growing up" and
- "the period of life from puberty to maturity terminating legally at the age of majority."

Notice how these definitions imply a lack of maturity. It wasn't always this way. Not so many generations ago, young men barely in their teens were performing important tasks in farming, in business, and at home. Many young American men helped their fathers clear the land with hand-saws, axes, and black powder. Barns were festooned with the farmer's name followed by "and Sons," signifying the importance of the young men in running the operation. Even the local fishmonger, piano maker, and tool-

maker recognized the importance of youth in their business by adding them to the signage. Some examples include:

It is clear that young men—both those specifically detailed earlier in this chapter along with countless others, known and unknown—have routinely achieved important things that had real value for the people and community around them.

But in recent decades, the stage of life called adolescence, rather than being a time of growing up and developing as a person and a man, has morphed into an excuse for *not* maturing and for having lowered expectations of behavior, as in "We can't expect too much from him. He's just a teenager."

Worse than that, however, is how the stage *between* adolescence and full adulthood has evolved and extended into a period that sociologist Michael Kimmel calls Guyland.* In his book of the same name, Kimmel defines

---

*In the research for his book, Kimmel interviewed four hundred men aged sixteen to twenty-six. However, I believe that there are men who are in the midthirties whose maturity levels and aspirations quality them as residents of Guyland.

Guyland as a life stage where "in order to avoid the responsibilities of adulthood, young men retreat into a homosocial world, a social space and a stage of life where guys gather to be guys with each other, unhassled by the demands of parents, girlfriends, jobs, kids, and the other nuisances of adult life."

The Nature of Masculinity

Let's take a moment to talk about the birds and the bees. It is a biological imperative for the continuation of the human species that males need female partners to procreate. This desire begins when we reach puberty. They must attract females for this to happen. The same holds true for all nonhuman males: In most animal species, the alpha male (the animal that best displays the external masculine characteristics of strength, virility, aggressiveness, and so on) usually attracts the best females. But the human condition is a bit more complex because the father plays a key ongoing role in the well-being of his family, whereas in the animal world the male typically has a minimal role in the family unit after the offspring are born.

Men who inhabit Guyland mistakenly believe that outward displays of masculinity will attract the finest females. They disregard the eternal truth that women desire a partner with vital but less visible traits, such as intelligence, wisdom, empathy, caring, and kindness—in other words, virtues that are not considered "macho."

In addition, some misguided men like to use their apparent "alpha male" characteristics to bully, intimidate, and dissuade other males in order to elevate their own status within their group and to appear more desirable to females. This behavior is straight out of the animal kingdom. It is ridiculous for humans—who have minds, intellects, and the ability to think and speak—to act as if their only appealing value is in acting out some over-the-top definition of masculinity. If you feel you have to act macho, chances are you will only attract females who do not have the intellect to see real virtue in a man.

Even though they are physically men and are often obsessed with being fully "masculine," they shirk the responsibility of real manhood. They strive for "fun" in their activities and relationships. Emotionally, they are little beyond children in their degree of seriousness about life, with their posturing and bravado and their inflated sense of entitlement and self-worth.

Our media, marketers, and culture at large exacerbate this problem. Their unending emphasis on short-term pleasure and fun is masking the truly valuable and important things that males should be seeking. The result? Far too many young men today are disillusioned and damaged. They are mere shells of the men they could be, their goals and achievements limited in scope and oriented almost entirely around self-satisfaction.

Examples of men stuck in Guyland are all around us. Do you remember Olympic swimmer Ryan Lochte, whose widely publicized immature antics were mentioned in the introduction? Clearly he was an individual who was still loitering in Guyland, despite his amazing talents as an athlete and the promise of being so much more. Rob Lowe is another clear example.

In 1988, Rob Lowe was experiencing the heights of movie stardom and professional recognition. By age twenty-four, he had already starred in eight feature films and was politically active in the Democratic Party presidential campaign. The night before the party's convention in Atlanta, he met and picked up two females, ages sixteen and twenty-two, at a bar. He videotaped their sexual adventures that night. (Luckily for him, the age of consent in Georgia was fourteen at that time, or he could have been charged with statutory rape.) Of course the women made off with the tape, which later received wide distribution. Lowe's career tanked, agents and directors stopped calling, and it was two long years before another movie with him in it was released. It took many more years for his career to fully recover. On the bright side, Lowe appears to have learned his lesson, admitted responsibility for his actions, and rehabilitated his career. His story provides clear evidence that a man can grow, mature, and leave behind the shallow antics of life in Guyland.

Previously I mentioned how culture often promotes Guyland-like behaviors. Shows and movies such as *Friends*, *Seinfeld*, and *The Big Lebowski* often feature characters who are portrayed as ostensibly lovable, free-spirited men but who are merely self-interested, lazy, and without meaningful long-term relationships with others. The long-running television program *Two and a Half Men* is a prime example. The main character, Charlie Harper, is a freelance jingle composer who lives in a luxurious ocean-front home and rarely gets up before noon. He is constantly drinking, smoking, gambling, and womanizing. His probable drug use is never portrayed but left to the viewers' imaginations. If you want an example of a man who exemplifies a selfish individual with few redeeming qualities, it is Charlie Harper. Of course we're speaking about a character in a television show. It's just entertainment and fantasy. But the man who played Charlie Harper was in many ways playing his real self. Here are some of actor Charlie Sheen's life "highlights":

- In 1983, Sheen was expelled from high school for poor grades and attendance.

- On May 20, 1998, Sheen suffered a stroke after overdosing on cocaine and was hospitalized.

- In January 1990, Sheen accidentally (and nonfatally) shot his fiancée, Kelly Preston.

- On December 25, 2009, Sheen was arrested for assaulting his wife at the time, Brooke Mueller.

- On November 17, 2015, Sheen publicly revealed that he was HIV positive, having been diagnosed roughly four years earlier.

- In April 2016, it was announced that Sheen was under investigation by the Los Angeles Police Department stalking unit for threatening to kill his former fiancée, Scottine Ross.

The fictional Charlie Harper dies by being run over by a subway train. We'll have to see what the ultimate fate of Charlie Sheen is, but both Charlies focused their lives on having "fun," which led to their downward spirals.

Inundated by examples such as these, it's easy to see how young men are affected by a culture that encourages them to engage in immature behavior, behavior that is the complete opposite of an Awesome Man's behavior. Have you felt influenced by the messages that our culture sends you? How about your friends and peers? Do some of them seem fully committed to living in Guyland?

Important Notice!

I want to share an important bit of information: I love fun! I realize it may not seem that way, based on how I'm talking in this chapter. But I really do believe that fun is good, fun is healthy, and fun is positive. What I am saying is that as you get older and become a young man, fun should not be a goal in and of itself. And for the Awesome Man (as well as for most mature adults), fun comes from doing positive things in an enjoyable way. That's what delivers real satisfaction and fulfillment.

I realize it can be hard to put away childhood things. I was once a child myself, after all! And on top of the problems with our culture discussed in the introduction, sometimes parents over-coddle their children. Parental love and protection are vital, of course, but they must be balanced with preparing a child to face the stings of failure and disappointment too. Not everything in life is fun.

One can see why so many young men find it easier to stay in this state of super-adolescence, or Guyland, where all the surface pleasures of manhood are available, but the deeper pleasures derived from shouldering responsibility and achieving worthy goals are not. The culture has told them that having fun is the true objective of life and that any activity that is not fun should be avoided.

The Awesome Man skips or quickly transits through Guyland because he has his eye on a fulfilling future. He sees the big picture, has a positive vision for where he wants to go, and can't wait to get started. He realizes that, as Saul of Tarsus stated, "When I was a child, I spoke as a child, I understood as a child, I thought as a child. But, when I became a man, I put away the things of a child." No matter what your age, if the primary goal in your existence is to have fun, you will never realize the important objectives and successes in your life, the things which will provide you with true happiness, joy and contentment.

I've got a few important questions I want you to ask yourself. Take your time and think hard about them.

- How much of your time right now is focused on having fun? How about your friends and peers? Are they the same?

- Do you believe you are here on earth to have a "good time," or do you feel you have a more important destiny? If the latter, have you thought about what you should be doing today—and every day—to build toward that inspiring future? To become an Awesome Man?

You *Can* Change Who You Are (Thanks to the Power of Brain Plasticity)

I see four primary challenges that you as a young male may face on your path to becoming an Awesome Man:

1. You are comfortable with your current set of inappropriate, self-defeating behaviors. ("I like the way I am. It works for me.")

2. You do not believe there is any reason to change these self-defeating behaviors. ("I am free to do what I want. It is my choice. You can't convince me to change who I am.")

3. You do not believe you *can* change your negative behaviors. ("This is the way I always have been. I cannot change, even if I wanted to. You just have to learn to accept me.")

4. You resent how people who care about you keep pushing you to change and "grow up." ("Why can't the world accept me the way I am? Why does everybody want me to change?" Hint: They see the potential in you, which you are suppressing.)

Each of these challenges is a problem of the mind, of how you perceive yourself and others. But these self-limiting beliefs are not set in stone; in fact, there is now scientific proof that behavior change is possible for every human being. The field of neuroscience has made great strides in understanding the remarkable phenomenon of brain plasticity. If you have never heard this term, let me tell you what it means, because this information can change your life.

Numerous books and studies have shown that the brain has the ability to change its patterns and structure, its vast and complex network of neural connections. In short, brain plasticity refers to your mind's ability to change. It's what allows you to grow, learn, and evolve—to develop new patterns of thought and behavior. To become an improved person.

Brain plasticity means that the way you are right now is *not* because nature "locked your mind" into the person you are. Rather, the way you are right now is because of all the decisions and choices you have made to date that have wired your brain. And the great news is that if you don't like certain aspects of yourself, you are capable of "rewiring" your mind to behave differently. That is the immense power of brain plasticity.

For example, I have noticed that the more I write, the better I become at writing. In a very real sense, I am rewiring my mind to become better at translating my thoughts into the written word. I have no doubt that you, too, have trained your mind to do something very well. Can you think of something that you're good at? Perhaps it's math, or a particular athletic skill (pitching a baseball, shooting a basketball), or puzzles? You didn't start out being good at that thing. But you became good, over time, by practicing it over and over. Your brain is like a muscle, and you trained it to get strong at that particular skill.

If you don't like certain aspects of yourself, you are capable of "rewiring" your mind to behave differently.

Although it's true that the more you do something the better you become at doing it, there is a darker side of this that we must discuss. Because of the way certain stimuli work on the brain, the more you consume these stimuli, the harder they can be to stop. This is how addiction works. The stimuli can be visual, tactile, chemical, or other types. As hard as it is to quit smoking after five years, it is much more difficult after forty years of smoking. Similarly, it can be very difficult for a mind accustomed to constant video game playing or the consumption of pornography to release itself from these activities.

So what does this all mean for the Awesome Man? First, the brain can unlearn time-wasting and self-destructive behaviors and learn new behaviors that promote growth and maturation. Let that statement sink in for a moment. You can rewire your brain to drop your bad habits or your continual focus on having fun, and program yourself to enjoy new, more meaningful activities. With effort, it is quite possible and realistic for you to achieve things in terms of mental ability that you do not think are doable.

Second, the Awesome Man comprehends that things that appear to give him pleasure are really the brain reacting to neural stimuli. If these pleasurable experiences are inappropriate for an Awesome Man, they can be replaced by appropriate pleasures, which will help him achieve success and happiness.

If you do not like to

Read, read more.

Play sports, play sports more.

Shave, shave more.

Study, study more.

In terms of brain activity, whatever you do not like to do will become easier and more enjoyable the more you do it. Conversely, whatever is bad for you, stop doing it! And the best way to stop is to stay away from the situations that trigger bad habits.

Drinking too much?
Stay away from bars and liquor stores.

Wasting too much time on video games?
Get rid of the controllers.

Not getting enough sleep?
Turn off all the technology and go to bed.

Because of the way in which brain plasticity works and the ability of the brain to change itself, you'll find that this method works.

Use Small Steps to Reprogram Your Brain

Most people, no matter how well-intentioned, set ambitious initial behavior goals that are unachievable in the short term. Understanding this, members of Alcoholics Anonymous do not have a goal to stop drinking for the rest of their lives. Their goal deals with today only. "Today I will attempt to not drink. If I fail today, I will start again tomorrow."

If you wish to change an inappropriate behavior to an appropriate behavior, start by setting a one-day goal. One day at a time should be your mindset. Understand and accept that there are likely triggers to your inappropriate behavior, and if you can become aware of those triggers and avoid them for just one day, the chances of success the next day, and the following day, become far more likely.

Any behavior can be formed and unformed with a combination of the right circumstances and awareness of what triggers your behaviors. If you want to stop playing video games so you can use your time for more important pursuits, figure out a way to avoid playing video games today. Have somebody hide your game consoles and devices away where you cannot easily access them. Do not associate with other gamers today and stay off the gaming websites. Most importantly, fill your day with nongaming activities. Schedule other fun things to do, like going to the movie theater or taking a day hike. If you remove the tempting triggers from your environment and stay engaged with other types of enjoyable activities, chances are very good you will reach your goal of not video-gaming today.

Tomorrow is a new day, so review the reasons you want to stop playing video games and once again plan a day of positive activities. If you lapse, think hard about what triggered you to break out the game console and try to avoid that trigger tomorrow. And remember, you have to fill your day with positive activities to replace the void created by no video games.

It is hard at first, but taking small steps one day at a time works. I cannot emphasize enough that you must set small, achievable, measurable goals for yourself. The grandiose goals most people have, such as to lose forty pounds, stop drinking forever, get a job, or graduate in three years, are rarely achieved.

Many young men who want to become Awesome Men often do not start out with a history of success in setting and achieving goals. It is so important for you to be successful, and fulfilling simple goals can significantly boost your confidence in your ability to achieve the bigger things you want in life. So start by focusing on small things: Eat an apple instead of a bag of potato chips today, go to the movies instead of a bar this evening, complete a résumé and drop it off at a potential employer, do your homework completely tonight. These goals may take some amount of effort, but they are completely within your means to achieve, and they are great first steps on the path to success.

A psychotherapist friend once told me that when treating people who had serious depressive illness, he stressed the crucial importance of getting up in the morning—simply getting out of bed, shaving and showering, and getting dressed. Even if they spent the rest of the day on the couch, they had made progress by not lounging around all day in their pajamas. The therapist had one patient go to a mall for one hour a day. At the mall the patient could be relatively anonymous and did not have to interact with

Set small achievable and measurable goals so you can consistently get wins under your belt.

others, which helped him build confidence in facing the world. The patient would report proudly to the therapist that he had gotten dressed, eaten breakfast, and had gone to the mall three times in the last four days. The patient made great progress, considering where he had started from, but the key point is that this progress was achieved in small, gradual stages.

Another of the therapist's clients was addicted to online pornography, watching a minimum of three hours a day. The patient gradually reduced his daily viewing time by twenty-minute increments and spent his newfound time on productive, fulfilling activities. In a matter of weeks he realized he could go a whole day without porn, something he achieved step by step.

In conclusion, set small achievable and measurable goals so you can consistently get wins under your belt. If you need guidance, don't be afraid to ask for help. Plenty of good people are willing to mentor and advise you.

Remember: Focus always on tiny victories.

The Rewards of Being an Awesome Man

An Islamic teaching states, "Whoever does good, will see the result of his goodness, and whoever does bad, will also see the result of his wrongdoing," which is to say goodness is its own reward. But there are truly tangible rewards to being an Awesome Man, some of which are

happiness and joy

contentment

peace of mind

respect

self-confidence

love

fulfillment

wisdom

These rewards are truly valuable and priceless, and rich or poor, each male is capable of earning them. History has shown that nobody ever regretted being an Awesome Man. Nothing in Guyland can even come close to measuring up to these rewards, and they are available to men now—no waiting, no purchase necessary, and no expiration date.

A Deeper Look: Today Is the Most Important Day in Your Life

You should know that today, the present, is the only day you have any control over. Why? Because yesterday cannot be changed and tomorrow will be affected by what you do today. *Today is the most important day in your life.* The things you do today can make a huge difference to your future self and to those you love—hence the expression carpe diem (seize the day).

There are so many examples in life where a simple choice to do good or to do bad has had huge impact and consequences in men's lives. Vince Lombardi, the famous football coach, once told his players that the result of a football game (winning or losing) often turns on merely one or two plays. Unfortunately, no one ever knows ahead of time when that crucial play will unfold. That is why it is paramount that each player gives full effort, focus, and concentration on every play—just as you must do each and every day of your life.

In the real world, we never know when our next action will have a dramatic long-term impact on our life. Understand that every course of action you take, either good or bad, is important and significant, and the things you do now connect the you of today to the you of tomorrow.

Some Awesome Men understand rewards through the concept of karma, a Buddhist term that comes from Sanskrit and relates to fate and action. It teaches that you alone are responsible for your actions. It is the law of cause and effect, an unbreakable law of the cosmos. You deserve everything that happens to you, good or bad. You created your happiness and your misery. One day you will be in the same circumstances in which you put someone else. The Hebrew Bible expresses the same concept with these simple words: "Whatsoever a man soweth, that shall he also reap."

For thousands of years, moral philosophy always and unequivocally has said that being a person of values, goodness, and character—an Awesome Man, in other words—is rewarding and beneficial and far surpasses any other alternatives. This life awaits you. Start being the Awesome Man.

Awesome Man Profile: Thomas Truxton

Thomas Truxton was born February 17, 1755, near Hempstead, New York, on Long Island. The only son of an English country lawyer, he lost his father at a young age and was placed under the care of a close family friend, John Troup. He joined the crew of the British merchant ship the Pitt at the age of twelve.

Having proved himself adept at seamanship, at the age of twenty Truxton garnered command of his own vessel, the Andrew Caldwell. He operated as a US privateer during the American Revolution, commanding the ships Congress, Independence, Mars, and St. James. Truxton was highly successful in capturing enemy ships during this period. After the war, he returned to the merchant marines and retired from active duty in the US Navy in 1800, at the age of forty-five. His resiliency as a young man allowed him to overcome the loss of his family and his lack of formal education. His powerful drive to learn and improve, coupled with the effort he expended in his early teens, resulted in a life of achievement and happiness. Truxton was clearly a man who knew how to seize the day.

3

Fear Strikes Out

If you want to conquer fear, don't sit home and think about it. Go out and get busy.
—Dale Carnegie, author and motivational speaker

"The Only Thing We Have to Fear Is Fear Itself"

As President Franklin D. Roosevelt so eloquently expressed in the words above, fear* is our greatest enemy. Fear is a very powerful inhibitor in becoming an Awesome Man. Why is this so, you might wonder? Perhaps the answer to that question, in large part, is that the fears that hold us back come in many shapes and forms. Here is a list of some of these shapes and forms. You may find you are familiar with many of them, and you'll probably notice they all have one thing in common. They prevent you from taking action.

Fear of Losing What You Have (Yes, I'm Stuck in a Rut, but I Am Comfortable in It)

Did you ever have the feeling you could be better than you are? Have you ever dreamed about truly excelling at something? Really giving it your all? Striving like an Awesome Man to get to the next level in your life? But then you told yourself, "Yeah, that would be nice, but things really aren't

---

* As a young boy, I was aware of Jimmy Piersall, who retired in 1967 after seventeen years as a center fielder in the Major Leagues. His autobiography was titled *Fear Strikes Out*, and I dedicate this chapter to his bravery and efforts to overcome the adversity and stigma of bipolar disorder.

that bad right now. I better play it safe and not risk a big move that could backfire on me."

Does that internal dialog sound familiar? It does to me. Many men have gone through the same self-defeating thought cycle. And I bet you have too. We humans are never *totally* miserable and unhappy, so even when we know we have great potential to be more, we often convince ourselves to stay put, to not make a move that could jeopardize the life we do have, mediocre as it may be.

When you consider matters from this vantage, you can see what the problem is: You are afraid of losing the things you have and enjoy, even if those things are meager and relatively unfulfilling.

> **Part of becoming an Awesome Man is understanding that you have to let go of things that, in the past, may have been very important to you.**

For example, if you go off to college for several years, you may lose touch with your girlfriend. If you start volunteering at the YMCA, you may lose some sleep. But if you think about it, you do not have to lose anything that is important. If the girl is important, you can maintain a vibrant and satisfying long-distance relationship with her. If sleep is important, you can do fewer of the unimportant things in your life and get the sleep you need. You can do it all. It just takes planning and effort on your part.

An important element in becoming an Awesome Man is understanding that you have to let go of things that, in the past, may have been very important to you. Sometimes you must move on. Why? Because there are even greater things in your future. It can be scary to make that leap into the future, but most times, after making that leap, we end up asking ourselves, "Why didn't I do this sooner?"

Fear of Ending Up Worse Than Where You Started (Lack of Confidence)

"What if I do the right thing and end up worse than I am now?" Ask yourself, "Worse in which way?" For example, if you turn down a promotion and transfer at work to stay local so you can take care of your dying mother, you may end up somewhat financially poorer. Emotionally and mentally, you may be much richer taking care of your mother in her final months. If you are promotion-worthy now, some company will recognize your value and reward you in the future.

Fear of Making a Mistake (Lack of the Desire to Learn)

Nobody wants to make a major life choice and find out later they did the wrong thing. In reality, though, whenever we decide to do the right thing, to do good, to be a person of character, integrity, and value, it is impossible to do the wrong thing. Nobody ever lay on their deathbed and said, "I valued and loved too much. I did too many good and virtuous things. I helped and cared for too many people." When you make the decision to be an Awesome Man, your moral compass will guide you and you'll make the right choices.

However, often we fear making an incorrect choice or, more often, make no choice at all, simply because we lack the desire to learn. We wallow in ignorance, limiting our own knowledge and understanding of life. This ignorance, the product of a lack of effort to learn about the world, leads us to suffer from more fears. And these fears paralyze us when we need to act, when we need to make big decisions.

Imagine for a minute you are a prehistoric man out hunting for food and you come across a number of chickens. You have never seen chickens before. You are ignorant of the fact that chickens can provide food and eggs and that their bones can be used as needles and fine implements. You have a choice: You can run away in fear, scared off by the chickens' loud cackling, pointy claws, and rustling feathers. Or you can observe and learn about the behavior of chickens. You can learn they are docile in most cases, cannot harm you physically, and can be controlled. Being a hunter, you can learn even more by killing and cooking one, discovering that it is quite tasty and nutritious. In the future, this knowledge you earned means that you will not be afraid when you come across chickens again. You may even take some home to raise. On the other hand, if your fears prevented you from gaining this knowledge about chickens, you have missed out on important information about your environment, much to the detriment of you and your people.

Here's another example—a composite of actual incidents I have witnessed—about how lacking the desire to learn leads to fear of making a mistake. When Chris was a senior in high school, the local Red Cross was offering a first aid/CPR course after school. Despite his classmates laughing at him for signing up, Chris completed the course and received certification. That summer, while at a pool party, a classmate tripped on the pool deck, smashed her mouth, and was knocked unconscious. All the other kids stood around in shock and fear, some screaming, not knowing what to do. They were afraid to do the wrong thing and make the situation worse. Because of his training, Chris was able to control the bleeding and provide CPR until the paramedics arrived. The girl lived and made a complete recovery because Chris had a desire to learn and was not afraid to fail when the time came for him to act.

Life is filled with examples where Awesome Men did awesome things because they had learned skills or acquired knowledge in the past that made a difference today. What skill and knowledge can you acquire today that will make a difference tomorrow?

Fear of Failing (Needing a Psychological Safety Net)

The fear of failing—which can be considered a variation of the fear of making a mistake—can be found often in sports and similar types of events where the participant needs to perform well. As a young performer, has there ever been a time when you did not give a 100% effort because you knew that if you failed, you could always use the excuse that "I really wasn't trying"? This is a more common excuse than many would believe. It allows the young man to have a second chance (in golf, such do-overs are called mulligans).

What the performer is doing is holding back on effort, in case he needs a viable excuse or safety net to justify his so-called failure. The point is the young man, by clinging to this psychological tether rope, goes through much of his life doing less than his best, never unleashing his full energy and abilities. He lives a restricted life that limits his sense of fulfillment and prevents him from maturing into an Awesome Man.

When you think about it, failure in life is a great learning opportunity because it reveals what doesn't work. In fact, for many, failure has been the path to success. And as a bonus, it helps develop mental ruggedness and fortitude. The great inventor Thomas A. Edison once said, "I have not failed. I've just found 10,000 ways that won't work." Now there was a man with an indomitable spirit who clearly knew how to embrace failure and use it to his advantage. You can do the same in your life.

The Fear of Embarrassment

Before we move on, let's discuss another factor at play related to the fear of failing. One of the regrettable aspects of modern society is that people who fail are often laughed at. Sometimes they are even viciously ridiculed, which creates a great deal of embarrassment for the person attempting the activity. On YouTube, there is even a channel where they post the "Fails of the Week." This site's videos typically get over a million views!

Yes, suffering embarrassment isn't fun, but it's often a by-product of your making those necessary first attempts to achieve something. Chances are you'll fail the first time or two! Remember, failing equals learning, which is very good. And it's all relative. For example, in the world of pro basketball, if for your career you fail at 50% of your three-point-shot attempts, you will likely go to the Hall of Fame and be considered one of the greatest shooters of all time.

When I was beginning my off-road motorcycling hobby, I was told that if you don't fall, you really aren't trying very hard. The second thing I learned was that I should not take myself too seriously. I fell a lot as I learned, and I laughed at myself even more. My riding buddies laughed at many of my "get-offs," as I did at theirs—but it was in respect to the effort we were all making in trying to improve. I was embarrassed, but ultimately I didn't care because it was a small price to pay for becoming a proficient motorcycle rider, something that was important to me.

Another part of this topic is dealing with the often juvenile criticism of peers and others who are less mature or less knowledgeable than you. Not all of us grow and develop at the same rate and in the same way. You may be my best friend and have greater skill at basketball, and I may be able to read better. If you want to go play basketball and I want to go to the library, I would hope you would not laugh at me for my choice. The reality of it is that when people laugh at or ridicule us, even when we are making good choices, it is usually because they do not understand our choices or they are afraid the choice we are making reflects badly on them—perhaps because they fear being left out or left behind.

If my friend ridicules me for going to the library instead of playing basketball, it's probably because a number of things are going on in his mind. Perhaps he feels I like books more than I like him, or he's worried he won't have anybody to play basketball with, or he's embarrassed about his poor reading ability. If I wanted to be an Awesome Man, I could tell him, "Why don't you come to the library with me and we can see if they have a book on basketball for you to read? Then you and I can play basketball this evening." If I include my friend, he will not feel abandoned and would have no reason to ridicule me. This may seem like a simplistic explanation, but it is a very realistic portrayal of what happens daily in society.

As a last option, it is important to realize that if your friends do not respect the good choices and decisions you are making, even after you've made an effort to involve them, it may be time to consider looking for friends who are more in sync with what you are trying to accomplish.

And if people laughing at you causes you to feel embarrassment, ask yourself this question: "Why do I let somebody else's behavior negatively affect me?" If you want to achieve significant things as an Awesome Man, you must learn to block out distractions. Do you think LeBron James, Cam Newton, Henry Ford, Steve Jobs, and Bill Gates were much concerned with the people who laughed at and ridiculed their efforts? Not likely! They had big goals in mind and could not care less about the jeering detractors standing on the sidelines of life.

One of the characteristics of an Awesome Man is the ability to continue on in the face of adversity of any kind. Speak to any man who has accomplished anything of value in life. Ask him if at times people laughed at or ridiculed him. Odds are strong that did indeed happen. Next, ask him if he *allowed* embarrassment to stop his progress. No, he didn't! The Awesome Man does not allow other people's poor behavior or negative commentary to hold him back from reaching his goals!

Fear of Failing (Defeatism)

The fear of failure has been real for me, especially when it involves a commitment of my personal time, money, and/or heavy physical effort.

Recently, I had a chance to attend a beginner's Tai Chi course. Not many men sign up, in large part because many of them have enrolled in similar physical activity programs in the past and ended up quitting. So with a defeatist attitude in place, they tell themselves "Why bother?" whenever a new opportunity comes up, and therefore never partake in healthy exercise activities.

I had the same doubts myself at first, but my reliable Awesome Man voice spoke up and reframed the situation: "What do you have to lose? Other people can make the commitment—so can you. If you give it solid effort, you may find you really enjoy it. Even if you try it and do not like it, you will be better off for the experience of learning something new." Well, I listened to my Awesome Man voice and attended the class. I am still not very good at Tai Chi, but I am learning and enjoying the physical activity. I even signed up for the next session.

Have you ever had that same negative, self-defeating voice inside your head, nagging you not to even try something new? If you do, step back for a minute and listen carefully to what's going on inside your head. Do you hear your Awesome Man voice? You may be trying to ignore it, but it's there also, insistently urging you to try and achieve and grow. Do not ignore that voice.

To get going, try to set a series of small intermediate steps on your path to your ultimate goals. Even if you fail, use the experience as a learning opportunity on how to do better. Was the goal set too high? Did you underestimate the effort required on your part? Remember, Rome was not built in a day, and most of the things you may have viewed as failures were actually just learning stages. Some people may say defeatism is not technically a fear, and they are probably right, but it inhibits so many young males from becoming Awesome Men that you need to be aware of it. Silence that "no hope/why bother trying?" voice in your head. It is not your friend.

Fear of Making a Real Effort (Laziness)

The Awesome Man is motivated and works hard. It takes time to fully develop these traits, but many young men, sadly, never even take the first few crucial steps in that direction because they do not want to make the necessary effort. They are satisfied with existing in their comfort zone. That zone's scope is limited, but at least it's comfortable enough and doesn't require much exertion.

But the hard truth is that to move forward in life, you must expend effort—a lot of it. You need to plan, prepare, and execute consistently and diligently to achieve your objectives in life and to grow as an Awesome Man. You are capable of more than you realize. Do not let laziness hold you back!

Fear of Losing Connection with Our Friends (Lack of Ambition)

Sometimes we do not do the right thing—even when we know it is what we should do, and it is what we want to do—for fear our friends and peers will not accept us anymore. We fear they will laugh at us or mock our achievements. Perhaps they will even unfriend us.

Here's an example: Let us say you and your good buddies are slackers when it comes to schoolwork. But you happen to very much enjoy one subject: science. You are intrigued by how the world works, and you enjoy how science provides answers. A school science fair is coming up, and you have a great idea for an exhibit. In fact, with some effort, you think you've got a chance at winning a prize.

But suddenly doubts creep into your mind. What will your friends think and say to you? Will they ridicule your efforts? Will they act as if you are rejecting their slacker standards? Will they be angry and jealous of your efforts and success?

As these questions flood your mind, I hope that you'll ask yourself one other, much more important question: "If my friends are going to act that way, are they really my friends?" Here's the answer: Real friends, the sort of friends you deserve, will support your positive efforts and achievements, not ridicule them. Be aware that in underachieving to please your friends, you are really not doing them any favors, because you are influencing them away from developing into Awesome Men themselves. By being the best you can be, you will be a positive model for them, and you will develop your skills as a leader.

Let's think about ambition a little bit. I have known many students and employees whose aspirations are to be average. Society calls them slackers. They think that any result that's better than average means they have been

Doing the Thing We Don't Want to Do Is Often the Thing We *Need* to Do

Let me tell you a story about a young man I know, Scott.

Scott attended a very exclusive private high school in our area. He always had an interest in sports, so he decided to join the high school football team. One afternoon the players, instead of a regular practice, were told they were going to be divided into groups and each group would be assigned to one of six local nursing homes. The young men would then interact with the residents, making cookies, conversing, playing cards, or reading to the seniors.

Scott thought this was a stupid idea; he had no interest in old people, especially ones who could not care for themselves. However, the coach explained that there would be many benefits to the team, and they would talk about it after they returned. Scott was absolutely sure he was going to hate this trip.

When the team returned to campus a few hours later it was as if a transformation had taken place. The young men were amazed how happy the residents were to have them as guests (some of the residents had not had visitors for years, and others had not spoken to teenagers in decades). The young men felt that the time they had spent was very meaningful to both the players and the residents. Scott was amazed by two things. First, he was surprised by how pleased the residents were to see him and how interested they were in him specifically. One elderly man in a wheelchair even spoke of his own high school football exploits. But the second and more profound effect on Scott was his realization about how good he felt about himself after visiting the seniors. He was not sure how or why he felt this way, but he couldn't ignore the feeling.

Initially, Scott did not feel like going to the retirement home. He saw no benefit for himself and felt he had nothing in common with the old people. He even contemplated skipping practice that day so he could do something more enjoyable. When it came to giving of himself for others, Scott was lazy. He did not care to see that being of service to others was also a great benefit for himself. Fortunately,

Scott listened to his Awesome Man voice and tried hard to follow the coaches' guidance and instructions. He made a genuine effort to listen and relate to the seniors. In hindsight he realized that his initial fear and laziness had nearly kept him from having a meaningful experience. He planned to visit the seniors again in the future.

Plenty of organizations in your own community would be thrilled to have you volunteer to help them: parks, community and recreational associations, food pantries and food banks, homeless shelters, Habitat for Humanity chapters, local libraries, animal rescue shelters, museums, political or environmental campaigns, the YMCA and similar groups, retirement homes, the Red Cross. Will you follow in Scott's footsteps and listen to the Awesome Man voice inside you?

working too hard. Now think for a minute and put yourself in the position of an employer or a school administrator. What kind of employees or students do you want? Whom are you going to devote your precious time and resources to? Whom will you nurture and support the most? Who is going to make your school or organization better or more successful? Who gets the letters of recommendations, the scholarships, the promotions, and the raises? The average guy? No way!

By aiming to be average, in terms of ambition and expectations, you are aiming to be last—and you will deservedly receive few benefits for your minimal efforts. Is your life to be based on getting participation ribbons? (Now there is nothing wrong with participation ribbons, if you gave your very best effort. But if you just slacked along, that is a problem.) The misguided average slacker seems to believe that he is born with a limited supply of effort to expend, and that by expending less effort during his lifetime he will receive some big prize at the end. On so many levels this is just wrong and dumb. Your personal capacity is near limitless. In fact, medical studies have shown that there is a positive correlation with effort expended on healthy physical activity and one's long-term physical well-being. Men who use their minds and mental capabilities are less likely to suffer from diseases of the brain as they age. Unmotivated, underperforming slackers live shorter lives, have more accidents, suffer more illnesses, and do not receive any of the benefits of being Awesome Men.

Fear of the Unknown (Lack of Vision)

Have you ever experienced a situation where you had an opportunity to do something but were fearful of what you were getting yourself into? Here's an illustration: Gabriel has an opportunity to begin an agricultural program on scholarship at a university in Minnesota. Gabriel grew up on a farm in a small, largely Hispanic California community. He doesn't like big cities, has never has been out of his own state, and has heard only bad things about the climate in Minnesota. To cement his scholarship opportunity, he has to raise his grades in a couple of subjects; if he fails to do this, he will lose out on the scholarship, without which his family cannot afford to send him to college. His father, who can barely read or write, does not see the value of higher-level education for a farmer. He told Gabriel that the price they sell a basket of strawberries for will not change if Gabriel has a university degree. Gabriel's high school guidance counselor, however, holds the opposite view. She says a scholarship for a college education is a wonderful opportunity and he should go for it. Gabriel is torn by ambition on one side and fear of the unknown on the other.

The best way to deal with fear of any type is to study it and understand it.

Have you ever been in a situation like Gabriel's? Maybe there was a certain class you wanted to take, but the professor was rumored to be a hard grader. Or perhaps you had a chance to take an internship at a local company that would give you great experience but also thrust you into a new situation with lots to learn and do. Did you go ahead and make the move? Or did your fear of the unknown hold you back? If the latter, don't fret. Everybody on earth has experienced a fear of the unknown at one time or another.

Very often, we do not go forward with good choices and great decisions because we do not know with certainty what the outcome will be. We focus on the risk. The easiest choice for Gabriel is to stay with his family working on the farm, avoid the cold winters in Minnesota, and forget about obtaining a university degree. Gabriel does not really know what impact accepting the scholarship will make in his life, and because of this he is leaning toward not going forward with the scholarship.

The best way to deal with fear of any type is to study it, understand it, and overcome it by controlling and minimizing the risk. We will never know the results of all our choices before we make them. But we know if we make good choices based on values, reason, and knowledge, dealing with the results will be manageable if things do not turn out as we had hoped. Fear should never stop you from doing the right thing.

Awesome Men are often referred to as fearless. But this is not exactly true; they have fears like every other human being. What separates them from non–Awesome Men is their ability to recognize, understand, and deal effectively with their fears. Fear is a natural part of life, a warning sign for recognizing risk. By managing the risk factors, the Awesome Man can achieve so much more for himself and society.

How the Awesome Man Deals with Fear

I have always been fascinated about how warriors and soldiers deal with fear, especially when failure can mean serious injury or death. Soldiers often don't have the luxury of dealing with their fears in the common ways most of us deal with them. They cannot run away from what they may fear, and often they don't have time to wait it out or think it over. Getting drunk or high and hiding are not practical alternatives either.

So how do they control and manage fear? And for that matter, how do risk-takers and high achievers in general move forward toward their objectives, regardless of their anxieties and fears? After some research, I discovered several key tactics they use, tactics that are directly applicable to your efforts to become an Awesome Man.

Prepare and Practice

The number one way warriors, as well as many other high-performance people, deal with fear is to practice and prepare. This could be drilling or rifle practice or intense training on piloting and ship navigation. They optimize the knowledge and skills they need to perform their tasks.

Boxers and Ultimate Fighting Championship fighters are famous for their dedication to practice and training. A boxer in a 12-round title fight will spend at most thirty-six minutes in actual combat with his opponent. However, you can be certain he will have been training eight hours daily for years to prepare for those crucial thirty-six minutes. Olympic athletes, too, will spend years of their lives preparing for their big moment at the games. For most of them, fear will simply not be a factor during their performance.

Examine your own life. Chances are the only times you were fearful and worried before an exam were when you knew you hadn't put in the effort to fully study and prepare for the test. Being prepared and practicing doesn't eliminate risk—you still might do poorly on the test—but it does *minimize* the risks. And more importantly, it reduces or even negates that nagging, energy-draining emotion of fear.

Let me give you a simplistic scenario to illustrate this idea of managing risk (and thus reducing fear). Let's say I'm on the upper level of an old building. I want to go down a long set of stairs to the lower level, but the stairwell is dark and I can't locate the light switch. The risk I face is that if I try to descend the stairs in the dark, I might misstep and fall, injuring myself. Quite understandably, my awareness of this risk is creating fear in my mind. But I also realize that because I'm alone in the building, I can't very well wait for someone to rescue me. I need to conquer my fear and go down the stairs myself, in the dark.

Here's where, even in this limited scenario, preparation comes into play. I make a plan to securely hold the handrail as I go down. I plan to descend slowly, placing one foot down gently and feeling for solid support, so I do not step on something that will cause me to fall. Then I'll do the same with the next foot and so on. After each step, I will listen carefully, just in case there's a particularly concerning creaking that might indicate weakened wood.

By carefully planning out my course of action, I find that my fears have mostly disappeared. I've dispelled the unknown by preparing in every way I can. Yes, there's still risk involved, but my careful planning has controlled the risk and brought calm focus to my mind.

Laugh in the Face of Fear

He laughs at fear and is not dismayed; and he does not turn back from the sword
—Job 39:22, *New American Standard Bible*

The Old Testament quotation above is usually interpreted to mean that Job was so brave that he had no fear. However, there's another interpretation that might be more accurate. We now know that one of the best ways of dealing with fear is to make fun of it. Gina Barreca, PhD, states:

> We can use humor to put our fears into perspective. Humor addresses the same issues as fear, not to dismiss them, but to strengthen our ability to confront them and then laugh them away from the door.
>
> Humor is, of course, the one thing that fear cannot abide: Laughter banishes anxiety, and can help replace fear. Laughter is a testament to courage, or at least a manifestation of the wish for it, and courage is stronger than fear. We need a strong and healthy dose of focused humor in our lives every day.[*]

Much the same way people laugh and scream on amusement park rides, think of times and places when you have used humor and laughter to calm your anxiety and steady your nerves. Laughter is like a magical potion of strength. Use it to banish your fear in risky situations.

Breathe, Deeply and Slowly

Next time you are watching athletes in a batter's box, or at the free throw line, or concentrating on an important move, observe them closely. What do they almost always do?

They stand still and take several slow, deep breaths. Breathing deeply for about five seconds will calm your nervous system, saturate your blood with fresh oxygen, and help you regain control of your natural physiological responses to fear. This puts your intellect back in control and mitigates your anxiety. It's just like using software to control the hardware in your computer. The programming is in charge of the machine, not vice versa—just as your mind is in control of your body.

This is a simple but very powerful tip. Use it!

Let It Out and Talk About It

Most of us keep our fears and anxieties bottled up inside us. We do not want anyone to know our fears because we have been taught that to be strong is to be silent. Wrong!

I want to let you in on a secret: Fear is a big scaredy-cat. It cannot handle being exposed and out in the open. Talking about your fears to a friend

---

[*] Gina Barreca, "Laughing at the Scary Stuff: Humor and Fear," Snow White Doesn't Live Here Anymore (blog), *Psychology Today*, April 1, 2013, https://www.psychologytoday.com/us/blog/snow-white-doesnt-live-here-anymore/201304/laughing-the-scary-stuff-humor-and-fear.

or mentor or confidant is a great way to confront those fears. Chances are you'll learn that once it's out in the open, your fear is not so debilitating. Other people have fears, and often together you can deal with them, both yours and theirs.

Keeping your fears bottled up will allow them to grow and fester, and they will soon paralyze your mind and prevent you from taking action. Get them out in the open, and like a vampire exposed to daylight, they will shrink and fade away.

That Stupid Voice in Your Head Needs to Be Told to Shut Up!

A little later on in the book, I am going to speak about a concept called negative self-talk. At this point in life you may have realized that there is a voice in your mind constantly spouting negative and derogatory phrases such as "You're a loser," "You can't win," "You will fail," "You're stupid," and so on. This voice can be called the voice of fear and failure.

But with a bit of practice, you can easily defeat that voice and shove it out of your mind. You do this by loudly drowning out that bad voice with phrases such as "I will succeed," "I am prepared and I will overcome," and "If one person can do it, so can I." Use positive self-talk to reframe your mentality by focusing on positive experiences and your past successes, rather than on possible setbacks. Call it your Awesome Man voice.

Meditate

As hard as it is to believe, the US military has introduced programs such as Warrior Mind Training, which provides meditation practices customized to meet the needs of the armed forces. This program offers new recruits and seasoned veterans alike the opportunity to benefit from a technique that has been shown to provide tremendous mental health benefits. When you think about it, the martial arts have for centuries used meditation and mind training as means to control fear and anxiety in combat.

Meditation really works, and if fear is part of your everyday life, it's something you should strongly consider. To learn more about meditation and how it can be an important part of your life, search on the web, at your library, or in a bookstore. A number of organizations in most communities provide meditation instruction as well. Even YouTube offers a number of meditation channels. Remember that meditation is not necessarily associated with any religions or cults, and you can tailor your meditative practices to your situation and lifestyle. It's worth a try because the benefits of a calmer, more focused mind are worth the effort.

Keep Pushing Your Boundaries

Intense efforts and emotional experiences are good for you. The more you have, the less anxiety and more confidence you will have. It is the old "get back in the saddle if you have fallen" theory. Setbacks, tough challenges, and adversity are the pathway to confidence and achievement. Just as you cannot forge great steel without lots of fire and hammering, so, too, you must forge your character with heat and effort. The exposure to and overcoming of the things you fear is profoundly empowering and a real emotional rush—better than any drug. Try it. Challenge yourself and see how you grow.

Concluding Thoughts on Fear

A big part of becoming an Awesome Man is dealing with fear. Nobody enjoys fear, but it's a part of life and can't be avoided. However, as this chapter has shown, it can be managed—quite effectively in fact. Use fear as a beacon to increase your own awareness of how your mind works. When you feel fear, analyze, study, and apply the tactics described in this chapter to master your fear and use it to your advantage. If you do this, more often than not you will realize that what you thought you feared is in reality irrelevant and inconsequential, just a bump on the road toward your Awesome Man life.

Awesome Man Profile: Dale Carnegie

I refer to Dale Carnegie several times in this book. Dale Carnegie, through his actions and achievements, was always striving to be an Awesome Man. And he had a particularly effective technique for dealing with fear. His famous maxim on what to do when confronted with a challenging decision or situation was "First ask yourself, what is the worst that can happen? Then prepare to accept it. Then proceed to improve on the worst."

In his writings, Carnegie states that many people are paralyzed into inaction because they choose to dwell on their fear of the worst possible outcome in a given situation. Carnegie's refreshing approach was to accept terrible outcomes before they happened, thereby coming to emotional terms with them and quashing fear. Once your fears and emotions are thereby subdued, you can make adjustments to make that worst-case outcome bearable. And if you keep thinking about and improving those plans and adjustments, there's a good chance you can turn the merely bearable into the positive. For example, every time a driver gets into his car to go somewhere, he risks death or grievous bodily injury. But by obeying the rules of the road, ensuring that the vehicle is in good mechanical condition, wearing a seat belt, and never driving impaired, he greatly reduces the risk of driving.

Carnegie's technique to control fear and uncertainty is somewhat advanced, and it's definitely not a "happy thoughts" approach. But it does help you rationally analyze and understand your fears and risks, work to moderate them, and point to a way to move forward.

This technique definitely paid huge dividends for Carnegie and his life. He was a prolific and accomplished public speaker and the author of *How to Win Friends and Influence People*, a book that propelled him to global fame. Carnegie confronted a great many challenges during his life and always accepted them with grace, vigor, and a can-do attitude.

Part Two:
Principles and Concepts

4

Attitude Is the Paintbrush That Colors Your World

Your problem isn't the problem, it's your attitude about the problem.

—Ann Brashares, novelist

You Can't Be an Awesome Man without an Awesome Attitude!

The chapter title is a phrase I learned as a young man from a very astute supervisor. Of course I did not quite understand what he meant so I asked him to explain. He said that how we see, perceive, and react to the world is based on our attitude and that attitude works like a paintbrush. If we perceive the world as dark, scary, and ominous, we have painted the world that way. If we see the world as light and sparkling, our brush (our attitude) is bright and sparkling. We get to choose what mindset we have about people, the world, and its issues. We can see situations as problems or opportunities, we can react to new people as threats or potentialities, and we can perceive setbacks as failures or learning stages.

I believe the most important aspect in becoming an Awesome Man is attitude. I do not mean in the sense of "He's got *attitude*." I do not mean someone who is contrary, or truculent, or adversarial. I mean attitude in terms of clear thinking and outlook. He has a good attitude.

As we grow in the broadest sense of the word from infancy, we are shaped by everything that we have experienced and by everything that we have inherited from our ancestors, both culturally and through our DNA.

We can have all the things society thinks are important—wealth, fame, good looks, athletic ability—yet still be empty and shallow human beings. Please remember that things like fame and fortune are not measures of awesomeness and will not necessarily lead to happiness. It is not the things we possess, but our attitude that determines the quality of our existence.

I was listening to ex-NFL quarterback Ryan Leaf being interviewed the other day. As a young man, Leaf was a bright, handsome, and gifted athlete. He believed the world was telling him he was very special—even exceptional. He felt entitled, was egocentric, and thought he had everything figured out when he received a full scholarship to Washington State to be the football team's quarterback. Leaf had a successful college career and earned All-American honors. In 1997, he, along with fellow quarterback Peyton Manning, was among the finalists for the Heisman Trophy.

Leaf and Manning entered the NFL draft together in 1998. Manning was drafted first by the Colts and Leaf second by the Chargers, who signed Leaf to a four-year contract worth $31.25 million, including a guaranteed $11.25 million signing bonus, the largest ever paid to a rookie at the time. The Colts picked Manning because there were rumors that Leaf may have exhibited signs of immaturity compared to Manning.

And here I've hinted at why you may never have heard of Ryan Leaf: He failed miserably at the professional level of the sport, flamed out of the league after four seasons, and is considered by many observers to have been the number one "draft bust" in NFL history. Leaf possessed all the physical skills—and then some—that you could hope for in a quarterback. What he lacked was a mature attitude and the willingness to learn and grow emotionally. He was not yet ready to behave like an Awesome Man, something that successful NFL quarterbacks, with all the leadership expectations their teams put upon them, generally do.

In the interview, Leaf admitted how he had sabotaged himself. His profound sense of entitlement due to his accomplishments on the football field had fostered an attitude that was completely focused on himself and his pleasures. It was selfishness.

This poor attitude conflicted with the lofty demands of professional football. Leaf exhibited poor emotional maturity and judgment; he was continually embroiled in conflicts with teammates, team management, fans, and the media; and he was constantly partying and abusing alcohol and drugs. He was the "can't fail" college prospect who did.

Out of football, Leaf continued his downward spiral, with no change in his personal attitude and no desire to learn and grow emotionally. His empty life included suicide attempts, arrest warrants in at least three states, and a seven-year jail sentence. Even in prison Leaf got into trouble because of his outlook and his attitude.

Finally, with the encouragement of his cellmate, he began teaching illiterate prisoners how to read. "I did it begrudgingly," Leaf says. "But I went and I went back the next day and the next day. Before I knew it I was sleeping better, I was talking to my family, I was more personable. The key was that I was being of service to another human being for the first time in my life." This marked a turning point in his life, and since that time Leaf has dedicated himself to the betterment of others, especially those suffering from addiction and substance abuse.

In a speech, Leaf explained what happened: "The only reason I'm still here standing in front of you is because I made a choice to change my life 180 degrees. This was going to have to be the foundation of what I did, or nothing would change. It had to be about other people. It couldn't be about me ever again."

It took a long time, but Leaf eventually became aware of his own attitudes and outlooks, most especially the selfish and destructive ones. Leaf's personal motto is "How are you being of service today? I defy you to be of service to another human being and not have the most peaceful night of sleep." He is now well along the path to being a better man.

We must all do what Leaf did, which is adjust our thinking to focus on being of service and value to others. The important thing is you do not have to be locked in a prison cell when you decide to be an Awesome Man. You can become that man right now.

Mindset

This is probably a good place to pause for a minute and talk about mindset. Mindset is a theory researched and further expanded by world-renowned Stanford University psychologist Carol Dweck during decades of study of achievement and success. She has written about the topic extensively in books such as *Mindset: The New Psychology of Success* (2007) and *Succeed: How We Can Reach Our Goals* (2010).

In her early research, Dr. Dweck noticed that some students rebounded while other students seemed devastated by even the smallest setbacks at school. After studying the behavior of thousands of children, Dr. Dweck coined the terms *fixed mindset* and *growth mindset* to describe the underlying beliefs people have about learning and intelligence. When students believe they can do better scholastically, they understand that *effort* makes them more successful in school. Therefore, they put in extra time and effort, and that leads to higher achievement.

Individuals with a fixed mindset believe their basic qualities, such as their intelligence or talent, are locked in from birth and unchangeable. They spend their time excusing themselves for their intelligence or talent instead of developing them. They also believe that talent alone creates success—*without effort.* These people often explain their behavior and actions with phrases such as "That is the way I am," "Why do you want me to change?", "I am sorry you do not like the way I am, but that is your

> **If you have a fixed mindset, you will never achieve the full measure of happiness and achievement you deserve.**

problem," "I cannot fulfill your expectations because that is just not me," and "I am just not good at that."

As you may have guessed, the theory of mindset is highly relevant to becoming an Awesome Man. If you have a fixed mindset—meaning you believe that the way you are now is the way you always will be and that the world and your abilities, feelings, attitudes, and outlooks are locked and fixed—you will never achieve the full measure of happiness, joy, and contentment you deserve. Just as Ryan Leaf finally developed a growth mindset and discovered that his life was going to be of value only by his being of service to others, each of us has to believe in and be open to personal growth, whichever direction that growth may lead in.

The fixed mindset causes us to give up after every setback and to come up with excuses such as "I can't do it," "I didn't want to do it in the first place," "See, I told you I was no good," "I always fail," and so on. When dealt setbacks, the Awesome Man, however, will likely use phrases such as "I need to prepare better," "I have to work on my curve more," "I better get some coaching help," "Let me look at the video to see what happened," and "I have to go in with a plan next time." Do you notice the difference between the two sets of phrases? The Awesome Man takes responsibility and responds to setbacks with an attitude of resilience and self-improvement.

People with a growth mindset know and believe that their most basic abilities can be developed further through dedication and hard work. This attitude creates a love of learning and a resilience that is essential for great accomplishment. Virtually all Awesome Men and all great people (and by great people I mean everybody from the volunteer at the homeless shelter and the man teaching English to newcomers to the past statesmen of our country) have had these qualities. I have yet to meet or learn of any person who has accomplished anything of any real significance without a growth mindset. Please remember that fame and fortune are not measures of awesomeness and will not necessarily lead to happiness for you.

You Can Change Your Mindset

If you've diagnosed yourself as having a fixed mindset, you might be thinking, "I have a fixed way of thinking. Does that mean I can never change? Does that prevent me from becoming an Awesome Man?" Read on! Good news awaits you.

The research results on mindset mesh well with our ever-increasing understanding of brain plasticity, which we discussed in chapter 2. We now know that the connectivity between neurons can change with experience. With intentional practice, neural networks can grow new connections, strengthen existing ones, and build insulation that speeds the transmission of neural impulses (thought). These neuroscientific discoveries have shown us that we can increase our neural growth by the actions we take, such as using good strategies, asking questions, practicing, and following good nutrition and sleep habits.

Researchers then saw the link between mindset and achievement. They learned that if you believe your brain can grow, you will behave differently. As well, they learned that we can indeed *change our mindset from fixed to growth*, and when we do, we can increase motivation and achievement. In other words, it's not your brain that needs fixing—it's your attitude.

In the practical application of this knowledge to becoming an Awesome Man, keep the following in mind:

a. Believe you can grow your brain and behave better and more effectively.

b. You will have to work at it and it will take effort.

c. The results will be far greater for you than you thought possible.

The way you are in terms of intelligence, talent, and achievement is not locked in. You can make significant improvements in those abilities and reap the benefits. It all depends on your mindset, which you control.

You Can't Get Better without a Better Mindset

As humans, we have a tendency to make generalizations and assumptions about situations and people based on our historical experiences. If the last time I went to the library I was asked to leave for being too noisy, I may assume that the librarian does not like me and will ask me to leave again if I go back. This is an unwarranted assumption on my part. It could well be the case that the librarian is a welcoming person and would be delighted to see me come back (assuming I behave myself!).

As you see these generalizations and assumptions lead us to create stereotypes about situations and people (including ourselves). The benefit to having these generalizations and assumptions is that they reduce the load on our mind because we do not have to learn and relearn things. For example, when walking across a cow pasture a second time, you remember from the first time that you have to watch where you are walking to avoid stepping in cow droppings.

However, a danger lurks within the mind's reliance on "shortcuts" based on prior knowledge or experience. These shortcuts can sometimes lead us to conclusions that are not necessarily valid in a given circumstance. Here's an example:

Let's say that in grades nine and ten you struggled in your math classes. There's a good chance that you will begin grade eleven with the belief that you will not be successful in math yet again. This belief is based solely on your recent past experiences. But is it even accurate?

What if you took a step back, analyzed what happened in grades nine and ten, and came to the realization that

- your poor grades were the result of not paying enough attention in class,

- your poor grades were the result of not putting your full attention and energy into your homework and other assignments, and

- you never made the effort to ask for help, even though the teacher made a frequent point of offering it.

- Here's where the growth mindset can do wonders for you. What if you began grade eleven's math class with the following mindset?

- I'm going to keep a positive attitude toward mathematics and try to do the best I can.

- I will pay attention in class.

- I will do my homework and assignments to the best of my ability.

- I will ask for help when I have difficulty with any aspect of the class.

If you changed your mindset in this way, you'd almost certainly experience much better results. Failure or success in your endeavors is almost always the result of your own attitude, which drives your effort and determination.

Fear, Scarcity, and Reframing Failure

"Hurry, while supplies last." "You need to protect your family." "They will bankrupt the system." "We have to protect ourselves from this threat." "Time is running out."

How many times in your life have you heard marketers and politicians use phrases similar to the ones above, expressing sentiments such as these to play upon our deep concerns about fear and scarcity? And listen closely to the people around you. How often do they express opinions or take actions based on fear and scarcity? How often have *you* done the same?

In chapter 3 I discussed fear, but here I want to delve into how fear intersects with the concepts of attitude and mindset. If our attitude is based on fear and scarcity, everything we do will be negative. Our proverbial paintbrush will be filled with black paint. On the other hand, if our mindset is bright and sparkling, our world will be filled with assurance, calmness, faith, happiness, joy, and trust. Here we are painting a world filled with glorious color, full of possibility.

If you exhibit a positive attitude, you'll find that some people will be irked by your confident, enthusiastic mindset. Such people love to comment about how the world is full of hate, cruelty, insufficiency, and abuse. And I agree—many bad things do exist in our world. But there are also many great and wonderful things in our world, such as beauty, sufficiency, love, and kindness. The world is also full of great people striving to make it a better place.

The Awesome Man understands and accepts that failure is a step in the learning process.

The Awesome Man chooses to face the world with a mindset that all good things are possible. He goes forward with a positive attitude and a growth mindset. But he is in no way dismissive of pain or unfairness or misfortune, whether it be his or another's. The Awesome Man understands, for example, that crying is a natural and healthy human response to pain and suffering. And he knows that big men do cry, and it is appropriate to cry when terrible things happen. Throughout our life, we will cry again and again, and that is a good thing too.

Most importantly, the Awesome Man understands that fear is a natural by-product of being alive. He accepts that and does not fight this basic aspect of existence. But he does not succumb to his fears. He sees how so many of us fear failure as much as or even more than death. The Awesome Man understands and accepts that failure is a step in the learning process. Rather than a judgment or an evaluation of ourselves, failure is the cornerstone of future success. He does not fear failure, because he knows that without failure, real success is unlikely.

Let me give you an example. I took clarinet lessons when I was in eighth grade. I thought I was a pretty decent musician, so with the support and encouragement of my music teacher I entered the local Kiwanis music festival. There were about six or seven other contestants besides me, but I was quite confident in my ability. I did my best, but as I listened to the other contestants play their instruments, I became much less confident about my chances of winning. When the adjudicator handed out the results, I came in last with a score of 75%.

I was crushed! As I stood at the bus stop waiting to go home, I cried my eyes out. I was hurt, angry, disappointed, frustrated, bitter, embarrassed, and humiliated (some of my peers from our local band had competed and surpassed me). As I slumped back to my classroom the next day, my teacher asked me how I did. I replied "Not very good" and showed her the adjudicator's report. Her reply was surprising and enlightening: "Wow! You got 75%! That is a good mark. Way to go, Dennis."

Instantly I learned that failure is a matter of perspective. What I perceived to be a great failure, my classroom teacher saw as a great success. From her perspective, I was a boy who was learning a musical instrument, the only one in class doing so. I had stepped up and been willing to compete and be evaluated by an impartial judge, and I got a decent score, even though I didn't win. I never did turn into a great clarinetist, but I stuck with it, and musical performance has continued to be part of my life to this very day.

I absorbed important lessons from this event. I learned that to have enjoyment, satisfaction, and pleasure from any endeavor, you do not have to be better than others. What you have to do is

- try (overcome your initial fears about trying something new),

- learn from your mistakes (failure is part of life; don't fear it, accept it, and use it to grow),

- try again (and again and again),

- expend effort to be the best you can be (be resilient), and

- never consider failure as a label but as a step in learning and growing (have a great attitude).

My teacher, Mrs. Soulliere, had the wisdom to understand that failure was only relevant as a stepping- stone for learning, and I thank her for that. Her attitude about me points to the importance of how we evaluate others. We must accept that at times we all are emotionally fragile beings.

Therefore, it is so important that those of us who evaluate others (parents, teachers, coaches, mentors, supervisors, etc.) act in a positive way. This includes *you*, perhaps in how you engage with younger siblings or classmates who are experiencing fear about their grades or trying something new.

Too often we crush the people around us by emphasizing their weaknesses and inadequacies rather than recognizing and encouraging effort and success. It is so very important that we support everybody we can in their path through life.

When I think about this subject, Theodore Roosevelt's great quote comes to mind:

> It is not the critic who counts; not the man who points out how the strong man stumbles, or where the doer of deeds could have done them better. The credit belongs to the man who is actually in the arena, whose face is marred by dust and sweat and blood; who strives valiantly; who errs, who comes short again and again, because there is no effort without error and shortcoming; but who does actually strive to do the deeds; who knows great enthusiasms, the great devotions; who spends himself in a worthy cause; who at the best knows in the end the triumph of high achievement, and who at the worst, if he fails, at least fails while daring greatly, so that his place shall never be with those cold and timid souls who neither know victory nor defeat.

A Deeper Look: Being the Best Version of Yourself

Each of us should try to foster attitudes that are positive, developmental, externalized, and forward thinking. By externalized, I mean our attitude should be open to life, people, and the world. We should not swagger or act as if we are above others.

Most of us have developed our attitudes, outlooks on life, or perspectives based on our past learning and experience. If you grew up in a wealthy family, your view of life is likely much different from that of someone who grew up extremely poor. It is ludicrous for me to tell someone who lives in poverty that he should smile and be happy and that everything will be wonderful. That's BS. Difficult and challenging life experiences often lead us to adapt and evolve in ways that other parts of society might find puzzling or inappropriate.

Let us say that so far life has not dealt you a very good hand. However, you still possess an intellect that allows you to make choices, just like anybody else on earth. The most important choice you have to make is what your attitude, or mindset, is going to be. Because that choice will affect every other choice you make from this point on. If your attitude is "I'm bad-ass, and I don't give a f*ck about anything or anybody," you, unfortunately, will never develop into an Awesome Man. But since you're reading this book, I don't believe you're that sort of person.

When it comes to mindset, the important thing is to not accept your status quo. Many of us believe that we have to be "ourselves." However, if being your "authentic" self means you do not strive to be an Awesome Man, do not grow, and do not develop a growth mindset, then being yourself means you are satisfied with being a mere shell of the person you can really be. When you really think about it, what you are now—the current version of *you*—is really what you were *yesterday* and the days before. But what comes today and tomorrow could be different and awesome. The only thing holding you back is your attitude.

I get flak from some readers when they think I say they should not be themselves. What I am really saying is that we should be the *best possible versions* of ourselves. For example, if I am having a bunch of friends over for a BBQ but have been drinking all day without moderation, when I begin to grill there is an excellent chance that something will go wrong. I will overcook something, undercook something else, drop something on the patio, say something stupid, and (based on past experience) quite likely burn myself. I am being myself, but it is an intoxicated version of myself and truly far away from the best version of myself as a chef and host.

It is important to realize that a negative attitude about life in general is very easy to develop and maintain, as it involves little in the way of intellectual effort. Remember the old saying: "To eliminate darkness you only have to light one candle." You have to learn to light that candle in yourself. In your attitude self-analysis, try to uncover any underlying fears or false impediments that may be present. Look at your life. Is there darkness and its companions, hopelessness and futility? If the answer is yes, study and analyze them. Once you understand them, it will become much easier to, in time, discard these negative feelings and attitudes. Striving to be the best version of yourself is a virtuous task, so why would you settle for anything less? Why not go ahead and light a candle in your life right now? Give your life meaning and value and you will be on the path to being an Awesome Man.

Here is a small list of "candles" you can light right now:

- Call or contact someone you care about and tell them that they are important in your life.

- Call or contact someone you have hurt, apologize, and ask for forgiveness.

- Shower and shave; wear clean clothes.

- Do the laundry.

- Clean your room; pick up garbage in the yard; clean up some graffiti.

Words the Awesome Man Does Not Use

Words matter very much, in both what words we say and how we say them. The way we speak communicates a great deal about our mindset and attitude. What is truly miraculous is that the words we use also can subtly change how our mind formulates our mindset. If we speak defeatist and negative words, we will nurture a defeatist and negative fixed mindset. However, if we speak words of hope and confidence, our attitude will become hopeful and confident, and we will develop a growth mindset.

Look at the people around you. Listen to genuinely happy people; they do not use or express negative words, language, or thoughts. They know that to achieve happiness, they need to use the right language to foster the right attitude.

Here are some phrases to avoid using:

"I'm no good at . . ."

This common phrase is so debilitating. Here you are stating—even before you have attempted a task—that you are not competent. Usually this statement is based on previous negative experiences (failures) and can prime you for failure again. Stop this and instead say, "I can learn to be better!"

"I just . . ."

This is usually the beginning of an excuse justifying poor or inappropriate behavior. Do not behave poorly or inappropriately. Never start a sentence with "I just."

"I don't like to . . . I don't want to . . . I don't feel like it . . ."

People use these phrases when they want to justify laziness or selfishness or fear. Avoid them like the plague.

"I can't . . ."

Always replace "I can't" with "I haven't yet." You do not know what you can do until you have been taught, learned, or tried with genuine effort. You'll find that there aren't that many things that you truly cannot do if you put in the effort.

"I don't get it . . ."

You were not paying attention when it was discussed, did not bother to prepare, or made minimal effort to figure it out yourself. You must ask for clarification.

"It is hard . . ."

Of course it is. If it was easy, anybody could do it. No matter what your goal, if it is worthwhile and meaningful, it will be hard, challenging, and difficult. However, with effort, action, and determination you will achieve your goal.

Filler words and obscenities

I am amazed how often celebrities and personalities appear in the media and begin speaking, yet they make little or no sense at all. The reason is their speech is filled with meaningless sounds. Example:

> Interviewer: "George, great game today. How does it feel to be going to the finals for the first time in your career?"
>
> George: "Well, like, umm, it's really, really great. You know we showed those rubes from Ruleville. Like I said, man, that is so bad! We really gave them the beating they deserved. Okay, so in the next series, we are going to do what we have to do, really. I mean totally, you know what I mean?"
>
> Interviewer: "Thanks."
>
> George: "Anytime."

Don't be like George. Show some class. Be awesome, not subpar.

Words the Awesome Man Should Use

Please understand that just because you use positive words, the world is not going to turn all sweet and wonderful. But when you are dealing with the challenges and burdens the world presents you, your positive attitude will make those tasks much more achievable. Use words that reflect that attitude.

"Yes."

One of the first words we hear as a child is no. It is the beginning of negativity in our world. That is why yes is so powerful. The Awesome Man uses yes as often as he can: "Yes, I will help you," "Yes, I can do that," "Yes, I will make that better for you," "Yes, I will be there," and so on.

"I care."

The Awesome Man knows that telling others that he cares about them is powerful. More than just words, "I care" implies that he backs them up with actions. He knows that actions speak louder than words and his deeds prove he cares.

"I am sorry."

You may be surprised to see this phrase in the list, but its use signifies a positive attitude. To make a mistake or an error is human, and sometimes others get hurt by what we do. The Awesome Man knows that when he stumbles in striving for his goals, he has to acknowledge the pain he and others may have caused or experienced.

"I am responsible."

These are probably the most powerful words the Awesome Man utilizes. He states he is the one to take charge, show leadership, and fulfill his duties and the roles expected of him. He is dependable, conscientious, and in all cases accountable.

"It will not happen again."

The Awesome Man is aware that sometimes things do not work out as planned. He studies what went wrong and makes the required changes so it will not recur.

"If someone else can do it, so can I."

Often we come across tasks that we are really not sure we can accomplish. We may be overwhelmed by them and start to doubt ourselves. In these cases, the Awesome Man asks himself, "Has somebody else done what I am contemplating? If somebody else has, then with the proper preparation and effort so can I."

"I have a question."

How often have you sat in a classroom or a lecture and not understood some idea or concept that was presented? The lecturer asks if there are any questions, and nobody raises a hand. Afterward, many in the audience will speak to one another about the things they did not understand, having missed the opportunity to ask the lecturer directly in the classroom.

Ask thoughtful and meaningful questions whenever something is not clear or when you wish to clarify your understanding.

"Thank you."

Be grateful and gracious and show appreciation for every little kindness and blessing you receive. Acknowledge the generosity of others and tell them you recognize their efforts. This is especially important to those who are closest to you.

"He who never undertook anything never achieved anything."

This fourteenth-century French proverb summarizes a basic conviction of the Awesome Man: Without starting out and without effort, nothing of value or importance is ever achieved.

A Deeper Look: Words Matter

We have all heard the expression "If it looks like a duck, swims like a duck, and quacks like a duck, then it probably is a duck." In this chapter, I focused on "quacks like a duck." The words we use in language affect us and those who hear them. By using unwarranted, counterproductive, and negative words and phrases, we actually and very specifically damage ourselves and others. Rather than lighting candles, we are blowing them out.

Listen to your own speech patterns and see if the things you say are hurting you or those around you. Remember, just because something is true is never justification to hurt, offend, or damage anyone. Why? Because when we injure others we are also injuring ourselves. Words express attitudes, and attitudes have impact on life. Using the right words results in the right outcomes.

Is your world filled with negative words, phrases, and attitudes? If so, please install a mental "firewall" to filter and block all the negativity that may pervade your life. Understand that by using negative and closed language, you cloud and obscure your true potential and ability to be all that you can be. If you adjust your speech pattern and phraseology to reflect a mindset of growth and development, you have a great chance to make a positive impact on your life and the lives of others and will proceed at a faster pace down the path to becoming an Awesome Man.

Awesome Man Profile: Can You Name This Man?

I've listed below some facts about an Awesome Man that you are probably very familiar with. See if you can guess who he is before you reach the end.

- He was born in Beirut in 1964 to an English mother and a Chinese-American father.

- His father abandoned the family when he was three.

- His father ended up in prison as a heroin dealer.

- He moved with his mother from Beirut to Sydney, Australia, then to New York City, and finally to Toronto. His early life was quite unsettled.

- He attended four different high schools in four years, was expelled once, and never graduated. His educational challenges may have been partially due to his dyslexia.

- He did have a talent for acting, first performing at the age of nine. At seventeen he moved to Hollywood.

- He had success as an actor, but his personal life was filled with tragedy. His sister developed leukemia, and his girlfriend died in a car accident. He lost his best friend, River Phoenix, who died at twenty-three from a drug overdose.

- The characters he plays are not evil so much as they were hardened by evil. Mostly, they're destined to save the world.

- His fans believe that he is the "the most wholesome person alive" and that he should have been the *Time* magazine Man of The Year.

- He has been extremely successful financially but is known for his kindness and humility, and he is a very generous (and anonymous) philanthropist.

If you knew this was the bio of Keanu Reeves, you might know that in the thirty years he has been an actor and celebrity he has avoided the usual pitfalls associated with fame, money, and success. He has worked very hard, overcome adversity, and avoided the lure of decadence, all the while being aware of and helping others.

5

Effort

The "Luckiest" People Are Actually the Hardest Workers

Have you ever heard someone say things like the following about another person's achievements?

- "He is lucky to be able to do that."
- "He was lucky to come in first."
- "He has all the luck."

Have you ever said such things yourself? I know I have, from time to time in moments of weakness. But is it true that some people are just luckier than others? I don't believe so. In fact, I have yet to discover anybody who ever achieved anything of significance and worth who did not work hard and persevere through numerous challenging periods in their lives.

Tommy Emmanuel, one of the great guitarists of our time, was once approached after a concert by a young man who stated he wanted to play the guitar as well as Tommy did. He asked Tommy for some guidance. Tommy inquired if he practiced much, to which the young man replied, "Yes, an hour a day most days." Tommy informed that young man that he practiced *eight hours*, every day. Tommy knew that amount of effort was required for him to achieve and maintain the level of skill he now had.

Sometimes we want to be great without putting in enough effort. The Awesome Man knows that approach will *never* work out. There is simply no substitute for earnest, consistent time and effort. There are no shortcuts or hacks to cheat your way to the top.

It does not matter how positive or appropriate your attitude is: Unless you invest significant effort into reaching your objective, you will not be happy with the outcome. That effort may be in the form of preparation, energy expended, learning and study, physical struggle, or a combination of these and more. Rarely in life do good things happen by just waiting. We all have heard the expression "Just don't stand there. Do something!"—and it makes perfect sense. Without effort, the Awesome Man cannot exist. Why? Because if effort was not required in life, then every male would be an Awesome Man. And we know that's certainly not the case.

> **"I am a great believer in luck, and I find the harder I work the more I have of it."—Stephen Leacock, author, professor, and humorist**

Have you ever been in a situation where an instructor was supposed to teach or demonstrate something to you, and you got the distinct impression he was just going through the motions? He wasn't putting in the effort and wasn't particularly interested in truly assisting you. Did you feel like you were being treated as if you were not a human being of worth but just an annoying interruption that the so-called instructor had to put up with?

This not uncommon situation is the result of a person not making an effort to be the best he can be. And it's not just you, on the receiving end of this shabby treatment, who is frustrated. The really sad thing is that this individual is not receiving any satisfaction in his life either, all because of his pathetic lack of effort. When you do as little as possible, in any endeavor, you are not only depriving everybody who comes in contact with you of any satisfaction, you are also depriving yourself of any satisfaction that might be gained from doing a first-rate job. Effort yields happiness.

Let us imagine you are a dentist repairing a cavity. If you do not do your best, use the right amount of freezing, remove all the decay, make sure the filling is smooth, and clean all your instruments, your patient will likely

The Sin of Sloth

If you have ever seen the film *Se7en*, starring Morgan Freeman, Brad Pitt, and Kevin Spacey, you will know about the Seven Deadly Sins. Just to refresh your memory, they are

- sloth
- lust
- gluttony
- greed
- wrath
- envy
- pride

Christians believe that all vices and therefore all sins originate from these seven. The one I want to address is sloth, which is the opposite of effort.

The French theologian Réginald Garrigou-Lagrange noted that sloth is "a disposition by which one refuses effort, wishes to avoid all trouble, and seeks a *dolce far niente* [i.e., carefree idleness]." I concur that sloth encompasses far more than just laziness and lack of effort; it also encompasses mental lethargy and apathy.

Some slothful, misguided individuals even cultivate a "don't give a damn" attitude, falsely believing this will help inoculate themselves from the problems and disappointments of life.

Wise individuals understand and recognize that sloth in all its permutations destroys the individual on many levels. In her books *Vainglory: The Forgotten Vice* and *Glittering Vices: A New Look at the Seven Deadly Sins and Their Remedies*, Rebecca Konyndyk DeYoung describes how sloth prevents us from fully engaging in relationships of love and sacrifice with other people. This is tragic because it is only in these sorts of relationships that we can find deep fulfillment. Being slothful in any of its forms, besides leading to frustration and despair, denies you any chance at becoming an Awesome Man.

suffer from discomfort, pain, and misery. You will not be proud of what you have done. No matter what excuses you come up with, you would know inside that your shoddy work was a direct consequence of your poor effort. And there never is a defense for poor effort.

So often we hear in the news of some disaster where the root cause comes down to somebody not doing what they were supposed do at the right level of effort. Examples are the Chernobyl nuclear (1986) meltdown and the sinking of the Italian cruise ship *Costa Concordia* (2012).

You always reap the benefits of a great effort, chief among them being a fulfilling sense of satisfaction.

It even happens in sports. In 2019, Australian tennis pro Bernard Tomic was fined his full Wimbledon prize money for not meeting the "required professional standard" during his lackluster fifty-eight-minute first-round defeat by Jo-Wilfried Tsonga. Tomic was assessed a $56,000 penalty for his limp performance, the shortest men's match at Wimbledon since 2004. Specifically, officials penalized him for a lack of effort and professionalism after failing to chase down balls and appearing indifferent to the result. In his post-match press conference following the defeat, Tomic looked like he'd rather be anywhere but there. Slouched in his chair, avoiding eye contact, and rubbing his face with his hands, Tomic was asked if he thought he might be fined. Tomic's response: "What for?"

When humans do less than their best, everybody suffers. Sometimes we can escape the results of poor effort on our part, but that is rare. However, you *always* reap the benefits of a great effort, chief among them being a fulfilling sense of satisfaction.

Even the famous members of the rock band the Rolling Stones expressed frustration in their hit song "(I Can't Get No) Satisfaction" about how they couldn't get any satisfaction. Well, let us see what the singer of the song was doing that resulted in getting no satisfaction.

The lyrics claim the young man is driving his car, listening to the radio, and later he is watching television. He seems to be conscious of the incessant commercials, but never mentions the content of the actual programs he is listening to. He also laments about his poor experiences with women. One female gives no reaction, and another dismisses him to maybe come back next week. At the time the song was released in 1965 (I was 16 then), everyone believed the song was about a lack of sexual satisfaction and the resultant frustration. Many radio stations would not play it for that reason. On the other hand, one wonders what kind of a woman would be interested in a guy who, based on the description in the song, didn't have much of value going on in his life.

Driving around, watching TV, smoking, and trying to pick up girls are not tasks that involve any effort so it is not surprising they do not provide long-term satisfaction or happiness.

By the way, in their prime the Rolling Stones would spend four to six hours a day for two or three months rehearsing together before they went on their tours. Despite the lyrics in their song, they know you cannot be good without effort. The tremendous energy and enthusiasm they have for their craft is the very antithesis of slothfulness.

In my life I have been fortunate to meet world-renowned inventors, authors, athletes, and race car drivers. I also have met a great many other outstanding individuals who, though they have not received world acclaim, have achieved a level of happiness and contentment that we all wish for. One common characteristic that these Awesome Men have is the effort they put into their activities and lives.

Whatever they do, from the least important task in their daily lives to truly world-shaking activities, they do it with a level of effort, attitude, and commitment that is truly inspiring. These people rarely avoid the task at hand or shirk responsibility and duty. They tackle life with gusto and vigor, and they always expend the effort required for the successful completion of any task, assignment, request, or obligation.

No Effort = No Reward

Sadly, I also meet some young men who believe that the ideal way to live life is with the least amount of effort possible. Somehow they believe that all the effort (aka dedication and work) they do not expend performing useful tasks will somehow be stored up for them and they can cash it in for some type of reward in the future. That is if they actually think about the future.

A Deeper Look: With Effort, Everything Is Possible

From time to time, I meet sad and frustrated young men who have experienced a setback, some sort of disappointing result or outcome from their endeavors. It may be a failed exam, a defeat at an athletic event, a lost sale, a demotion at work, or, worse, a suspension, expulsion, or termination. The young man is usually upset and angry and often feels he has been treated unfairly. Have you ever had this experience yourself? I know I have.

All I can say to you is **do not be upset by the results you did not get, from the work you did not do.**

Perhaps that sounds harsh, but hear me out. I would venture to say that 90% of the setbacks in our lives have been the result of poor or insufficient effort on our part. Too often we have a goal or an objective, but we do not calculate the true amount of effort we need to expend to reach that goal. Instead, we tend to set our effort level first—which is often too low to achieve our objective—and then hope it will be enough to reach our goal. This is a backward approach, as anyone who's a real pro at goal-setting will tell you.

Let me give you a personal example. If I am tasked to write an opinion column for my local newspaper, my real goal is to write a really good column. I do not say to myself, "I am going to do this writing assignment in two hours and then move on to something else." Nor do I say, "When I hit five hundred words I am going to stop." Rather, I set out with the goal of writing an excellent column to the best of my ability, regardless of how long it takes and how many rewrites and edits I have to do. I *will* expend the effort necessary to reach my goal. You see, I've learned the hard way (which, by the way, is how most of us learn!) that by taking the approach that you will do all that is required to reach your objective, your chances of success increase exponentially.

This same "all-in" approach applies to your life. Let's assume you are in school and have a test coming up. What guarantees you a better chance of success: studying for a predetermined limited period and then calling it quits, or studying until you are fully prepared and confident you will achieve an excellent result? I think you will see the answer is obvious. Your level of effort must match what is required to accomplish your goal.

Now perhaps it's the case that you feel you have put in the right amount of effort to succeed but have still been frequently disappointed by poor outcomes. Perhaps you may have become apathetic (remember the definition of sloth) and feel that it is no use. Perhaps you feel that no matter your effort, it won't make any difference.

If you're in this position, I'll give you some insight into how to overcome that slump. One of the virtues of the Awesome Man is honesty, especially about himself and his behaviors. He will carefully examine and contrast his own efforts against those of his peers who are succeeding, and he will ruthlessly analyze his shortcomings, because he knows the problem lies within himself and only he can provide the solution. He knows that the only way out of his current quagmire is to be painfully honest about where he is falling short and then make the needed adjustments.

So far in this book, we have read several examples of individuals, many not much different from you, who worked harder than you might believe is possible to achieve their goals. They are the proof that reaching goals and aspirations is mostly a function of effort and dedication. So the next time you achieve a goal, no matter how small, reflect for a minute about the effort you gave and how that effort made the goal a reality.

The reality is that without effort there can be no satisfaction and happiness in life; that is the wisdom I am trying to share with you now. By effort I do not necessarily mean drudgery and heavy physical exertion, though that may be required. The Awesome Man always works smart, and he always is working toward his goal.

Many young men eventually work out of their "slump" and start putting in the time and effort required to build a good life. Unfortunately, some underachievers become complacent and accept the "fact" that they are not going to achieve much. They come to believe that what little they have achieved so far is totally acceptable and adequate. They are quite comfortable with their lack of accomplishment and see no downside to this attitude (there is that word again). When questioned about their lack of achievement, they often behave in a passive-aggressive manner.[*]

This lack of effort sometimes is linked to the fears of failure or defeatism, articulated with the belief that "No matter how hard I work or how much effort I expend, it does not make any difference in the results." Such young men may also be of the opinion that the effort required to progress in life is not rewarded adequately. Sadly, they cannot see that the effort they are expending currently is far less than what is really required to achieve anything of value. They often refuse to learn and grow as individuals, and in fact their outlook and attitude appear locked into a youthful time trap. Many males who inhibit the mythical world of Guyland still enjoy doing the things a fifteen-year-old would, such as playing video games, "chilling out," and "hanging with buds." They have no goals. They have no strategy for their lives. The only plans they have usually revolve around the next meal, game, holiday, or movie. When a friend confronts him with this reality, the young man often accuses the friend of trying to control his life.

> A young man should strive to be the best version of himself. He should strive to become an Awesome Man.

The problem is that this underachieving male is highly unlikely to make any changes to his life because he has become quite comfortable with the status quo and does not see any need to change his attitude and behavior. He has become quite skilled at telling anybody who will listen that he has the right attitude regarding life and can prove it to you. He sees himself as somewhat of an expert on human behavior, and he is adept at pointing out other people's shortfalls, especially their unwillingness to do the right things. Finally, this individual often has an inflated image of himself. He cannot see or evaluate himself objectively. He has a certain level of charm

---

[*] Passive-aggressive behaviors involve acting with indirect aggressive rather than with direct aggression. Passive-aggressive people repeatedly exhibit resistance to requests or demands from family and other individuals, often by procrastinating, expressing sullenness, or acting stubborn.

The Solution for Homelessness? More Awesome Men

An extreme example of people who show defeatism or lack of effort could be the homeless men who populate our cities. What has caused these once active, healthy, and vibrant young boys to self-exile themselves from society?

We know about 90% have mental health issues. If they have been diagnosed and prescribed medication, they often do not take the medication because "they do not like what it does to them." Many self-medicate with alcohol and street drugs instead.

Examined closely, most homeless people usually ended up on the streets because of a number of tragic circumstances that occurred in their lives. Their mental health issues may be the result of a myriad of causes such as post-traumatic stress disorder (PTSD), criminal behavior, or sexual abuse. But not dealing effectively with these issues compounds their difficulties.

Often they have not had a support system to help them in their hour of need. Their reliance on inappropriate coping strategies such as drugs, alcohol, and crime continues the downward spiral in their lives. Because of their lifestyle and lack of proper food, clothing, and housing, they become susceptible to further medical issues that rob them of a quality life.

Some anecdotal research points out that for addicts and the mentally ill, the most important factor in recovery and reintegration into society is personal engagement with caring individuals, such as mentors, counselors, and life coaches. Surprising as it sounds, people who have appeared to reject human and personal interaction are the ones who need it the most to get healthy again. This points to the need and value of the Awesome Man acting outwardly in the community with care and concern for others. This is exactly what Ryan Leaf discovered.

and charisma and feels that he gets along with most people, therefore, in his mind, he is average and okay. What he refuses to do is look at all the talents and abilities he has, and that lack of self-analysis combined with his lack of effort in striving to achieve worthwhile things results in emptiness in his life.

It can be difficult to help a young man to see the value and reward of effort and work, especially if years have gone by. In fact, he may feel quite

> **The Awesome Man knows with effort he can achieve things in his life that others will not. Without effort, nothing of value can be gained.**

defensive about his choices; in his mind, were he to admit he needs to change, he would be repudiating all the choices and decisions he has made in the past. Nobody wants regrets. The first problem is that the young man quite probably *really does believe* he is expending effort, has a growth mindset, displays resilience, is constantly learning and growing, and is achieving worthwhile goals. Second, he really feels the only failures he has experienced have been things outside his control. Third, he may be working or going to school, does not do drugs, and is not in jail, so in his own judgment he is doing okay. By some standards that is true. There may even be some apologists among his friends and family who say, "He's okay. Not everyone has to be an overachiever."

My response to all of this is that a young man should strive to be the best version of himself. He should strive to become an Awesome Man. Otherwise, he will not receive all the happiness, joy, and contentment he so richly deserves. And he will not be the very best he can be in terms of being of service to others.

Ordinary men can be heroic. Ordinary men can be awesome. They just need to adhere to the Awesome Man Formula:

Awesomeness = Determination + Effort + Perseverance + A Bit of Luck (the harder you work, the "luckier" you are)

Role Models and Heroes

What can help a young man stuck in an underachieving rut, this fixed mindset, break out and see the world of possibilities before him? Heroes or role models can help. I sometimes ask young men who their hero is. Chances are their hero will be an athlete or a celebrity who had a number of successes and achievements in his life. If they have researched their hero's background, they will have learned that the hero had to work hard to achieve his success and likely had difficult challenges and obstacles to overcome.

I find that many young men are astonished to discover how many hours and years of preparation and effort their hero required to achieve his success. The all-stars in any endeavor practice daily, constantly honing and expanding their skill sets. Amazingly, most males who have far fewer talents and abilities do not actively grow and develop their own skills through practice and learning. Once they reach a certain level of competence, regardless of the field of endeavor, they coast. No matter what endeavor I considered, I found that the individuals who were the poorest performers and who were the most likely to benefit from more learning, practice, and effort were the very ones least likely to do so. In school, most students who want to raise their grade from a B to an A have to increase their effort level greatly. On the other hand, to go from a D to a C requires proportionally less effort and is sometimes just a matter of handing the work in on time. The reality is that the student currently with a D who will benefit greatly from a grade improvement often does not do what is required.

Let me briefly relate the story of Rudy Ruettiger, upon whose life the film *Rudy* was based. His is a real success story. Lacking in intellectual and athletic gifts, Ruettiger, through effort and hard work, was able to achieve his goal of playing for the Notre Dame Fighting Irish football team. True, he participated in only three plays, but that was a tremendous achievement and deeply satisfying for him. Young males can similarly set goals that are appropriate for their situations, and with effort they can achieve those goals.

Daniel Ruettiger (nicknamed "Rudy") had a hard time in school because he was dyslexic. He was the third of fourteen children in his family. He attended Joliet Catholic High School, where he played for locally famous football coach Gordie Gillespie.

83

Ruettiger joined the United States Navy after high school. After his discharge he applied to Notre Dame, but due to his marginal grades he had to do his early college work at nearby Holy Cross College. It was during his time studying at Holy Cross that Ruettiger discovered he had dyslexia. After two years at Holy Cross, in the fall of 1974 Ruettiger was accepted as a student at Notre Dame on his fourth try.

Ruettiger harbored a dream to play for the Notre Dame Fighting Irish football team, despite being undersized at 5 feet 6 inches and 165 pounds. Head coach Ara Parseghian encouraged walk-on players from the student body. For example, Notre Dame's 1969 starting center, Mike Oriard, was a walk-on who was eventually nominated for a Rhodes scholarship and offered an NFL contract with the Kansas City Chiefs.

After working as hard as possible and showing that he was willing to make the required personal sacrifices, Ruettiger earned a place on the Notre Dame practice squad that helped the varsity team practice for games. Merv Johnson was the coach who was instrumental in keeping Ruettiger on as a scout-team player.

After the 1974 season, Notre Dame coach Parseghian stepped down and former Green Bay Packers coach Dan Devine was named head coach. In Ruettiger's last opportunity to play for Notre Dame at home, Devine put him into a game as defensive end against Georgia Tech on November 8, 1975.

In the movie *Rudy*, Devine is given a somewhat antagonistic role, not wanting Rudy to dress for his last game. However, in actuality, it was Devine who came up with the idea to dress Rudy. In the final play of Ruettiger's senior season with the Fighting Irish, he recorded a sack, which is all his Notre Dame stats line has ever shown. Ruettiger actually played for three plays. The first play was a kickoff, the second play was an incomplete pass, and on the third (and final) play he sacked Georgia Tech quarterback Rudy Allen. Ruettiger was carried off the field by his teammates following the game.

Awesome Man Profile: Kenneth Bishop

To be an Awesome Man does not require great intelligence or unique physical ability. An ordinary man can do awesome things while others just stand and watch. But being an Awesome Man does require effort, sometimes more effort than one believes is possible.

Most people prudently are very wary of fire. Imagine if you witnessed a gasoline fuel truck on fire. What would you do? What effort would you expend to save a man's life?

As you will read in the account below, Kenneth Bishop instinctively understood that to act effectively and decisively would require more than a "so-so attempt" or a "good try'" or an "I'll wait and see" attitude. He knew and understood that to achieve significant results, significant effort is required. His efforts were based on total commitment of his emotional and physical strength to succeed in his goal of saving another's life.

Kenneth Bishop earned Canada's highest civilian and bravery award, the Governor General's Cross of Valour.

His citation reads:

On March 30, 1974, when a fuel tanker and freight truck collided and burst into flames at Vegreville, Alberta, Kenneth Bishop withstood severe burns to his body to save the life of a man who lay helpless in the midst of flames and explosions. On impact, the man was flung from his truck and suffered a serious injury. Some 7,000 gallons of gasoline from his ruptured tanker ignited and surrounded the driver within walls of fire. No one but Kenneth Bishop dared attempt to save the victim and as he approached the inferno, the rescuer was thrown several feet by an explosion. His clothes caught fire but he refused to turn away. Already severely burnt, Mr. Bishop protected his face from the blistering heat and snaked his way to the victim. Taking a firm grip of the man, under the arms, he dragged him safely away from the conflagration. Although aware that his deed might cost him his own life, Kenneth Bishop exhibited the finest example of selfless courage and humanitarian concern to save a complete stranger.

We are often faced with challenges, stress, and crises, and frequently the best solution necessitates abundant effort. The Awesome Man knows with effort he can achieve things in his life that others will not. Without effort, nothing of value can be gained.

6

Perseverance and Self-Discipline

The man who moves a mountain begins by carrying away small stones.

—Confucius

You Cannot Win If You Do Not Finish

Perseverance is one virtue that is constantly overlooked in our instant-results, instant-gratification world. It is amazing how many men give up on meaningful goals and objectives when the results they are seeking do not come right away. Research has shown that it usually takes a minimum of six weeks to learn a new skill, or develop a latent talent, or change a habit. Most men in Guyland feel that to stick to anything for six weeks is totally unreasonable. Predictably, this mentality results in unfulfilled goals and a lack of satisfaction.

The Awesome Man's perspective is completely different. He knows that very little of value in life is achieved quickly and easily. He welcomes the challenges that worthy endeavors bring. The Awesome Man understands that you should persevere until you have reached your goal.

But is it ever okay to give up on a goal or quit a project? If the goal or project is worthwhile, the answer is no. As mentioned previously, we often underestimate the time and effort required to achieve a goal. When we get to the point where it is obvious things will take longer than anticipated, we are presented with a momentous choice: We can reformulate our strategy and redouble our efforts, or we can quit. Awesome Men do not quit because they know quitters never win and winners never quit. If the achievement of the goal is still a valuable objective, they will simply keep working and adjusting until they win the day. They will persevere.

So, what does it really mean to persevere? Here's an example: You may not be familiar with the disease polio. Why? Because the disease was conquered by the first effective vaccine, a vaccine that is still in use today. It was invented by Jonas Salk. How long did it take him and his team to do it? Seven years!

Christopher Columbus and his brother spent twelve years planning and raising funds for his trip to the New World. After it launched the first American, Alan Shepard, into space in 1961, it took the United States eight years to land *Apollo 11* on the moon. J.K. Rowling started working on the story seven years before the first Harry Potter book was published. It took musician George Thorogood about ten years before he recorded "Get a Haircut " after he had acquired the rights to the music (George wanted to improve his guitar ability before doing a studio recording, a great example of planning ahead).

"Actually, I'm an overnight success, but it took twenty years."—Monty Hall, TV game-show host and philanthropist

History also provides a number of tremendous examples of perseverance by groups or countries. Starting in 1945, a little third world country, Vietnam, consecutively defeated two world powers, France and the United States. The United States had the greatest military strength in the history of the world at that time. The goal of the Vietnamese rebels was to unify their country, expel foreign occupiers, and gain full independence for Vietnam. In 1975 they at long last accomplished their goal. The thirty-year war that achieved their goal is an example of what effort and perseverance can accomplish on a national scale. Similarly, two hundred years earlier a British colony in North America defeated the greatest military power at that time and formed the United States of America. If you are an American citizen today, it is because of the effort and perseverance of those colonialists. You too are capable of the effort and perseverance these individuals had.

As you can see from these examples, perseverance means doing meaningful and important tasks to get the desired and appropriate results. Quite often this process involves starting over or changing your approach—in fact, adaptability is often a key factor in achieving ultimate success. But it never involves quitting or giving up.

Think for a moment about the longest amount of time you ever spent on any project or goal. Perhaps it was a lengthy school assignment, or building a complex model airplane, or writing a poem, or learning to throw a curve ball. Did you accomplish that goal? If so, can you recall what motivated you to persevere through the project's ups and downs until you completed it?

Conversely, have you ever set a meaningful goal but failed to achieve it? What caused you to quit? What was lacking that had been present in the goals you did achieve? You can learn a lot about yourself by understanding why you stopped. Be honest with yourself. Was it too difficult or too hard? What was so difficult about it that it overwhelmed you? Was it beyond your ability to complete? Did you ask for guidance or assistance? Or was it just more work than you were prepared to do?

As a football coach at rookie camp, I often did not tell the players what drill we were about to do. I had previously discovered that if I told players they would be doing this or that drill or running a mile as a means of developing endurance, their first comment would be "I can't do that." And some would even drop out. So I just told them to start running slowly around the football field. Using this approach, it was amazing how many rookies, not knowing what they were doing, had run a mile (four laps) for the first time in their lives—something many would not have thought possible. Our minds put more limits on our achievement than any other factor.

Our minds put more limits on our achievement than any other factor.

In the world of Awesome Men, time is not measured in seconds or minutes but in days and years. There is always more than enough time to do awesome things. Developing mental toughness, a strong sense of personal honor and pride, and an iron determination to succeed will help you reach all the important goals in your life in good time. The rewards always far exceed the effort in the long run.

I cannot emphasize enough about the importance of finishing what you start. Do not be one of those men who says "I almost did," "I just about," "I nearly did," "I could have, if only . . . ." Be perseverant and reach your goals.

Obedience and Self-Discipline

I believe that understanding and practicing obedience and self-discipline are directly related to the Awesome Man's life. He knows that adherence to values, principles, and authority is the basis of freedom and responsibility. He knows that if he doesn't stand for anything, he stands for nothing. He knows that for society to work best, individual freedom requires great responsibility, and that responsibility is manifested through obedience and self-discipline.

> **To be obedient means to control ourselves according to external standards; to be self-disciplined means to control ourselves according to our internal standards.**

Obedience and self-discipline are linked and both involve control. To be obedient means to control ourselves according to external standards; to be self-disciplined means to control ourselves according to our internal standards.

The Awesome Man believes in and practices obedience and self-discipline because those behaviors allow him to simplify his life by focusing on the important things. His stress levels are reduced because he has fewer unimportant decisions to make when he follows the rules. Does this seem strange to you, that obedience and self-discipline make life simpler? If so, consider this:

- How would your driving experience change if all drivers could decide when to obey traffic rules? No one would know what the other drivers were thinking or planning. Talk about a stressful commute!

- Even worse, imagine the chaos if every pilot chose his direction and altitude to fly and ignored the air traffic controllers' instructions. How would you feel taking an airplane trip in that situation?

- What if your doctor doesn't adhere to the rules of hygiene and the sterilization of medical instruments? Sure, he obviously is aware of those rules—but he lacks the self-discipline to regularly wash his hands and tools.

- Can you imagine the planning involved on your part if you wanted to go to a concert where nobody had to comply with the assigned seating arrangements? To compound the problem, what if the starting time of the concert was not set, and the musicians could play any chord they felt like, or freestyle anytime they wanted, regardless of how the song was composed?

Many of us do not obey our bosses, teachers, and parents. That's just the way it is, because to one extent or another we all have the freedom to do whatever we want. It's the "my life, my choice" attitude so common today. In Western society, the virtues of obedience and self-discipline are now often regarded with scorn and disapproval. Perhaps you share that sentiment. But before you get all twisted up about obedience and self-discipline as a restriction on your freedoms, take some time to consider the many positive aspects obedience and self-discipline have on your society and therefore your life:

- In a representative democracy, we need obedience and self-discipline to maintain a functioning society and ensure freedom for all. People in authority who exercise that authority justly and properly benefit society and help to make life a little simpler for each of us.
    - What kind of judicial system would we have if judges did not have authority?
    - How could we protect our families if there were no rules?
- Obedience and self-discipline become virtues when we obey authority, even when we think we know better.
    - To claim these virtues as ours, we often have to minimize our desires and wants for the benefit of others and society overall.
    - Self-discipline gives us a moral compass when we are confronted with ambiguous situations.
    - If more people exercised obedience and self-discipline, we would have no need for so many laws and legal restrictions.

- Obedience and self-discipline are based on trust, which is a key aspect of healthy relationships.
  - When we choose to obey, we trust that those in proper authority will guide and lead us correctly.
  - When leaders abuse their authority, they then lose our trust.
  - Our self-discipline will keep us trustworthy.
- Even though some (many) leaders have abused our trust, that does not mean all other leaders don't deserve our trust and obedience.
  - We as individuals in a society should not tolerate abuses of power, but when authority is properly applied, we all benefit by obeying. We must tolerate occasional errors in judgment. One teacher who makes a mistake does not invalidate the authority of all other teachers.

How much happier and less stressful our lives would be if everybody worked together to uphold our laws and standards through the prudent exercise of obedience and self-discipline. Imagine how your life would be if everybody obeyed the laws regarding theft and did not steal. We would not have any anxiety about being robbed. We would not need security systems or guards at malls, and our society's costs for courts and jails would be reduced dramatically. You could walk anywhere anytime without fear of being mugged.

Or imagine if everybody had the self-discipline to resist the lure and temptation of a quick score or easy money or refused to exploit others. It's hard to even imagine these scenarios, but all it takes is some obedience and self-discipline to create a better world for everybody.

"That's Not Who I Really Am!"

Some of you will be familiar with *Strange Case of Dr. Jekyll and Mr. Hyde*, a novella written by the Scottish author Robert Louis Stevenson, first published in 1886. This story details the experiences of a major personality change Doctor Jekyll underwent while under the influence of a potion. The highly respected Dr. Jekyll, who is conscious of evil tendencies within himself, developed and consumed the potion to remove these tendencies from his personality. Unfortunately, as often happens, experiments with

A Note to Those Who Are in a Position of Authority

Abusing your authority and being corrupt or dishonest are very great evils on your part. You were given authority to benefit others and society, not for the betterment of yourself. Using power for anything but good is a serious offense against humanity. You cannot be an Awesome Man if you do not discharge your authority honestly and justly. Remember, the Awesome Man does not have as his goals power, wealth, or fame.

In government, the opportunity for abuse of and by authority is constantly present, especially in the form of corruption. This can affect the Awesome Man in three different spheres of activity: as an elected official himself, as a government administrator or employee, or, most commonly, as a client of the government (a citizen). The Awesome Man does everything to peacefully and nonviolently resist and oppose all forms of abusive authority. He challenges all forms of bribery, graft, or influence peddling, whether he is the beneficiary or not. And regardless of his position, he discharges his duties honestly and fairly. He never rationalizes with phrases such as "I'm not hurting anybody," "Everybody else does it," "I am doing it for my family," or "I have no choice." He never attempts to corrupt or manipulate other individuals in authority either.

The Awesome Man conducts himself similarly when he is in a position of authority in the private sphere because he knows his personal character, integrity, and reputation are paramount in any role. He knows that in a free society supporting the rule of law and the justice it affords everyone is his greatest motivation, not personal gain. Only when all members of society are treated equitably, not just the rich and powerful, is there true peace and harmony for all. He is very aware that others will attempt to corrupt and dissuade him from the path of righteousness to the detriment of society and he has to be ever vigilant to resist their enticements.

Unfortunately, in everyday business life the Awesome Man encounters abuses by authority. Here's an example: Let's say your company is holding a sweepstakes contest for your customers. You are in charge of the contest, and you have arranged it so that all the company's customers have a fair and equal chance at winning. The day before the draw, the president of the company tells you he wants one of the company's largest customers to win. He implies that you are to fix the draw so that this will happen. What he is asking you to do is both morally and legally wrong. If you disobey him, you risk your career. But if you do obey him, you risk jail time and losing your integrity, in addition to your job.

Depending on the situation, the Awesome Man, when faced with this reality, would consider doing one of the following: He could explain to the president that it would be in the best interests of the company and all involved not to jeopardize their reputation, integrity, and positive customer relations by entangling themselves in such a seamy activity. Alternatively, the Awesome Man could consult with the company's legal department and ask it to provide a legal opinion on the president's request. The president would appreciate and likely take guidance from legal counsel on this matter, as it could save him grief down the road. If these alternatives are not possible, the Awesome Man would refuse the instruction, explain why, and be prepared to resign. Anything less would be participating in fraud and would violate his principles. The Awesome Man simply will not want to work for a company that demands immoral and illegal behavior from its employees.

Anybody with knowledge of human history will know that many of the great injustices and wrongs have occurred because good men were obedient to evil superiors and said or did nothing. They found it easier to stay silent and commit crimes and abuses. When held to account, these people falsely claimed they had "no choice."

But we always have a choice. The Awesome Man knows this, and he makes the right one.

concoctions and brews do not turn out well. Amiable Dr. Jekyll was transformed into the cruel, remorseless, and evil Mr. Hyde.

Although we humans don't drink potions anymore, we still can and do experience significant personality, attitude, and judgment changes when under the influence of drugs and alcohol or emotional tension. A survey of Canadian prison inmates found that over 80% of the inmates committed their crimes while under the influence of drugs or alcohol.* No doubt US statistics are similarly astounding. Clearly, we lose our self-discipline and moral compass and exercise poor judgment if we fall under the influence of drugs and alcohol.

The Awesome Man knows this. And he also knows that people who experience significant emotional (rather than chemical) stimulation or distress can also behave in a reckless way. This simply means that when we are angry, sad, frustrated, sexually aroused, or frightened, we often make decisions and choices that we would not normally make when we are in a calm state. We take risks we would otherwise avoid and do things we would never imagine undertaking when relaxed and unruffled. These are often the epitome of bad choices. There's a good reason we all have heard terms such as "crime of passion," "when enraged," and "under duress" to describe healthy, disciplined people who have briefly acted "out of their minds" when under great emotional stress.

In 2006, behavioral research scientists Dan Ariely and George Loewenstein published a paper called "The Heat of the Moment: The Effect of Sexual Arousal on Sexual Decision Making" in the *Journal of Behavioral Decision Making*.† They discovered that sexual arousal also has the same negative impact on decision-making. Good choices people would make when calm were left by the wayside in the heat of passion.

So what does this mean for you? It means you have to be extremely careful when you are drinking or using drugs (prescription or otherwise), or when you are angry, aroused, or in any other way emotionally charged.

---

* Canadian Centre on Substance Abuse and Addiction, *Proportions of Crimes Associated with Alcohol and Other Drugs in Canada*, 2002, http://www.ccsa.ca/Resource%20Library/ccsa-009105-2002.pdf.

† Dan Ariely and George Loewenstein, "The Heat of the Moment: The Effect of Sexual Arousal on Sexual Decision Making," *Journal of Behavioral Decision Making* 19, no. 2 (April 2006).

In these circumstances, you have to be particularly vigilant about making any choices that you may regret.

- I can certainly confirm I have made some bad choices when I was not my usual calm, sensible self. So I want to share a few ideas I've learned through experience that will help keep you safe:

- First, is there any—regardless how minimal—risk or danger to an activity you are planning? If so, make sure you do it only while clean and sober!

- Second, consider the consequences of your actions while you are still calm and collected. Otherwise it will be too late.

- Finally, if you find yourself thinking thoughts like "What's the harm?," "You only live once," "Go for it, big boy!," or "Don't be a chicken," then stop and calm yourself. Draw on your reserves of self-discipline to make good choices. Be the Awesome Man, right then and there.

You Can't Escape Your Emotions

Take note that even when you feel you are making rational and sensible decisions, you are still a human being, and emotions and feelings are still going to be a huge factor in your choices.

Let me explain. Let us say you want to buy a chair for your bedroom. Comfort and the durability are probably the most important rational factors in purchasing the chair. You notice that a particular chair you are considering has an ugly style and the wrong color for your décor, even though those attributes are irrelevant in doing the job of providing a place for you to sit. The chair in question is strong and comfortable, yet you turn away from it and move on to looking at other, more eye-catching chairs.

The point is that very few people purchase ugly chairs that are the wrong color. Yet many uncomfortable chairs are purchased if they look good. So even though having a comfortable place to sit is a key requirement, other emotional factors affect the choice and likely are more powerful influencers. In reality, people often buy higher-priced items that offer less comfort or durability because they are the right color and look good. This is what the whole fashion industry is based on. If you need further proof of emotional power in decision-making, just look at some of the shoes women wear.

The key point here is to be honest with yourself. If you are buying for style, looks, or other emotional factors, say so to yourself and everybody else. It is okay to buy for style or fashion, or to impress. But do not fool yourself and believe when you decide on something for emotional reasons it is for rational reasons.

And it's not just our personal lives—let me tell you about how emotions affect business and political decisions. Peter Drucker was one of the preeminent business analysts of the twentieth century. One of the many ideas he developed was the concept of "investment in managerial ego."

Often business leaders will support and promote a brand, product, or idea that has no real validity in the market, primarily because the leader is passionate about it. During the negotiations for the US government's bailout of General Motors in 2009, a number of politicians were upset with GM's sales forecasts, as GM predicated future revenue based on the sales of gas-guzzling trucks and SUVs. The congressmen who held the purse strings for the bailout funds were almost apoplectic that GM was not planning to transform into a primarily "green car" producer. These politicians were committed to ecological and green initiatives and found it very hard to bail out a company that had minimal commitment to these environmental goals. In the end GM got the money and, by selling the types of trucks and SUVs they were familiar with, became financially viable again and paid back all the funds it had received from the government. The politicians were passionate about the environment, much more so than the consumers of motor vehicles, who stuck with tried-and-true traditional vehicles. This is another example of where passion can cloud judgment.

> You are a human being, and emotions and feelings are always going to be a huge factor in your choices.

On a related note, the number one green car producer is Tesla, which was not financially viable for the first fifteen years of its existence. CEO Elon Musk's perseverance was demonstrated by his personal investment of millions in the company. In 2019 Tesla recorded it first annual profits and is opening two new plants worldwide to meet demand. Quite likely they have turned the corner to success.

Most of the challenges you will face in life require this
understanding.

You have to do it yourself,

But you cannot do it alone.

Stop waiting for others to do things or make changes for
you.

You always have to supply the Perseverance and Self-
Discipline.

You have to make the changes, and do what needs to be
done yourself.

Rely on others for guidance, assistance, support, and
encouragement.

Negative Self-Talk

One of the features of a fixed mindset or a self-limiting attitude is negative self-talk. It is often our own negative self-talk that convinces us to quit, give up, or stop before we reach our goals. At the crucial moment when we need to exercise self-discipline and perseverance, our negative voice inside is saying things like "It is too hard," "It's not worth the effort," "Nobody cares," "It's not important," "It's not fun," "It's too difficult," and "We can do it later."

Negative self-talk causes us to feel exhausted. It can make us feel hurt, angry, frustrated, depressed, or anxious. It destroys focus and concentration. It undermines our self-confidence so that we underachieve and fail to be what we can be. Perhaps the greatest challenge to being an Awesome Man is dealing with that voice in your head that tells you why you cannot be an Awesome Man. It is all but impossible to progress or achieve anything of value in any endeavor while negative self-talk is occurring.

It's important to understand how and why negative self-talk occurs. Usually, it is based in fear and poor past experiences. If a particular thing went poorly for you before, next time you are faced with the same situation your mind will probably tell you it will go bad this time as well. If, for example, last year you tried to eat healthy during the first week of January but couldn't sustain the habit into the second week, what do you think your mind will be saying when you try it again? Nothing positive, that's for sure.

Yet negative self-talk doesn't have to be crippling. In fact, if you simply recognize that past failures are usually due to a lack of preparation and not being fully aware of all the steps to achieve completion, then the negative self-talk will be much less strident.

The important thing is to understand that almost all negative self-talk is useless and counterproductive. It encourages laziness and sloth and discourages perseverance and effort. Let me share some of the negative self-talk I had before my first book was published, and how I countered it:

- **What makes you think you can be a writer?** I had read some pretty poorly written books previously, and this gave me confidence that I could not do any worse than those authors. I knew I had a story to tell, and I was passionate about it. I also realized I had articles and stories previously published in newspapers, which is how many authors start out.

- **What do *you* know about writing a book?** As a reader of books I knew what I liked, plus I knew a few authors whom I asked for guidance. I knew I could not do it alone and I did not hesitate to ask for help.

- **Nobody will buy a book you wrote.** Maybe, but I will let my publisher and the readers decide that. I will just try to write and promote my book the best I can, and I will accept whatever happens afterward.

- **You will never find a publisher.** In reality this was the hardest part in the whole process. As a writer, you are asking a publisher to invest a great deal of money and effort in your dream. You had better be committed, passionate, and convincing about your goal. I continued my efforts to find a publisher until I succeeded. It took over two years.

As you can see, I addressed the various negative voices that plagued me about my ability to be a writer with effort, perseverance, and a willingness to learn. I adapted as needed, kept plugging away (persevered), and was eventually rewarded with my book's publication.

So next time you have a task or a goal to achieve, be on the alert for negative self-talk. If it does occur, remember that you can control it with understanding and preparation. Replace that deflating mental chatter with positive thoughts and ideas. Reinforce your commitment by telling yourself that with effort, perseverance, and a willingness to learn you can and will succeed.

If the negative self-talk persists, reset the scenario and look at it from a positive perspective. If what you want to do is good and positive and the negative self-talk is still loud, you are probably still anxious about certain things you have not fully thought through yet. Pause for a moment to properly assess what's bothering you and make sure you fully understand the scope of what you are trying to accomplish. If you are feeling overwhelmed, cut the task or goal into little steps or stages and go forward one step at a time.

This exercise will have two benefits. One is that you will learn that most situations can have better outcomes than you initially anticipated. The other is that you'll have more confidence in your ability to positively control the outcomes of future situations by the way you prepare for these situations.

Here is an example: Rocco doesn't like visiting his aunt Helena. Aunt Helena has been a widow for many years, never had any children of her own, and often suffers from loneliness. Aunt Helena is eccentric. She feels she is very good at giving advice and telling Rocco how he should lead his life. When Rocco visits Aunt Helena, she is very hospitable but just talks and is boring.

Each time on the drive to Aunt Helena's house, Rocco's head is full of negative self-talk. By the time he arrives he is in a really bad mood. Rocco's only mental response is the wish not to visit Aunt Helena.

How should this scenario be reset to eliminate the negative self-talk? Let us consider how visiting Aunt Helena could be a happy experience for Rocco. Chances are if Aunt Helena is lonely, she is seeking company and friendship from her nephew. Rocco can provide this by learning about his aunt, asking her questions about her past, how life was when she was Rocco's age, what her parents were like, what did she as a young girl, and so on. It will take some effort on Rocco's part to be curious about Aunt Helena and her life, but you can rest assured she will have some interesting stories to tell. If Rocco sees visiting Aunt Helena as a learning experience rather than drudgery, the negative self-talk will disappear and visits with his aunt will become much more tolerable, and perhaps in time even memorable. (If you do not believe that you can learn much from older people, read *Tuesdays with Morrie* by Mitch Albom.)

The Awesome Man refuses to listen to negative self-talk. He knows with perseverance and self-discipline he can overcome the obstacles to his goals. He knows that with learning he can free himself of that harsh and counter-productive blather from the critic in his head and achieve the happiness, joy, and contentment he deserves.

Stop and Smell the Roses

From time to time young men can become too obsessed with their goals and lose sight of the beauty and joy that are present in their world right now. It is very important for you to stop, breathe, and be calm. Serenity is a feeling that you should enjoy when going about your day. No panic or obsession. You do not have to be "on" all the time. Just because you have important goals in your life does not preclude peace and tranquility from being a part of your day. Take some time for yourself. So really stop and smell the roses, have a coffee with a friend, go for a walk, and take time to recharge your batteries.

Awesome Man Profile: Tom Kelley

Tom Kelley is an Awesome Man, and not just because he earned the Congressional Medal of Honor in Vietnam for "conspicuous gallantry and intrepidity at the risk of his life above and beyond the call of duty." The fact he was severely injured and was rendered blind in one eye does not alone make him awesome. What makes him awesome was how he responded when, after recovering from his injuries, the US Navy deemed him unfit for service and planned to discharge him as a disabled veteran.

Kelley at the time was in his early thirties and felt in no way ready to end his navy career. He persevered and convinced the navy hierarchy to give him a chance. It was not easy, and he was confronted with many challenges that he faced head on. He moved up in responsibility and rank, eventually commanding the frigate USS *Lang*. He then became the chief of staff for the commander of US naval forces in Korea. Before he retired, his final assignment was as the director of Legislation in the Bureau of Naval Personnel. There he worked on enhancing the responsibilities and stature of enlisted personnel, while closely integrating minorities and women into mainstream navy assignments.

By his tenacity and example, Tom Kelley has shown that people with physical challenges can serve with distinction in both the military and civilian life. After retiring from another successful career serving as secretary of the Massachusetts Department of Veterans' Services, Kelley now provides meals for a homeless shelter and helps run the veterans ministry at his church. He also mentors students at Boston College High and is an active alumnus at Boston College.

7

Character and Ethics

To educate a man in mind and not in morals is to educate a menace to society.
—Theodore Roosevelt

Character and Ethics, the Pillars of a Good Life

The Awesome Man is usually identified by others based on his character and ethics. Too many men from all walks of life often sacrifice their character and ethics needlessly for some immediate gratification or pleasure, not realizing that without these values they will become a shell of a man. The Awesome Man knows that character and ethics go hand in hand to create a quality individual. As a responsible male, he knows that without character and ethics he has little value in the world. He understands deep inside that with responsibility, freedom and happiness follow.

So what exactly do I mean when I talk about character and ethics? The Josephson Institute of Ethics (JosephsonInstitute.org) defines ethics in terms of moral duties and virtues that flow from six core character traits, which the institute calls the Six Pillars of Character:

Trustworthiness. Ethical people are worthy of trust. Trustworthiness means being honest, telling the truth, having integrity, keeping your promises, and being loyal.

Respect. We must respect ourselves and remember that every person has the right to our respect.

Responsibility. We must be accountable for our own actions, practice self-restraint, and always do our best.

Justice and fairness. Fairness is one of the most difficult values, because sometimes it means doing the right thing even if others disagree. We must try to do what we know is fair and just.

Caring. Caring is concern for the interests of others.

Civic virtue and citizenship. Responsible citizenship means being involved in public service. This includes voting, reporting crimes, testifying as a witness, protecting the environment, and working for the candidate of your choice.

I am going to share with you a story that occurred when I was about fifteen or sixteen years old. I was working for about six months in a fast-food restaurant (it since has gone defunct) and was enjoying the job. One evening I was working with Perk (not his real name), a manager I had not worked for previously. But I knew his name because he had at one time owned one of the finer restaurants in our city. The evening was progressing normally when I noticed one of the junior guys outside in the parking lot. It was routine for one of the new guys to go outside regularly and clean up the parking lot, empty the garbage bins, and make sure everything was neat and tidy. What was unusual was my friend Freddy (not his real name) seemed to be picking up used fountain cups. Later I saw him in the back room washing about twenty or thirty cups in hot soapy water and drying them. I asked Freddy what was going on, as I had never seen this done previously. He told me that one of his duties when working for Perk was to collect discarded drinking cups, clean them, and then reuse them.

I was filled with confusion but went back to work and said no more to Freddy. After a while I figured out what was happening. The restaurant's accounting system factored the cost of each cup into the cost of the drink. For example, the cup itself might cost 2 cents, the drink cost 25 cents, and the labor cost was 13 cents for a total of 40 cents (assume the beverage was sold to the customer for a dollar). At the end of each shift, the number of cups used would be totaled to determine the costs. So if a cup was cleaned and reused, the costs would be recorded as zero, and that shift manager would record a more profitable shift.

What was happening was

a. The manager was consciously overstating the profits. Since he counted the receipts at the end of the shift, he could have kept the apparent overages for himself. At the time I did not recognize that was what was likely going on.

b. The reuse of the cups for customers was strictly against company policy.

c. If discovered by the public or competitors, reuse of the cups would have created extremely negative publicity for the restaurant.

d. Even though the cups that were reused were supposedly washed thoroughly, the health risk was still credible, as the restaurant used coated paper cups that were not designed to be reused in the way glass, ceramic, or plastic containers are.

So what did I do?

I was not as courageous as I could have been. What I did first when pulling cups from the dispenser to pour a drink for a customer was to carefully check each one to ensure that it was new and pristine. If it wasn't, I would put it aside so it would not be used. Other crew members began to do the same almost spontaneously. I also told Freddy, who was a friend, that I would not collect or recycle the cups, and if the manager told me to do so, I would refuse. I implied to Freddy that he should stop gathering and recycling used cups. I told him he should refuse if Perk asked him again. Other crew members whom I spoke with agreed with my point of view.

The next week when I came into work, I learned that Perk was gone. I never asked why. I never spoke of the matter again.

I learned two things. First, it is important to stand up for your values and ethics, because if you do not, your character and integrity will suffer. I certainly did not want somebody getting sick because I served them a drink in a contaminated cup. That was not something I wanted on my conscience. I also learned that when faced with ethical and character challenges, it is not always necessary to make a big issue or create a scene to effect change. Often a word in confidence, a suggestion, or an opinion can achieve the results required.

In conclusion, the easiest thing would have been for me to mind my own business and say nothing. But speaking to others and voicing my opinion about the wrongness of the situation somehow ended it. I cannot honestly say that my actions directly resulted in Perk's termination, and that was not my goal. My goal was to stop the reuse of the cups for health reasons, and I'm glad that goal was achieved. A half century later, I know I did the right thing.

As Children, We Think Only of Our Wants

It is a sad fact of life that many men allow character and ethics to go by the wayside as they pursue their objectives in life. Perhaps they never adopted these virtues in the first place. When we think only of what we want, we feel justified in doing and saying whatever is required for us to get what we want, with no concern for others or for the consequences of our actions. Far too many young men (and supposedly adult males) believe self-interest and self-indulgence are the justifications for their bad behavior. Let's spend a moment to consider how this happens.

As small children, we focus only on ourselves and our needs and wants. As infants, if we are hungry we cry, if our diaper is wet we cry—we have no concern with what is happening outside our little world. We as children soon discover that there are a number people in the world we can beg, implore, fool, deceive, trick, or manipulate. Our parents will likely be our first victims, soon followed by our friends and teachers. You, as a child, will likely lie to them, exaggerate, make up stories to escape responsibility, and use other tricks to get what you want from them. The more successful you become at being deceitful, the more likely you are to rely on those traits going forward and to avoid taking responsibility for your actions and the conditions of your life.

As you physically grow and leave childhood, it is expected that you will mature in character too. It is hoped that you won't feel the need to deceive people anymore, because as an adult you can easily acquire what you need in life by yourself without sacrificing your character or your ethics. Once you reach puberty you have the ability (and *need*) to put aside those childish practices and behaviors and take on the values of good character and ethical behavior for your own well-being. Young men who follow this path are on the way to growing into Awesome Men.

Unfortunately, a significant number of so-called adult males use their talents to get what they want (but do not necessarily need) inappropriately. Like children, they will lie, cheat, violate laws, and sacrifice their ethics to achieve their distorted view of success. They never realize that in the end they are only fooling and cheating themselves. There always comes a day of reckoning, usually much sooner than they ever imagined. This day of reckoning can take many unpleasant forms, from the loss of a coveted job to trouble with the law to the estrangement of friends and loved ones who hold themselves to higher ethical standards.

But until that day comes, such men will typically tell themselves—and perhaps authentically come to believe—that they are winning at the game of life. When questioned about their motives and behaviors, they will fall back to their childhood patterns of spinning webs of rationalizations to justify their actions and to try to soothe their consciences.

Take a look at the list of common excuses below. Do you find yourself ever using these or similar excuses or justifications for your behavior? If so, you have likely crossed at least one ethical line already. You may say, "So what?"—but saying that is just another excuse for ignoring ethics and character.

Everybody does it.	It not my fault—the people I fool are stupid.
I have a family to feed.	It's not personal, it's business.
If I do not do it, someone else will.	That is the way it's done. I don't make the rules.
It is not illegal.	I did nothing wrong.
There is no proof.	They had it coming to them.
What else was I supposed to do?	They can afford it.
They would have done the same to me.	What did they expect?
They budgeted for it.	You have to be pragmatic.
They have insurance.	I was provoked.

I was just playing.	They disrespected me.
I'm under a lot of stress.	They all do it too.
It was mine. I was just getting it back.	I had no choice.
I was just doing my job.	Lighten up.

If your objective is to lead a happy life, to be respected by yourself and your family, then you cannot achieve this goal by exploiting yourself and others through a lack of character and ethics.

The Fear of Scarcity

Not to dwell on the negative, but I think it's important to talk about one of the most pernicious varieties of self-involved, unethical men. In my view, the world can be divided into two main groups: those of us who think it is a world of shortage and those of us who think it is a world of abundance.

Those who believe in the world of scarcity are forever grappling with their fear of shortages, a fear that is usually not grounded in reality. These people are convinced there will never be enough of whatever they need; therefore, they must protect what they have already and, in addition, stop anybody from getting anything they might want. They suffer character defects that make them envious of others and feel justified in taking what is not theirs. But as demonstrated by the brief story that follows, the world has mechanisms to maintain its natural balance, and often those whose fear of losing something causes them to hurt others end up losing everything themselves.

Let me tell you the story of two men, Ken Lay and Jeffrey Skilling, who always wanted and needed "more." Their lack of ethics and character resulted in their company Enron's bankruptcy, which at the time was the biggest bankruptcy in US history. In total, twenty thousand employees lost their jobs, and in many cases their life savings. Investors also lost billions of dollars. Just think of that for a minute. These two men and their associates destroyed the lives and futures of thousands of families who depended on them to wisely guide their company.

This story vividly shows that boys and young men who enjoy an upbringing of privilege do not necessarily end up being men of character. Lay and Skilling came from good families and received quality educations. Both were gifted with intelligence and ability, and from running Enron they became very rich, likely billionaires. Yet still they wanted more and so led their company to ruin.

After the bankruptcy, Ken Lay was convicted of six counts of securities and wire fraud. He was facing up to forty-five years in prison, but he died of a heart attack on July 5, 2006, prior to sentencing. Jeffrey Skilling was convicted on nineteen counts of securities fraud and wire fraud and was sentenced to twenty-four years and four months in prison. In addition, he received a $45 million fine.

Lay and Skilling were two men who were publicly admired and honored for their wealth and apparent success. They were men who wielded power and influence in government and politics, yet they lacked the character or ethics to operate a public company for the benefit of all and met with miserable ends.

You may wonder how the story about Enron and the so-called leadership of Lay and Skilling relates to the topic of fear and scarcity. It goes to the root of the scandal, which was all about making more money for Lay, Skilling, and their friends—even though these individuals were richer than most Americans could dream of (in 2001 Skilling was paid $102 million in compensation by Enron). As crazy as it sounds, I believe these men truly were fearful about suffering from a scarcity of money. They did everything in their power to accumulate as much money and power for themselves as possible. How else can you explain their actions? Since antiquity and the myth of King Midas, the fear of not having enough money (greed) has caused the fall of many men.

In stark contrast, the Awesome Man strives to be a leader to all, and he accomplishes this by doing what he knows is right. As the Dutch business leader Paul Polman stated, "The basic skills of leaders are always the same: Be driven by a deeper purpose, be a human being, have a passion for what you do—and it's also about hard work and ethics."

A Deeper Look: Character and Ethics

Do you find character and ethics to be abstract concepts? Have your parents or mentors ever talked to you about them? Are you sometimes confused by the mixed messages that the media and society at large send you when it comes to values and the right way to act?

Thankfully, many great organizations—such as the Foundation for a Better Life—are working hard to get the character and ethics message out to the public. One of the things you can do is watch some of the foundation's video commercials at PassItOn.com. Another good website is that of the aforementioned Josephson Institute of Ethics: JosephsonInstitute.org.

In addition, being a writer, I recommend that you read a few of the many wonderful books on character and ethics, and perhaps some biographies of the individuals whose lives exemplified these traits. Thousands of such books are available, so I suggest you talk to your local librarian or bookseller and get some pointers. There are bound to be more than a few that suit your needs.

Above and beyond researching what other people say or write about character and ethics, it's important that you start thinking about these things yourself. A great starting point is to think about the choices you have made in the past. Were they the best examples of the values and ethics you want to be known for? Were you acting in the best interests of everybody or just yourself? Did you subjugate your character and ethics because of false wants, greed, or a fear of scarcity?

Then, after thinking about past your actions and decisions, spend some time analyzing the person you are now. Have you changed? If so, has the change been for the better, or for the worse? What areas of your character would you like to improve? Do you have a tendency toward laziness or perhaps toward being too abrupt with people asking you questions? Ponder these deficiencies, become aware of them, and try to change. You can do it!

I want to make it clear that improving one's character and ethics can be *transformational*. Evidence points to the fact that those who have good character and high ethical standards tend to be happiest in life. That is what being an Awesome Man is all about!

Being a man of character and ethics, however, requires action. It is not good enough to say nice things and think good thoughts. You must *live* your character and ethics, and they must be manifested in your actions. I have never met anybody who regretted being a man of character and ethics, but I have met many a man who regrets his lack of character and ethics and is now suffering the results.

Finding Meaning in Life

The Awesome Man realizes and accepts that becoming an adult male is a great thing, because it means he is now in a position to fully pursue happiness and develop a meaningful life. He knows that his character and ethics are cornerstones of achieving his goals in life and for conducting himself in a way that is open, generous, and honorable.

But what truly drives the Awesome Man is the potent energy he derives from having discovered the real meaning of his life. The particular form this meaning takes will vary from man to man, but for most men it involves not dwelling on your own suffering or condition and instead vigorously focusing outward to overcome challenges and build a better world for himself, his loved ones, and society at large.

Viktor Frankl, a world-renowned psychiatrist, author, and Holocaust survivor, developed the concept of logotherapy. The term is based on the Greek word *logos*, which stands for "meaning." The Viktor Frankl Institute of Logotherapy (viktorfranklinstitute.org) in Abilene, Texas, explains it as follows:

Logotherapy is based on the premise that the human person is motivated by a "will to meaning," an inner pull to find a meaning in life. The following list of tenets represents basic principles of logotherapy:
- Life has meaning under all circumstances, even the most miserable ones.
- Our main motivation for living is our will to find meaning in life.

- We have freedom to find meaning in what we do, and what we experience, or at least in the stand we take when faced with a situation of unchangeable suffering.

The human spirit referred to in logotherapy is defined as that which is uniquely human. Though in no way opposed to religion, the term is not used in a religious sense.

According to Frankl, "We can discover this meaning in life in three different ways:

- by creating a work or doing a deed; and/or
- by experiencing something or encountering someone; and/or
- by the attitude we take toward unavoidable suffering and that everything can be taken from a man but one thing: the last of the human freedoms—to choose one's attitude in any given set of circumstances.

On the meaning of suffering, Frankl gives the following example:

Once, an elderly medical doctor consulted me because of his severe depression. He could not overcome the loss of his wife who had died two years before and whom he had loved above all else. Now how could I help him? What should I tell him? I refrained from telling him anything, but instead confronted him with a question, "What would have happened, Doctor, if you had died first, and your wife would have had to survive you?" "Oh," he said, "for her this would have been terrible; how she would have suffered!" Whereupon I replied, "You see, Doctor, such a suffering has been spared her, and it is you who have spared her this suffering; but now, you have to pay for it by surviving and mourning her." He said no word but shook my hand and calmly left the office.

I believe Frankl helped this sad doctor recognize that his life had meaning by sparing his wife her pain, and now the doctor had to accept that because he did something wonderful for his wife, he would suffer and mourn for her. His depression would vanish as the doctor understood the meaning in his life.

Frankl also saw the powerful relationship between freedom and responsibility when he stated, "Freedom, however, is not the last word. Freedom is only part of the story and half of the truth. Freedom is but the negative aspect of the whole phenomenon whose positive aspect is responsibleness.

In fact, freedom is in danger of degenerating into mere arbitrariness unless it is lived in terms of responsibleness."

The Awesome Man knows that for him to achieve his goals of happiness, joy, and contentment, he has to lead a meaningful life. He has to be a difference maker in the world by doing exemplary work or performing good deeds, by experiencing something or encountering someone, and by taking the attitude that suffering is unavoidable. His character and ethics underpin both his inward and outward behavior. Through his practice of and dedication to Trustworthiness, Respect, Responsibility, Justice and Fairness, Caring, and Civic Virtue and Citizenship he will become an Awesome Man.

Larry and Tito

Each of us has a fundamental choice to make. We can try to lead a life where our objective is a life of pleasure. Or we can try to lead a meaningful life that will help us reach happiness. Let me illustrate this by comparing the lives of two young men, both aged nineteen.

The first is named Larry. Larry wakes up in the morning, checks his texts and email, and has breakfast. He then goes back to his room and plays video games for a couple of hours. As he becomes hungry again, he goes down to the local burger joint and has the Man-Buster Combo for lunch. He then goes back to his room and watches some porn until about 4:00 p.m., when he realizes he is horny. He texts his "friend with benefits," Mandy, and asks to come over. He takes a couple of joints, which he offers to share with Mandy if she will pleasure him. She agrees, and after she gets him off they smoke the joints.

Now they are hungry so they go out for beers and BBQ. Soon Larry has nothing to talk about and drops Mandy off at her girlfriend's house. He goes to the local sports bar to watch the game and hang with his buddies until closing time. He then goes home.

Larry has had a perfect day. He has done exactly what he wanted to do, including all the pleasurable activities he desired. Yet as he lies in bed trying to fall asleep he feels empty. He reminds himself to drink more next time so he can fall asleep faster.

Tito also wakes up. He tidies up his room and makes breakfast for himself and his little sister. He then goes to junior technical college where he is learning to be a welder. After school he plays volleyball on an intra-mural coed team. After the game he goes home and has dinner with his family. That evening he goes to the local library where he volunteers one hour a week as a tutor for disadvantaged boys. On his way home from the library he stops by his girlfriend's house, where she has some relatives over, and visits with them. Tito arrives home about 11:00 p.m., goes to bed, and falls asleep, satisfyingly exhausted.

Tito is not leading a life where pleasure is his goal. He is leading a mean-ingful life, which to him includes being of service to others, socializing with others in a positive way, and being both mentally and physically active. His time is used in a positive and purposeful way.

Of the two, Larry and Tito, who do you think is on the road to happiness and to becoming an Awesome Man? The answer is obvious, because our actions tell more about us than anything we say. By our actions we show our character and ethics and our understanding of what is truly mean-ingful in life.

Religion, God, and Spirituality

One common feature I have discovered in many of the Awesome Men I have met is their strong spiritual foundation. They may be committed to and active in one of the great organized religions, or they may have a spiri-tual center of their own that allows them to understand how the universe is organized and what role they, as Awesome Men, have to play.

I can claim to have read only a small portion of the many thousands of books written on this subject (I've even read a few books that have denied the need or even existence of religion, God, or spirituality). From my personal experience and the research I've done, I believe the world is divided into three groups:

- those who think about their spiritual or religious existence, are active in their beliefs, and whose beliefs affect their lives in a meaningful way each and every day,

A Deeper Look: Living Your Life as the Person You Want to Be

"It takes courage to grow up and turn out to be who you really are."
—E. E. Cummings, poet and essayist

Do you have trouble understanding and accepting the concept of life having meaning? If so, you're not alone. Acquiring that understanding is a difficult and challenging process. It requires that you expand your awareness and consciousness beyond your own personal mini-world so that you can become aware and accept that there is more to life than just yourself and your immediate surroundings.

You may feel some or all the ideas for personal change I am suggesting fit the category of "That ain't me." And perhaps that's true, at least for the you of here and now. But what you have to understand is that "you" are whatever you *choose* to be, and the you of tomorrow may be a very different person from the you of today.

Let me give an example. If I go out and rob a bank, I become a bank robber and a thief. I am no longer an author, a football coach, and a mentor. My behavior and actions transform me into a new persona. The same thing applies to you as well: *How you behave is how you become.* If you develop a gambling problem, you are a problem gambler; if you stop gambling, you cease to be a problem gambler. It doesn't matter what you say you are, because your actions speak the truth. If you act with character and ethics, you are a person of character and ethics.

I am a great believer that given the opportunity, each and every person can make a positive difference in the world. These positive differences do not have to be spectacular things like curing a disease but small things like helping your mom at home or assisting a child to do better in school. If everyone did small good things—what you might call the "lighting one candle" phenomenon—the world would be a much better place and the people in it would have much more meaning in their lives. By performing meaningful actions and displaying character and ethics in your everyday life, you will become the person you aspire to be.

One day not too long ago, I saw a new mother struggling to push a baby in a stroller up a little hill. Two young men were standing watching her in her difficulty. One man did nothing to help. Although I of course couldn't read his mind, it wasn't hard to imagine what he may well have been thinking: "She can make it. She doesn't need my help. In any event, she should have been smarter and taken the safer long way around." And so he watched and did nothing. But the other young man said nothing and ran up the hill to help the mother and child safely reach their destination on the top.

Maybe for you, life has little meaning beyond the next fun and pleasurable experience. Could it be that you still have the mindset of the child you once were, avoiding life's responsibilities, challenges, and efforts in an attempt to maximize fun and pleasure? Or, perhaps, is being "cool," laid-back, and apparently uninvolved in life's drudgery your vision of the perfect existence? I, too, had a period in my life when my main goal was for everybody to leave me alone and let me do what I wanted to do and be who I wanted to be. Luckily for me, that phase was very short, because I realized quickly that was not who I wanted to be. I was able to understand that although there are certainly times and places to have fun or "chill," those activities must be postponed when they supersede or replace leading a meaningful life.

Poets and romantics tell us to "be true to yourself" and to "follow your own star." And I agree with them 100%. But make sure you *choose* how you act, which means choosing who you are. Use your intellect and reasoning to come to the choices that lead you to a meaningful life complete with happiness, fulfillment, and achievement. With those goals in mind you will make the right choices. Do you have the courage to be an Awesome Man? It starts with small action steps.

- those who spend little or even no time contemplating the spiritual or religious aspects of their lives (e.g., Christians who attend church services at Christmas and Easter only), and

- those who deny any spiritual or religious needs whatsoever and who speak disparagingly of people who try to fill their lives with spiritual or religious faith.

Let me say that religion, spirituality, and God make no sense in a logical analysis. Anybody who tries to explain or understand these topics on a strictly rational basis will fail and never understand the true essence of the concepts. Any intelligent person knows that each human has a brain that is made up of two hemispheres. The left brain is logical and analytical, while the right brain is not. Research has shown that for most tasks, humans are most effective when they use both sides of the brain. That is why using left brain analysis (logic, rationality) always fails when contemplating spirituality, God, and religion. However, when you use both sides of the brain, most especially the right brain, you get a much different result. It is my theory that religion, faith, and belief have existed since the beginning of humankind and to this day are manifested in the lives of billions of people because they have understood that when both sides of the brain are used, spirituality is embraced.

Can you get through life with no religious or spiritual convictions? Of course you can, but research has shown it is less likely you will achieve all the happiness you deserve. So what is the downside of fostering the spiritual aspect of one's life, and is it enough to profess spiritual conviction without action? I had a teacher who explained the risks and benefits of maintaining a spiritual aspect to one's life quite succinctly this way:

> Let us imagine for a minute there is no Heaven or Hell, no afterlife, no God, no religious or spiritual requirements to lead a good life. If you do lead a good and righteous life and die and that is the end of existence, you have led a good and righteous life and you have not lost anything. On the other hand, if you live a life of selfishness, dissipation, excess, and indulgence and there is a God, and there is Heaven and Hell, you will suffer the consequences.

This explanation sounds simplistic today, but it is really powerful in its implications about choices and consequences and about wisely using your freedom and taking responsibility for your life.

There are those who profess spiritual or religious convictions but whose actions do not manifest their beliefs.

As a young man, I once met a fellow who appeared to be living a life of self-indulgence. As we were speaking he told me he was a Catholic. Astounded to hear this, I asked him how he could profess to be a follower of his faith and yet live the life he did. He explained that he had been baptized and went to church every Christmas. Further, his children had been baptized and attended Catholic schools. In his mind, he had checked off all the necessary boxes for living a spiritually respectable life.

Did this fellow really have a spiritual or religious aspect to his life? Despite his statements and token professions of faith, the way he lived his life and how he interacted with his fellow man spoke volumes. So before you smugly profess your spiritual and religious beliefs, ask yourself if you are really living that life and if your life actions are in sync with your stated beliefs.

From time to time you'll encounter people who attempt to disparage all religions, faiths, and beliefs by pointing out that evil things have been done in the name of God. Counter this by observing how much good has been done in the world by people of faith and belief. It by far outweighs the evil perpetrated by false prophets and gurus of malevolence. It is the obligation of each believer to be good and do no harm. If you discover individuals doing harm in the guise of religion, you must act to oppose them.

Fifteen Great Principles Shared by all Religions

In the book *Oneness: Great Principles Shared by All Religions*, author Jeffrey Moses quotes directly from the scriptures of Christianity, Judaism, Islam, Hinduism, Baha'i, Buddhism, and other religions. His book strips away the superficial differences between faiths by showing that the great spiritual and ethical principles are expressed almost word for word in every religion. The Dalai Lama, in commenting on the book, states: "Every major religion of the world has similar ideals of love, the same goal of benefiting humanity through spiritual practice, and the same effect of making their followers into better human beings."

Below are the fifteen common ideals found in most religions and belief systems throughout the world. Each ideal is consistent with the goals and aspirations of the Awesome Man. If those who reject religion or even the idea of a spiritual center of their own also reject these ideals, their road to becoming an Awesome Man will be very difficult.

1. **The Golden Rule / Law of Reciprocity.** The cornerstone of religious understanding. "Do unto others as you would have them do unto you."—Christianity

2. **Honor Thy Father and Mother.** Knowing them is the key to knowing ourselves. The day will come when we shall wish we had known them better.

3. **Speak the Truth.** "Sincerity is the way of heaven, and to think how to be sincere is the way of a man."— Confucius

4. **It's More Blessed to Give Than to Receive.** Generosity, charity, and kindness will open an individual to an unbounded reservoir of riches.

5. **Heaven Is Within.** "Even as the scent dwells within the flower, so God within thine own heart forever abides."—Sikhism

6. **Love Thy Neighbor / Conquer With Love / All You Need Is Love.** Acts of faith, prayer, and deep meditation provide us with the strength that allows love for our fellow man to become an abiding part of our lives. Love is a unifying force.

7. **Blessed Are the Peacemakers.** When people live in the awareness that there is a close kinship between all individuals and nations, peace is the natural result.

8. **You Reap What You Sow.** This is the great mystery of human life. Aware or unaware, all of us are ruled by this inevitable law of nature.

9. **Man Does Not Live by Bread Alone.** The blessings of life are deeper than what can be appreciated by the senses.

10. **Do No Harm.** If someone tries to hurt another, it means that he is perceiving that person as something separate and foreign from himself.

11. **Forgiveness.** The most beautiful thing a man can do is to forgive wrong.—Judaism

12. **Judge Not, Lest Ye Be Judged.** This principle is an expression of the underlying truth that humankind is one great family and that we all spring from a common source.

13. **Be Slow to Anger.** Anger clouds the mind in the very moments that clarity and objectivity are needed most. "He who holds back rising anger like a rolling chariot, him I call a real driver; others only hold the reins."—Buddha

14. **There Is But One God / God Is Love. Nature, Being, The Absolute.** Whatever name man chooses, there is but one God. All people and all things are of one essence.

15. **Follow the Spirit of the Scriptures, Not the Words.** "Study the words, no doubt, but look behind them to the thought they indicate; and having found it, throw the words away, as chaff when you have sifted out the grain."—Hinduism

Awesome Man Profile: Jimmy Carter

Most politicians are chastised for not being honest and not telling the truth. However, one US president served only one term because his honesty and openness about social responsibility, human values, and world peace created tremendous animosity among vested interests in his country.

Life was not easy for Jimmy Carter growing up in Georgia farming country during the Depression. Carter studied hard in school and worked with his parents on the farm. Eventually, in 1943 he became a naval officer and trained for the first nuclear powered submarines. He looked forward to a long and successful naval career. Then his father died and Carter returned home to take over the family farm. Initially, the going was tough. There were crop failures, and Carter was still learning how to be successful in the farming business. In fact, he and his family lived in public housing for a year. But owing to his dedication and strong work ethic, he took courses and read and learned all he could about agriculture and in time became a successful peanut farmer.

School segregation was a big issue at the time. Carter was for social tolerance, but many white farmers opposed his stance and boycotted his farms and businesses. Carter's beliefs eventually caused him to turn his eye to politics, which he did with great success. He became Georgia's governor and then, in 1977, president of the United States.

Carter's underlying spiritual faith has always underpinned his political views and desire for social justice for all. Just one of his achievements was the 1982 founding of the Carter Center, a nongovernmental, nonprofit organization with the purpose of advancing human rights and alleviating human suffering, including helping improve the quality of life for people in more than eighty countries.

As of this writing, the ninety-five-year-old Carter is recovering from surgery to address the complications of a fall he had while building houses for Habitat for Humanity. Carter, even at his advanced age, did not just talk about housing for the poor—he took action and as always through his life has made a difference. Jimmy Carter is an Awesome Man, in my view.

8

You Are a Social Being

The purpose of life is to grow and to share. When you come to look back on all that you have done in life, you will get more satisfaction from the pleasure you brought to other people's lives than you will from the times that you outdid and defeated them.
—Harold Kushner, rabbi and writer

When We Are Connected to Others We Are at Our Finest

Realizing that happiness and pleasure are not the same, the Awesome Man accepts that what is necessary for happiness is finding meaning in life. And he knows that to have meaning in life it is necessary to be connected directly with other human beings in a positive and caring way. If we lose that social connectedness with other humans, we cannot possibly achieve meaning and happiness in life. People are biologically wired to be at their best when interacting with other people in positive ways. This is fact and not to accept and encourage this biological predisposition in yourself is fruitless.

Social connectedness is defined by frequency of contact with others, personal relationships, and engagement in the community.

On the next page is a photo of fans at a football game. You can tell just by their expressions that they are connected with the team, each other, and the experience. They are sharing the thrill of the game with their team and with each other, relishing every bit of the joy. This is a good and healthy (and exuberant!) expression of social connectedness.

David Morris

Unlike most members of the animal kingdom, each of us—in ideal circumstances—is born into a close-knit family. We have two parents and four grandparents. We may have uncles and aunts, brothers and sisters, and cousins as well. We share our DNA with these people, and through that physical connection we also have an emotional connection. Why has nature provided us with these relationships? And why should we treasure and foster these connections? Understanding the answers to these questions is a key to understanding ourselves.

Human beings are the most complex and sophisticated creatures on earth. No other life-form is as multifaceted and intricate as a human being. We have one of the longest life spans on the planet and one of the longest time periods before we reach physical maturity and are able to reproduce. *Because the nurturing and development period is so long, we need help when we are young. Children are not self-sustaining for many years.

Besides our physical needs, we humans have a great requirement for emotional support and nurturing. Through bonding and relationships we hopefully grow our emotional selves. The Awesome Man finds meaning through his social connectedness. The first level of connectedness for the

---

* At the other extreme are Pacific salmon, which die after reproduction (sort of one and done!). Baby salmon do not need their parents to cherish and help them grow and develop.

Awesome Man is with his immediate family. He sees his parent(s) not as a source of resources for his gratification but rather as adults who also have needs and deserve understanding and respect. If he fosters an adult relationship (he knows there is no happiness in being a forever child) with his parents and siblings and is attuned to their needs, his family relationships will become so much richer and more genuine.

The next phase in expanding his circle of positive relationships involves going beyond the immediate family to the extended family of grandparents, aunts, uncles, and so on. The Awesome Man knows he can gain much from these relationships, because the breadth of experience these people have will give him even a deeper and broader understanding of himself and the world. By being of service in very small ways, such as making regular phone calls or short visits, he will enhance the lives of his extended family and his own life. And he benefits, too, in ways beyond the emotional warmth this brings him. The Awesome Man has come to develop a core of people who care about him. They will be there to provide him with support and security in his times of need, just as he will do for them.

The next ring in the Awesome Man's expanding circle of relationships involves his academic, community, cultural, sporting, and/or work relationships. The Awesome Man is conscientious about helping his peers, fellow students, and coworkers achieve success. He will especially endeavor not to be a burden on them or his mentors and supervisors. By helping others attain their full potential, the Awesome Man is well on the way to achieving his own.

Finally, the Awesome Man strives to interrelate with diverse people and groups, because he knows he will not fully develop if he restricts his interactions. Much like a person who only eats bananas will not have a healthy body and will not experience the richness and pleasure of diverse foods, by limiting your relationships and interactions to only certain social, professional, or cultural groups, you, too, will not experience the richness and pleasure a diverse array of human relationships brings.

There is one big caveat that I wish I did not have to mention. Choose your relationships wisely! The greatest source of introduction to criminality, drugs, and substance abuse is through friends and peers. Even guys you hang out with in your neighborhood have the potential to lead you away from your goal to be an Awesome Man. Judge well.

We Are at Our Worst When We Are Isolated

Once we accept that being connected with family and friends, associates, and good groups is necessary to fully develop and grow on the path to become the Awesome Man, we have to take action. Yet there is a common reason why many young men fail in this endeavor: self-imposed social isolation.

Isolation has a profound effect on the human mind. We know that one way to "break" captured terrorists is to isolate them, allowing them no communication with anybody. In fact, in prisons "solitary" is referred to as the "hole" and is considered the worst punishment an inmate can receive.

Here is what Canadian Senator Kim Pate—speaking in May of 2019 during a debate in the Canadian Senate on a "Bill to Amend the Corrections and Conditional Release Act"—says about the practice (which is called "segregation" in Canada):

> Over four decades, I have spent countless hours kneeling on cement floors outside segregation cells, pleading through meal slots in solid metal doors as someone's loved one—someone's child, sibling, parent, or partner—smashed their heads against cement walls or floors, slashed their bodies, tied ligatures or put nooses around their necks, tried to gouge out their own eyes, mutilated themselves in sometimes unimaginable ways, or smeared blood and feces on their bodies, windows, and walls. I have heard indescribable sounds of torment and despair that reverberate and haunt me.

These compelling words hint at the powerful effect isolation can have on the human mind. Sadly, there are many outside the penitentiary, out in society, who experience something similar—profound *social* isolation—and who suffer deeply as a result. We have all seen and heard words and terms that society uses to describe the less fortunate among us: "loner," "with few friends," "socially isolated." These people can never attain happiness and fulfillment in life unless they—or we—break the bonds of isolation.

So if social interaction and connectedness are so important to becoming an Awesome Man, why do many young men view it as unimportant and voluntarily avoid it? For some, the reason is that they may feel socially awkward or have convinced themselves that nobody "gets them." Others may live in rural areas where they are physically isolated. Some young men simply lack a supporting, caring family and social structure and have never been able to develop close social relationships.

However, regardless of our particular circumstances, in the end each of us has a choice to make: Are we going to make the effort to foster healthy and meaningful relationships with family, individuals, and groups, or are we going to self-isolate and suffer the consequences?

Since we know social isolation is harmful and nature has provided us with the resources to be connected, why is it that so many suffer from loneliness and self-segregation? What can you do to help yourself to avoid the dangers and pitfalls of disconnectedness?

The first step to helping yourself is to carefully analyze the choices or behaviors you make when it comes to interacting with other people. Are some of those choices or behaviors contrary to fostering connectedness? Here's some food for thought:

- When we are selfish and think first of ourselves and our desires, we will not likely reach out to others.

- When we are close-minded and insist on our own opinions being the only right and valid ones, we shut out others. A Palestinian Arab once told me, "The Jews and the Arabs agree on ninety-five out of one hundred issues, but we disagree on about five issues. We have a choice: Do we focus on what we agree on and thereby get along with each other, or do we focus of the few things we disagree about and fight?" My experience with families is much the same. Unfortunately, family members too often choose to focus on what they disagree about, and that results in much pain.

- When we are too busy with trivial and non-developmental activities to interact with others, we do not invest the time to develop human connection.

With the right attitude, we can choose to use the knowledge and skills we have and make the correct choices. The alternative is to condemn ourselves to isolation. You may wonder what I mean by "right attitude." Let me give you an example from my personal experience.

I love watch auto racing on TV. Many a Sunday while I am watching a big race, one of my sons or friends will pop over to visit. I have a choice:

a. I can say, "Come back later. I am watching my race."

b. I can say, "Come on in and watch the race with me."

c. I can turn the TV off and say, "Come on in and have a seat. Can I get you a drink? What's new?"

Which do you think is the right choice for me to make? If you were in the same situation, watching your favorite TV show, what would you do?

A Place Where You Will Always Be Welcome

If you feel you are somehow lacking in the requirements to connect with others, or your extended family is not available to you, consider volunteering at a charity or faith-based organization as a first step in your venture outside yourself. They are all very open and have lots of opportunities for you to connect with others and be of service.

"Why Won't You Leave Me Alone?"

Isolation is not the only problem confronting young men. The modern world offers many "shiny objects" that detract from our ability to form and maintain deep, connected interactions and relationships with others. And this is a shame, because what happens is that our relationships become superficial and lack depth, more like impersonal transactions that are bereft of genuine feelings and rapport.

Here's a list of some of the many (often digital) distractions that preclude successful human interactions in a man's life. Raise your hand if any of them apply to you.

- video games
- internet porn
- texting and other smartphone use
- Facebook, Twitter, Pinterest, and the like

- excessive behaviors such obsessive reading, television viewing, or binge streaming
- any activity that routinely precludes direct, meaningful human interaction

Why are these things bad for you as a social being?

To one degree or another, these tend to be merely superficial pleasure-giving activities that are not developmental in a social or humanistic way. Additionally, for young men at least, they are usually *solitary* activities. (And if you're wondering, no, interacting with a buddy over a gaming network is not at all the same as fostering a true friendship with that person.)

For example, video games are time consuming, are by design addictive, and involve only a limited range of your mind's capacities. They do little to develop a person into becoming a better human being and do not correspond to the real world's rich and dynamic experiences. In fact, there is a growing tendency for video games to take up truly significant amounts of time in a young man's life, diverting him away from school, relationships, and responsibilities. Since society sees video games as less damaging than other obsessions, they are often given a free pass. This is unfortunate, as many studies have shown the negative impact that video gaming has had on young men's achievement, motivation, and success in the real world. In particular, research indicates that dedicated gamers display poorer physical fitness, get less sleep, suffer from more mental health issues, receive poorer grades, and have lower graduation rates than their non-addicted peers.

Stern List

Let me be clear in stating that video games, when used appropriately for relaxation and recreation and in moderate amounts, are usually benign and for some males can have some positive attributes. It is the excessive and/or solitary use that may be detrimental to one's development as an Awesome Man.

Another example of a distraction that can impair social connectedness is internet pornography, a multibillion-dollar business almost exclusively targeted at males. The problem with internet porn is that it portrays the relationships between men and women in a totally unrealistic manner that doesn't relate to real life. It mostly depicts, as the basis of male–female relationships, the pleasure and satisfaction of the male, while largely ignoring

Suggested Reading List

In case you're interested in learning more about different types of activities that can become addictions, I've compiled a list of research you may find of interest:

Jory Deleuze et al., "Escaping Reality through Videogames Is Linked to an Implicit Preference for Virtual over Real-life Stimuli," *Journal of Affective Disorders* 245 (2019): 1024-31, http://www.uclep.be/wp-content/uploads/pdf/Pub/Deleuze_JAD_2018.pdf

Daria J. Kuss, "Internet Gaming Addiction: Current Perspectives," *Psychology Research and Behavior Management* 6 (2013): 125–37, https://www.ncbi.nlm.nih.gov/pmc/articles/PMC3832462/

Dustin L. Redmond, "The Effect of Video Games on Family Communication and Interaction," *Graduate Theses and Dissertations*, Iowa State University, 2010, https://lib.dr.iastate.edu/cgi/viewcontent.cgi?article&51&context=etd

Robert Weiss, "The Opposite of Addiction Is Connection: New Addiction Research Brings Surprising Discoveries," *Love and Sex in the Digital Age* (blog), *Psychology Today*, September 30, 2015, https://www.psychologytoday.com/ca/blog/love-and-sex-in-the-digital-age/201509/the-opposite-addiction-is-connection the woman's well-being. This one-sided portrayal often leads to poor interactions in the real world, which is never as ideal as the porn a young man views on his computer. As a result, the male feels frustrated and is drawn back to porn for the simple, undemanding "relationship" it delivers.

Second, much porn portrays females as subservient and obedient, there to please the male. It is fantasy of the poorest kind. This unrealistic portrayal again does not correspond to the real world and does not equip the watcher with the tools to navigate the complex relationships with women that make life so fulfilling.

It cannot be denied that the lure of pornography is strong and that real relationships with live human beings are complex and challenging, sometimes leading to pain. However, these real relationships are the only ones worth having. As pleasurable as porn can be for so many viewers, the fundamental fact is that the providers of porn are only motivated by getting your money. Nobody provides porn for the well-being of the viewer free of charge. If there was no financial motive, there would be no porn or the closely related sex trade.

In addition to potentially consuming huge amounts of time, incessant texting (as well as the use of any number of smartphone apps offering similar functionality) and social media sites such as Facebook, Instagram, and Twitter also carry the risk of unrealistic interactions. Instead of real human intercommunication—and with it all the subtleties of language, nuance, and nonverbal signals and cues—these sites offer a depersonalized mode of interaction, each with its own particular limitations (Twitter gives you only 280 characters to work with!). So much of the content on Facebook is reposts of commercial content generators. Other than selfies and pet and meal photos, very little of what is posted is of original reflection or offers much in the way of genuine insight into a person's life and character. Sure, it's possible to receive true and open feedback from social media connections. But more often than not, people posting real concerns and issues end up receiving responses that are flippant, superficial, or inappropriate.

In addition, many smartphone and computer apps provide for a layer of anonymity that allows the sender to express hurtful, disgusting, inappropriate, and damaging statements and outright lies. Millions of people daily are emotionally hurt and scarred through thoughtless and insensitive posts.

Thaninee Chuensomchit

I once personally experienced this veil of anonymity at work. I was in an organization where I interacted with a brilliant young woman who was extremely shy and reserved. Even though I made several attempts to engage her in discussions and an exchange of ideas, she remained aloof and withdrawn. I then connected with her on a social networking site and was amazed how she was now comfortable sharing with the world what I considered quite personal feelings and thoughts. I realized that for her, genuine face-to-face communication with other people had largely been replaced with interactions filtered through third-party technology. How can she learn to navigate the complex world of human interaction if her main tool for doing so is a keyboard and a computer monitor?

The great thing about face-to-face communication is how it allows the richness and fullness of the human experience to be *fully* shared. This is why the Awesome Man values, even cherishes, real human communication and socializing. If you disagree, ask any child if anything can replace a hug. Yes, face-to-face communication can be challenging for young men who don't have much practice with it. Nuances, subtleties, facial expressions, and voice inflections have to be noticed and understood when two people are talking. But as with so many things in life, your ability to speak and communicate directly with another person, while initially difficult, becomes better with practice.

Escaping the "Let's Hang Out" Rut

We men often limit ourselves to situations where we either feel in control or feel socially safe. Time and again, young men find comfort and relaxation in the company of like-minded males, where there is little chance of confrontation or critical thinking. Let me say that nothing is intrinsically wrong with hanging out with your buddies. Doing so only becomes a problem when it precludes personal development toward becoming an Awesome Man.

But at some point you will feel you've fallen into a rut and want to get out. Let me offer a few suggestions for expanding your social horizons and fostering new connections and friendships.

Many young men feel socially shy and awkward. If this is you, the first step is to develop some confidence in your ability to socialize and feel comfortable in new social situations. Try to understand the fact that most new situations are not that different from situations you have already experienced. Joining a new club or group is not that different from school. There will be some new people, there will likely be a leader (or teacher), and most of the people there will have some common interests. If you, too, share the same interests, connections will almost automatically begin to develop.

The easiest way to get going is to find groups focused on your interests. If you are interested in basketball, joining a basketball club will reduce your social anxiety considerably because you're already enthusiastic about basketball, just like the other people in the club. No matter what your interests are, chances are there are groups that cater to those pursuits. Here social media and technology can actually be productive tools, as they make it easy to connect initially with people and groups you want to learn more about.

Another idea is to take a friend along with you the first few times you get together with the new group. Bring a friend who has a positive outlook, and the experience will likely be better for everyone.

If discomfort remains, rehearsing may be an effective tactic to try. Rehearsing means playing the scene in your mind, much like an actor will go over the scene in a movie before the actual filming. For example, you might rehearse how you will greet the members of the club when you arrive. Just be sure you block out any negative self-talk while rehearsing.

The second step toward productively engaging with the wider world involves nothing more than developing a small but important perceptual shift—namely, that new and unfamiliar social situations provide a terrific opportunity for learning and growth! The wider and more varied your interactions become, the more confident and more successful you will become in different social settings and situations. Part of it is simply the result of "getting good" at trying out new things, and part of it is the experience and learning you get interacting with other interesting people. To expand on that last point, let me also encourage you to purposefully interact with people of all ages, because the richness of life is best manifested when we interact with people of different eras and experiences.

So many positive alternatives are available to you that have nothing to do with hanging out in bars or lounging at home in front of the computer all day. Try some new hobbies, volunteer to coach a young children's sports team, repair a broken fence, or just build something. Learn a new skill or further develop an existing one. Help somebody read, write, or play a musical instrument. Join a theater group. Get involved with community groups and service clubs. Just get out there!

The benefits are tremendous. You will

- meet new people with new interests,

- learn new skills,

- improve your social skills and confidence, and

- meet people of demographics different from that with which you would usually come in contact with.

Again, starting is always the hardest part, so I encourage you to start with just one, small step. All I ask is that this step points you down the path toward being an Awesome Man.

Masculinity and Peer Pressure

I believe that one of the greatest obstacles to being an Awesome Man can be peer pressure. This negative type of social interaction can take many forms, name calling being perhaps the most prominent. Have you or someone you know ever been labeled with one of the following epithets: bitch, chicken, creep, deadbeat, dyke, fag, fairy, girly-boy, homo, loser, man-whore, pansy, pervert, pretty boy, pussy, sleaze, or wuss?

The intimidator who calls another male one of these or similar labels (and who does so to establish his dominance in the group) is implying that the other person is somehow less than fully masculine. He is calling the target's masculinity and maleness into question. The victim's usual immediate response is denial, followed by his recounting of examples showing why he is not worthy of the label. For most boys, the threat of labeling and bullying and the pressure to conform to the "guy code" begins in elementary school. Any boy who excels scholastically, creatively, or artistically or does not meet expectations in demeanor or attitude will be focused on and ridiculed.

As a clarinetist who did not play any varsity sports in high school, I know of what I speak. Most boys in high school do not have the tools to deal with peer pressure, and they either adopt the style and attributes as set out in the guy code or experience high school as either a mildly unpleasant or miserable experience. As high school also provides an opportunity for a young man to take firm steps on his road to becoming an Awesome Man, it is important that high school offer a productive, positive experience for him. He needs the tools and skills to go forward and meet the challenges of peer pressure and verbal bullying.

What are the tools and skills that the young man needs? I recommend the following:

First, the young male must learn and understand that physicality has nothing to do with being a man. The Awesome Man in development does not have to be a star athlete. In fact, physical attributes are not preeminent in the development of an Awesome Man. All people grow and develop at different rates. The basis for much bullying and ridicule is focused on those who do not appear to have those stereotypical "manly" traits. Fortunately, most of those "manly" traits are of little importance in the twenty-first century.

Whatever your size or degree of physical strength, stand tall in your posture, make eye contact, and speak with a firm voice. It is okay to stand up to peers, and often your voice, speaking good sense, can carry the day. You always have the right to walk away from and not participate in what you perceive as bad situations. You also have the right and obligation to advise your peers on the dangers of their actions and attitudes.

Second, if a high school male is subject to bullying and abuse, he must understand that developing the social and mental skills to deal positively with this issue is an important growth step in becoming an Awesome Man. Although no one should welcome undue peer pressure or being the target of bullying, these challenges present a real opportunity for the young man to strengthen his inner self. As with most challenges in life, you cannot ignore the problem, but you can deal with it effectively.

- Speak openly with your parents and/or your teachers about the situation. Enlist their help and guidance.

- Speak to the bully; ask him why he feels it is necessary to abuse you. Do not grovel, beg, or whine. Act as his equal. Chances are he will be embarrassed and not enjoy your confrontation and therefore will avoid negative interactions with you in the future.

- If the bully remarks on some fact or issue he does not like about you, inform him you were born with that particular physical characteristic and you did not choose it. Explain how it is not really just or fair that he ridicules you for something neither of you have control over.

- Never deny anything he says. For example, if he says he bullies you because you are a nerd, do not deny being a nerd. Restate you were born that way, and not everybody can be the way the bully wants.

- Try to understand that the bully has his own issues and is likely abusing you to feel better about himself. Do not say this to him, though. However, do try to be empathetic with him.

- The key is always to be proud of yourself and have self-respect.

- In grades nine and ten I was bullied, long before adults considered it a problem. At that time it was appropriate to physically fight your tormentor, and in two cases I did. I do not believe I won those fights, but I was able to inflict enough punishment on my tormentors that they stopped picking on me. In grade twelve I decided to ignore my tormentor (fighting always led to expulsion at this private school) and act if he were nonexistent and insignificant. When he confronted me in a washroom with a truly inappropriate question, I nodded and

Explanations Are Not Excuses

Please note: Earlier in the book I rebuked people who say things like "That is the way I am" or "I can't help it, that's the way I was born" as an excuse for not growing and developing as a human being. Some readers may be puzzled when I suggest using the same expressions when dealing with bullies. The difference is whether the phrases are used as excuses or as factual explanations. This is something the Awesome Man is always mindful of.

Here's an example: I am color-blind, or, more accurately, color-deficient—that is the way I was born. I am explaining a shortfall in my physical ability. In no way am I using it as an excuse not to be the best I can.

walked away without giving him the response he was hoping for. He then realized that he would never get a satisfying response from me and stopped bullying me.

- Remember, the bully wants to do two things: intimidate you and elicit an inappropriate response from you, thereby building his self-esteem by reducing yours. By maintaining your dignity, restraint, equality, and self-esteem in front of him, you will thwart and frustrate him, and he will likely move on to less resilient targets.

Yes, this is easier said than done. As a high school counselor, I knew of a teenage boy who had some tissue removed as result of childhood cancer surgery. He was left with a significant disfigurement. It was not visible in normal situations, but word got out in the school and some boys began teasing him about the apparent deformity. His reaction was to deny it, which only increased the demand to "show us."

The boy came to me seeking guidance. After he explained the situation, I stated that many people have scars and have even lost body parts. The alternative to his surgery was death, so the result was a good thing for him. I added that the best course of action was to tell the truth and explain the circumstances and choices made at the time. He should ask his tormentors what they would have done in his place and speak from a position of honesty and strength.

Put People of Quality into Your Life

As you grow into adulthood, your parents, teachers, and other adults begin to yield less power over your thoughts and behaviors, and you become more aware of your peers' opinions. That is why it is important for you to develop tools, such as those mentioned above, that help you cope with this new set of influencers in your life and resist negative peer pressure (something even adults have to contend with).

I cannot say enough about the importance of associating with quality individuals, groups, and organizations to avoid the likelihood of negative peer pressure. Groups and organizations that have positive goals and objectives tend to have like-minded members.

Being around quality people is a force multiplier to becoming the person you want to be. These people of character and integrity may mentor you, become role models, and support you on your journey to becoming an Awesome Man. Becoming a member of a community association, a charity, a nonprofit, a youth organization, a service group, or some other unit of positive, proactive people dedicated to self-improvement and/or service to others will be one of the best things you can do for yourself.

For a young male, the struggle to prove one's masculinity to peers is quite real, and the fears of inadequacy, incompetence, and weakness are all too common. How you as a young man learn to cope with these pressures is crucial to your development as a person.

Previously in this book I have mentioned Michael Kimmel's book *Guyland*, which describes the prolonged period of immaturity many young men in today's society go through (and sometimes never emerge from). Kimmel offers the following suggestions, with which I fully concur:

1. Boys should have friends and interests outside their immediate high school classmates. This is an excellent way of avoiding the dangers of cliques. By reaching beyond the boundaries of his school, a young man will likely develop a richer, more diverse view of himself, his friends, and the world. Any activities that are outside the immediate sphere of his school are good.

2. Friendship on an individual basis is so important at this stage. Having a male friend outside the group or clique allows for the development of positive one-on-one relationships, much different from and much more beneficial than those that occur in a group or clique.

3. Having female friends is also a positive at this early stage in an Awesome Man's development. Being able to speak to and maintain a friendship with a girl is a great counter to the macho-shithead culture that he is being bombarded with everywhere. It will put him in a good place later on in life, since he already knows that he can have a great relationship with a woman that is not based on sex alone.

4. Kimmel also suggests having friends who are targets of bullies. The great advantage of this is that a young man will develop empathy, understanding, and humanity by embracing those who are also scorned.

Awesome Man Profile: Ryan Hreljac

Never doubt that a small group of thoughtful, committed, citizens can change the world. Indeed, it is the only thing that ever has.
—Margaret Mead, cultural anthropologist

One of the points that I have been hoping to make in this book is that there is no age restriction on when you can start on your path to becoming an Awesome Man. So why wait?

In 1998, six-year-old Ryan Hreljac was in first grade when his teacher told a story about the shortage of clean water in many parts of Africa and what a burden this placed on children and their families in terms of health, sanitation, and quality of life.

Ryan learned that for $70, a well could be provided for an African village. He determinedly went home that day and asked his parents for $70 to pay for a well. They said no. His parents, never expecting Ryan to persevere, stated he could earn the money by doing extra chores around the home. It took Ryan four months to earn and raise the $70! Ryan and his family arranged to donate the money to WaterCan, a charity that provided wells in Africa.

What Ryan then learned was that the $70 paid for the hand pump; the entire well cost $2,000! Most of us would be proud that we could pay for a hand pump, but resilient young Ryan was determined to overcome this setback and raise the entire $2,000. Recall that it took four months for Ryan to raise $70. It might take many years to reach this new, much higher goal. But Ryan had a mission.

Fortunately, people in his small town were becoming aware of the young boy who took on a huge task to make a difference in the lives of people he had never met. Small donations started flowing in, but more importantly other young men offered to help by doing extra chores and fundraising. Ryan had become an inspiration to others who wanted to join him in his goal and make it theirs. A sixty-year-old well-driller from Ryan's hometown got involved and persuaded other well-drillers throughout the region to participate.

In 1999, Ryan and his supporters had raised the $2,000 and provided a well to a school in Agweo, Uganda. But Ryan did not stop with this success. He set new goals. By the year 2000, he had raised an additional $61,000, and in 2001 at the age of ten, he and his family and supporters established Ryan's Well Foundation. The foundation has brought clean water to more than 892,725 people in sixteen developing countries, through 1,166 water and sanitation projects. In 2015, they drilled their 1,000th well!

What is most significant is that Ryan was connected with many people and groups of quality and compassion: his parents and family, teachers and students, other schools (where he gave talks), and his town and community members. Thanks to his social connectedness, Ryan's initial personal goal of raising $70 has grown to over $250,000.

Ryan Hreljac at the age of six began his journey to becoming an Awesome Man. He graduated from University of King's College in Halifax, Nova Scotia in 2013 with a degree in international development and political science and now works full-time as the CEO of Ryan's Well Foundation, which continues to do the good work he started many years ago. (Visit www.ryanswell.ca to learn more about his remarkable organization.)

9

Competence: The Key for Making Your Mark in the World

It is easier to do a job right than to explain why you didn't.
—Martin Van Buren, American statesman and president

Competence Means Being More Than "Good Enough"

The Awesome Man knows that there is one guaranteed way to be unique and stand out from the crowd, and that is to be competent. Not everybody can be a superstar athlete or a pop music celebrity, but with effort and perseverance, everybody can be competent and excel in their own field of endeavor.

Let me tell you about Chad Houser, a man you likely have never heard of. Through study, effort, and perseverance, Houser reached his culinary goal of becoming a top chef and restaurant owner in Dallas, Texas, and enjoyed great respect and financial success. Because of his high degree of competence, he had credibility and support in pursuing the next ambition of his life. After seventeen years as a chef, Houser sold his restaurant partnership in order to start Café Momentum. Café Momentum is a Dallas-based restaurant and culinary training facility that transforms young people's lives by providing a positive environment in which at-risk youth who have spent time in juvenile facilities receive intensive mentoring. Houser provides them with culinary, job, and life-skills training, enabling them to achieve their full potential. Houser's competence in culinary, business, and life skills was the essential factor that allowed him to make a transformational difference in the lives of many others, something that brought him tremendous satisfaction.

The *Oxford English Dictionary* defines competence as "the ability to do something successfully or efficiently." Let's first focus on the words "do something"—those words mean that action is required. The second key phrase is "successfully or efficiently." You *cannot* be competent if you are unsuccessful or inefficient in accomplishing the task in question. I believe that an Awesome Man manifests his competence by being proficient, capable, skilled, and adept at how he leads his life and in everything he does.

So how do you achieve competence? By action and effort! As Nike tells us, "Just do it." But how are you able to perform the actions in a way that results in success? First you have to acquire skills by learning. Humans do not magically acquire skills; they have to learn them, even rudimentary skills such as how to use a spoon, eat a banana, or brush our hair. Learning is a good thing and is the first step to being competent.

Freelance writer and content marketer Farheen Gani, in her podcast of July 11, 2017, titled "Top 10 Strategies for Learning New Skills," addresses the challenges of learning new competencies. With her kind permission, I have excerpted and condensed some of her most salient points here:

Make Learning Meaningful for Yourself

Finding meaning in our learning is key. Whatever you are trying to learn, you first have to make it meaningful for yourself.

Why? Because when things are meaningful and important to us, they become part of our being. Our level of investment in acquiring knowledge goes up dramatically when the knowledge is important to us. Learning to drive an automobile is a useful skill, but when you want to learn to drive so you can go on a camping adventure in the mountains, then it becomes a meaningful task for you. Learning to dance may be irrelevant, but it becomes very meaningful if you plan to ask a pretty classmate to the prom.

Learn by Doing

You are a natural learner and you learn best when you perform the tasks you are trying to learn. To be a competent cook, you have to actually cook, not just read recipes. If you want to write well, you have to write. If you want to become a skilled public speaker, you have to speak in front of other people. If you want to be a role model and leader to others, you have to lead. There is no substitute for actually doing the tasks at which you want to be skilled.

> **The Awesome Man manifests his competence by being proficient, capable, skilled, and adept at how he leads his life and in everything he does.**

Study the Greats, and Then Practice

One way I have learned to write better is to read a lot of books. I read for content and style, and when reading other authors I always consider how effectively they are communicating with the reader. If I'm impressed, I will even adopt some of their styles and techniques into my work. This approach is much the same way one could become better at free throws in basketball by watching how different college and NBA players do free throws and adopting their styles.

Teach What You Learn

One of the ways you can learn a new skill and ensure that you have it mastered is to teach it to someone else. That's right—even before you master a new skill, start teaching it to others.

This approach works because when we learn with the intention to teach, we break the material down into simple, understandable chunks for ourselves. It also forces us to examine the topic more critically and thoroughly, knowing that we'll have to explain it later to someone else. This helps us to understand the topic better.

Spend More Time Practicing Things You Find Difficult

In order to excel at any skill, you need to push yourself out of your comfort zone and practice things you aren't good at. As a tennis player, you will never get better by playing opponents who have equal or lower skill levels than your own. As a musician, you will never improve by rehearsing the same pieces you became skilled at last year. It is only by mastering the difficult, challenging, and demanding aspects of any skill do you become competent and proficient.

Take Frequent Breaks

The brain has two modes—focused and diffused—and both modes are equally important. While in focused mode, you're able to learn the nitty-gritties of a problem. In diffused mode, you're better able to see the big picture and bring all the elements together. It's important to let your brain relax for a while after a particularly intense session of study or practice, to give it time to connect the dots. Just like your body after vigorous exercise, your brain needs time to rest after hard exertion.

Test Yourself

Tests are an effective method in helping you learn. Most students reread notes before exams, but top students also spend time solving problems and taking practice exams. Testing is effective because it takes recall a step further by *demonstrating* how well you can use what you've learned, which is the ultimate goal of learning and the foundation of competence.

Find a Mentor*

Mentorship is perhaps the quickest way to take your skills to the next level. A mentor helps you navigate your field by offering invaluable perspective and experience. When reaching out to experts, describe what you have to offer, rather than what you will gain. Whatever services you can offer, be sure to let them know.

The key is starting—the worst a person can do is say no, so ask!

Be Curious

Nothing stimulates learning quite like curiosity! Instead of letting a textbook guide your learning, you take the lead. Seek answers from many sources. Don't merely memorize theories and techniques, think about why they matter and why they're relevant.

Chances are as a young boy one of your favorite words was *why*. Naturally you were inquisitive and curious, and wondered *why* and *how* about the world. You're older now, but that natural desire for awareness and knowledge still lives within you. That desire never went away—you just stopped using it. Use your competencies to open the door to greater understanding of the people and the world around you. See what you end up discovering![†]

---

*See part 3 for more on the importance of mentors, along with tips on how to find and meet them.

† Farheen Gani, "Top 10 Strategies for Learning New Skills," July 11, 2017, https://zapier.com/blog/learning-new-skills.

In the Real World, Being Just Okay Doesn't Cut It

In a previous career, one of my job tasks was to hire young people for entry-level jobs. I always looked at the hobbies and interests section of their applications to try to glean some understanding of the applicants to see if they were worthy of an in-person interview. I specifically was looking for competence in some area that indicated that the prospective employee had the ability to learn and do something successfully or efficiently. If I saw that competence in *some* field existed, I knew the applicant had the ability to learn and apply himself to the tasks and challenges of the position for which I was hiring. That was the person I wanted to employ.

I was amazed how many wrote on their résumé "music" as a hobby or pastime. As a musician, I knew that the determination, skill, and perseverance developed in learning to play a musical instrument were usually attributes that were transferrable to the work environment. You can imagine my chagrin when one applicant disclosed that his level of involvement in "music" was listening to music! Needless to say, it doesn't take a high level of competence to accomplish that. Not to be deterred, I asked if he had any deeper interest in music, anything that involved study or research on the subject. His answer was a simple no. And no, he did not get the job.

In my human resources roles, I once really hated having to fire an underperforming employee because I felt *we* had made the initial error, during the hiring phase. Or perhaps we did not properly train and provide the necessary motivation for that employee. However, over the years I experienced enough incompetence that I came to realize firings were a necessary but unfortunate aspect of my job. I also learned that some people did not care about being fired or even desired it. Some terminated employees would make comments such as "I wondered why it took you so long to fire me. I didn't like working here anyways." Or, "I wanted to be fired, so I had a reason to go to school."

One salesman working for me whom I ended up firing was Bill. Bill was a warm and personable guy whom I always expected to be an outstanding salesman. I liked Bill and did everything that I thought I could do to help him. I gave him extra coaching and encouragement, and I went over all his customer interactions and reviewed where he could improve. Sadly, Bill never strived to improve as a salesman. He had two obvious weaknesses, which I tried to help him with. Sometimes he got anxious in the sales process, and this lack of self-confidence was picked up by the customer. He was competent at some basic things, but when it got to the nitty-gritty of hammering out a deal with the client, he usually came up short. Bill's second weakness was he had no real desire to be the best he could be. He was a little too comfortable with and accepting of himself. The idea that he could develop new skills and be a top salesman was not something he could envision.

One day Bill was telling me he had taken up the sport of squash. I was pleased, as I felt (or, rather, hoped) that learning and playing a competitive sport would somehow strengthen him as an automobile salesman. Perhaps squash would foster a more aggressive and winning attitude toward his job.

About a week later, Bill came to me and said he had to go out for an hour for a dentist appointment. No problem. Then a couple of days later, he told me he had a chiropractor appointment. A few days after that, I was looking for Bill on the sales floor and asked where he was. One of the other salesmen said Bill had to go out for a little while. Then I started noticing Bill was frequently gone for more than an hour out of his five-hour shifts. As the weather warmed up and more customers were coming into the showroom, I became increasingly conscious of Bill's absences. On one very busy day, Bill was nowhere to be found. I phoned the local squash facility and asked for Bill. The person on the line said Bill was playing a game and asked if I could leave a message. I replied, "Yes, tell Bill his boss called and he should bring his company car and his keys back right away." In the car business this is how you knew you were terminated.

Bill was fired in part because he lacked competence in several key areas related to sales. But the real deal-killer was that he never really tried to learn and grow in his job. And he let me and his coworkers down when he failed to let us know his true whereabouts. He was not at the dentist or the chiropractor—he was playing squash.

Bill did not seem to understand that the short-term satisfaction he received from playing squash was in no way going to replace the loss of his job, his company car, and his self-respect. If he had been a moderately effective salesman, he might have gotten only a serious reprimand. But his lack of competence, when combined with his deceit, ensured that he was not going to get a second chance from me.

In the real world, every employer only wants the most competent employees. That's why being competent is the best and often the only form of job security you can have. As long as you are striving to be the best employee the company has and you are better than anybody else applying, chances are your position is pretty secure. If you drop down to average or okay, your job security diminishes very rapidly.

Fortunately, you already know how to become more competent. By learning, practicing, and developing your skills, you can avoid the fate of Bill and those like him, people who never invested the time and effort into getting better at what they do. All the job satisfaction and security you desire is available to you through acquiring knowledge.

Managing Your Time Well Allows You More Freedom to Do the Important Things in Life

A human being should be able to change a diaper, plan an invasion, butcher a hog, conn a ship, design a building, write a sonnet, balance accounts, build a wall, set a bone, comfort the dying, take orders, give orders, cooperate, act alone, solve equations, analyze a new problem, pitch manure, program a computer, cook a tasty meal, fight efficiently, die gallantly. Specialization is for insects.

—Robert A. Heinlein, author

I hope you now understand that being competent, being the best you can be, is a very important aspect of your working career. But more than that, competency is important for all the routine things we do in life. In fact, I have a mantra about this: Do ordinary things extraordinarily well. What do I mean by "ordinary things"? Quite a lot! Let's see how you answer these questions: Can you ride a bicycle? Can you fix a flat tire? Can you drive a manual transmission car? Can you sew a button? Can you repair a loose board on a fence? Can you ice-skate? Can you cook a tasty breakfast? Anything you can do competently is a credit to you. Plus, doing things well just feels good, not to mention that being competent makes your life run much more smoothly.

By also being competent in your roles as a son, a husband, a parent, and a friend, and in all the other important relationship roles you will have in your life, you will ensure that you will be living by the code of the Awesome Man. Sometimes in striving for competency in tasks and actions we neglect the very important human relational aspects of our lives. We are all familiar with celebrities, actors, and athletes who achieved significant skill and recognition in their fields of endeavor but who in reality are not very nice people and have a trail of broken relationships strewn behind them. Being a good son, husband, father, or friend takes effort and learning. You do not become a quality son to your parents just because "son" is your designation, no more so than if I put on a pilot's uniform and sat in the cockpit of an airplane would I become a competent pilot. It is a process of growing and developing the competencies necessary to be a good son. In fact, being competent in all aspects of your life is what ensures that you are becoming an Awesome Man.

With competence, your confidence increases—which brings all kinds of subsidiary benefits—and you will grow as a man. Possessing a thirst for knowledge and a deep desire to understand how things work, and then in time to master their mysteries—these are qualities of a real man. Remember, it is not that you are the best in the world at some particular activity that makes you special. Rather, it is the sum total of the skills, abilities, competencies, and internal strengths that makes you the unique person you are, an Awesome Man.

There is something magical when you reach your aspirations, whether the goal you accomplished was to pass a difficult course in school, install a new computer program for a friend, help make dinner for your family, or fix a broken window. The joy and happiness of stretching yourself and achieving through learning and effort will stay with you for the rest of your life. So enjoy the satisfaction derived from developing competence in every aspect of your life. When trying something new, do not let the lack of knowledge and ability hold you back. Learn and become competent, and you will soon overcome this lack. The results and the rewards will amaze you.

The most respected people are those who are competent and apply genuine effort.

Always aim to develop your competency at everything you do.

Guidelines That Can Be Helpful for Living a More Competent Life

- It always takes less effort and resources to do something right and properly than correcting or repairing it later.

- Be competent in your monetary expenditures. Most things you buy will end up being trash or garbage in a matter of time. Most of the things you "just have to have" will be old, worn-out, and thrown out in a few years.

- Keep learning—every day. The more you know, the more you will realize what you do not know. The minute you believe you know it all, you are in big trouble.

- Reading is the key to learning. Get a library card and read something worthwhile every day.

- Doing any task with the attitudes "good enough" and "average is okay" is a sign of impending failure. Banish those thoughts from your mind. Would you want a doctor operating on you who rated just 53% in surgery competency?

- You cannot be the best at everything, but you can be competent at many things. Do not worry about being the greatest. Just being solidly competent at a range of things is worthy and truly useful (to you and to others).

- Never make a major decision or perform a task while under the influence of drugs, alcohol, or strong emotions. These things crater one's competency and decision-making ability.

- Listen to and watch competent men. Use them as models of excellence and value. Choose your role models wisely, and emulate their best characteristics.

Rest and Time Management

"I'm too busy." "I don't have the time to do the things I want to do." "I'm so tired." Sound familiar? These are common refrains in today's society. Even though we have technology, automation, and other kinds of scientific advantages that previous generations never even dreamed of, we somehow seem to lack the time to rest and recharge or to engage in the activities we really want to do.

The Awesome Man knows that to sustain long-term success in life, we have to accept a few basic realities:

- We need to rest and take time to be still.

- We cannot "do it all" and shouldn't even make the attempt. No one is superhuman.

- We spend a lot of time doing unimportant and frivolous things.

- We must recognize what is important in our lives, especially that people are more important than things.

- We *can* take back command of our lives if we feel things are slipping out of our control.

- Daily adequate sleep is a necessity for a meaningful, productive existence.

- People and worthwhile human interaction are always more significant than worthless things and meaningless tasks. It's better to visit a sick aunt or call an old friend than to play a video game.

How can you take back control of your life?

Here are the three things you have to do:

- First, you have to decide what the important goals in your life are.

- Second, you have to prioritize accomplishing the tasks that will help you achieve your goals. All other tasks are of lesser importance.

- Third, you have to accept that you will not be able to do some of the things you have been doing because they are frivolous or incompatible with the goals you have set for yourself. This can result in a difficult period of adjustment as you let go of fond but unproductive habits, and you *stop wasting time*. But the positive glow from accomplishing truly worthwhile things will more than make up for it.

Changing your life for the better stems from doing the first step the right way. It is important to set goals for yourself that are achievable, that are practical, and that are of real value, either to you or to others.

People who set good goals and then prioritize and complete the tasks needed to reach those goals achieve more in life than others, and they have more fun and happiness while they're at it. These people also rest and take time out for simple and peaceful pursuits. This wisdom of maintaining a simple balance between rest and achievement means *they* are in control of their lives and are not governed by external forces or inner selfish desires.

Seven Virtues That Are the Pillars of Competence

The Roman poet and governor Aurelius Clemens Prudentius wrote an epic poem titled "Battle of the Soul" in which he describes the seven virtues of charity, chastity, diligence, humility, kindness, patience, and temperance. I fully believe that these virtues are as relevant today as they were millennia ago and that they are key aspects of the well-rounded personality of an Awesome Man.

But you may be wondering how these virtues relate to the subject of competence. The answer is simple: By practicing the seven virtues, you strengthen your character by creating strong "pillars" that are impervious to the chaos and setbacks that are part of life. These pillars are the mighty supports that anchor you to the ground below and allow you to build toward the sky above. With a solid base like this, building competency becomes a much easier task because you now have the strength to persevere and the wisdom to make the most of your relationships with other people. With your character based on virtue and competence, you will be able to deal with the challenges of life.

Charity

Charity in its traditional sense means generosity and self-sacrifice. Charity should not be confused with the modern use of the word, which means philanthropy or benevolent giving. Benevolent giving is indeed one aspect of charity, but only a small one. What charity really refers to is the sense of unconstrained loving consideration toward all others. Some believe it to be the ultimate manifestation of the human spirit.

The Awesome Man believes the eternal, fundamental heart of charity that underscores all else lies in defeating the selfish demon within each of us, so that our heart opens up to the plight of all people, whether they are newcomers who look different and speak with an accent or the various people we interact with all the time, such as family members, neighbors, and coworkers. We have a choice: We can be uncaring and selfish or we can manifest charity. Too often in our own families we shun and emotionally exile people and blame them for their misfortune, when they really need us to affirm our charity. It is this defeat of selfishness with charity that eliminates indifference, heartlessness, and self-centeredness from a man's character.

Chastity

Encompassing much more than just sexual restraint, chastity is the virtue that gives the Awesome Man the ability to refrain from being distracted and influenced by hostility, temptation, and corruption. Chastity is the virtue that allows you to be honest with yourself, your family and friends, and all of humanity because you never have to lie about, deny, or explain chaste behavior. It provides cleanliness through the cultivation of good health practices, hygiene and moderation from the excessive use and abuse of intoxicants, and discretion in sexual conduct according to one's state in life. Chastity is a foe of ignorance, which breeds suffering, while education embraces moral wholesomeness and promotes clarity in thought. Chasity is a bulwark against exploitation, slavery, and abuse.

Diligence

Diligence, which incorporates effort and perseverance, is the foundation of competence and achievement. This virtue encompasses an enthusiastic and careful approach to actions and work. By being diligent you will develop a positive work ethic and a steadfastness in belief, fortitude, and perseverance. You will budget your time and monitor your own activities to guard against laziness. Diligence is the strength to overcome indifference and apathy. The Awesome Man knows that with diligence he can accomplish important tasks.

Humility

Humility and self-confidence go hand in hand. Both are the opposite of arrogance, bravado, and conceit. Humility is not thinking less of yourself; it is thinking of yourself less. It is a spirit of self-examination and understanding toward people you disagree with. Humility provides the Awesome Man with the courage necessary to undertake tasks that are difficult, tedious, or unglamorous and to graciously accept the sacrifices involved. Humility instills respect for those who have wisdom. The Awesome Man shows humility

> **Humility is not thinking less of yourself; it is thinking of yourself less.**

by giving credit where credit is due. He does not unfairly glorify himself. Humility is being faithful to promises, no matter how big or small they may be. Humility also means refraining from despair and possessing the ability to confront fear, uncertainty, and intimidation. People who value humility refrain from "trash talk," teasing, put-downs, and bullying. Humility helps us to deal with our pride and arrogance, faults that have led to the downfall of many. It as well can be helpful in dealing with others' pride and arrogance by avoiding battles of one-upmanship from which no real victor ever emerges.

Kindness

Kindness is the virtue of charity, compassion, and friendship for its own sake, of offering empathy and trust without prejudice or resentment. By being kind the Awesome Man is unselfish and unconditional in concern and feeling for others, he maintains a positive outlook and a cheerful demeanor, and he seeks to inspire kindness in others. Kindness is especially valuable in dealing with the human and natural disasters that are all-too-common features of life.

Patience

Patience is about having a sense of stability and serenity rather than conflict, hostility, and antagonism. The Awesome Man resolves issues and arguments respectfully, as opposed to resorting to anger and fighting.

With this virtue you develop a tolerance that comes from moderation and enduring the seemingly unbearable with poise and dignity. Moderation is the elimination or reduction of extremes in one's life. We are all familiar with the phrase "too much of a good thing," which warns of the dangers of excessiveness. Moderation is important in areas of health such as medications and exercise as well in emotional reactions such as anger and disappointment.

Bearing the unbearable through patience is a magnificent trait. So often today we come across people suffering from apparently impossible burdens with grace and dignity. We admire people with disabilities and other life challenges who accept their burdens with resolute determination and go forward and lead amazing lives.

Patience gives you the ability to show forgiveness and be merciful to wrongdoers, miscreants, and those who lack knowledge and wisdom.

Temperance

The Awesome Man knows that temperance does not mean you can't enjoy life fully. Instead, he understands that temperance is an important tool for maintaining a constant awareness of others and one's surroundings. This is accomplished by practicing self-control, abstinence where required, and deferred gratification, with the wisdom to judge which actions are appropriate at a given time. Temperance allows for the proper moderation between self-interest and public interest. It permits the Awesome Man to evaluate the rights, needs, and demands of others. Temperance recognizes the value of sound judgment and specifically recognizes the bond between freedom and responsibility. Temperance is especially valuable in times when a clear head and common sense are required.

A Deeper Look: Becoming Culturally Well Rounded

One common trait of many people is their disdain for things, ideas, and concepts with which they are unfamiliar. They have a lack of interest beyond their own narrow boundaries and therefore miss much of the joy and pleasure the world has to offer them. The Awesome Man strives to be well rounded, open to the great diversity of life and culture. My favorite meal may be a sirloin steak, but that should not preclude me from trying vegetarian lasagna, or jerk chicken, or Szechuan spicy beef, or pierogies. Just because you have a favorite type of music, it does not mean you cannot enjoy other styles and genres. When it comes to music I enjoy everything from the Beatles to Motown, Donna Summer, Shania Twain, and Sheryl Crow. I also enjoy Mozart, military marches, gospel, boogie-woogie, and swing. Sure, some of these I enjoy more than others, but I'm more than willing to listen to them all to broaden my musical experience.

To be well rounded means you have a varied and interesting set of knowledge, skill, and abilities. Moreover, it indicates that you have a passion for learning new things or at the very least for being exposed to the unfamiliar.

You want to be able to enjoy the music of Mendelssohn, Michael Jackson, and Stan Getz. You want to be able to play and enjoy various and different sports, hobbies, and pastimes. You want to be able to support one political ideology but also appreciate the values of other political thought. You want to have the flexibility to grow and change.

Even though chocolate ice cream is your favorite, you can appreciate the nuance and flavor of a good vanilla ice cream cone. You may think mixed martial arts, soccer, and auto racing are silly sports, but at least try to learn about them and appreciate the skill and effort that others have put into mastering them.

I am constantly amazed how many men refuse to learn even the smallest amount about things that are not their primary interests. You cannot do or know everything, but it is amazing how much having an open mind and an interest in diverse learning can benefit you. That's one of the many amazing things about being human—nothing you learn, no scrap of knowledge you acquire, will be detrimental to your further growth and development as a person. As long as you use sound judgment in the application of your knowledge, learning will only benefit you. I have never heard any man complain he learned too much, knew too much, or experienced too much, and I doubt you have either.

Emotional Intelligence

Many people might be surprised to see me link competence and virtue with emotional intelligence (EQ), but in my mind the connection is obvious because how we think and how we act are directly related.

In case you're not familiar with EQ, here is its formal definition from PsychCentral.com:

Emotional intelligence (otherwise known as emotional quotient or EQ) is the ability to understand, use, and manage your own emotions in positive ways to relieve stress, communicate effectively, empathize with others, overcome challenges, and defuse conflict. Emotional intelligence is commonly defined by four attributes:

1. **Self-management.** You're able to control impulsive feelings and behaviors, manage your emotions in healthy ways, take initiative, follow through on commitments, and adapt to changing circumstances.

2. **Self-awareness.** You recognize your own emotions and how they affect your thoughts and behavior. You know your strengths and weaknesses, and have self-confidence.

3. **Social awareness.** You have empathy. You can understand the emotions, needs, and concerns of other people, pick up on emotional cues, feel comfortable socially, and recognize the power dynamics in a group or organization.

4. **Relationship management.** You know how to develop and maintain good relationships, communicate clearly, inspire and influence others, work well in a team, and manage conflict.[‡]

Not surprisingly, the attributes listed above for a high EQ are highly consistent and compatible with the aims and goals of the Awesome Man. Earlier in the chapter we discussed competence, which is the ability to do something successfully or efficiently. So much of one's success in life depends on self-management and one's ability to work well with others, all part and parcel of the four EQ traits above, which are also connected to concepts of virtue.

An important point I want to make is that the characteristics of competence, virtue, and EQ are not linked to traditionally defined notions of intelligence. Most things in life do not require the mental abilities of a rocket scientist (I have displayed less than perfect competence when trying to tighten a bolt with the wrong-size wrench because I was too lazy to check for the correct size). The point I am trying to make is that there is no relationship between competence and IQ. I have met a number of Awesome Men who were not geniuses; some had only minimal formal education. What they lacked in IQ they made up for in EQ.

The Awesome Man knows nobody wants to be dumb, and most people think they are pretty smart. Unfortunately, even very smart people do very dumb things. The first thing we all must understand is that intelligence, as measured by IQ tests, is only a very small aspect of true human value.

I would like to suggest a number of ideas for your consideration:

- You can increase your IQ scores just by reading and learning more.

- Your willingness and desire to learn, by being teachable and coachable, are very significant factors affecting your success in life. This is an EQ attribute.

- Talents and skills that can provide happiness and joy in life are not necessarily measurable in standard tests.

- The key is not how intelligent you are but how effectively you use the intelligence you have. As mentioned, plenty of smart people do dumb things.

---

‡ Michael Akers and Grover Porter, "What Is Emotional Intelligence (EQ)?," https://psych-central.com/lib/what-is-emotional-intelligence-eq/.

- Drugs, alcohol, fatigue, and stress will negatively affect your intelligence and make it easier for you to do dumb things.

It is imperative that you never refer to yourself as "not very smart." Using this phrase to describe yourself shows false humility and is an excuse for a lack of effort. I will tell you right now that an individual who is motivated, applies great effort, and has character will outperform and be more successful and happier in life than the so-called genius who lacks EQ and does not know how to apply himself to the task at hand.

Before You Start, Think About Stopping

Before you start on any path or endeavor, ask yourself honestly, taking into account others' experiences, "How hard will it be to stop?" I remember listening to a heroin addict state during an interview, "If I had any idea I would have ended up like this I would have never started." Yes, it's possible he may have been ignorant of the risks associated with heroin usage, but do you really think he didn't know? My point is this: Most of us do know how things might end up before we start them.

Even if you have never had a drink of alcohol, you know if you drink excessively, not many good things will happen. With very few exceptions, you already know sticking a needle in your arm will not likely have a great outcome. Falsifying documents tends to never work out the way you want. Providing recreational drugs to people who want to party may make you wealthy and popular, but that popularity may finally be with police, judges, and jails.

Always make sure before you start anything that it is a positive and good thing to do. Restoring an old bicycle is a good thing, stealing a bicycle is not. If you are filling your life with great activities and actions, you will have little or no time for any negative activities.

I've noticed over time that two specific factors always seemed to be present when I was about to make bad choices. First, I was not doing anything productive, usually just hanging out, chilling, or feeling bored. Second, so-called friends or associates would try to entice me in some way to "Try this, you may like it. If you don't, you can always stop." In one such situation, serendipitously for me, a stranger interceded before things went beyond the point of no return and could have altered my life completely. I was lucky; others were not.

What your are competent in matters. It is no value to you or anybody else to be a competent liar, thief, embezzler, or drunk. Most harmful things in life are a lot easier to start than to stop (or undo). Drugs, alcoholism, wars, hate, smoking, and lying are just a few examples. Before you start anything, be aware of and understand the consequences that follow. We all have to surround ourselves with good people and good pursuits.

Awesome Man Profile: Herbert Hoover

Hoover's father died when he was six years old and his mother died when he was ten. He was raised by relatives, and when he was thirteen he dropped out of school. He worked for his uncle in the family real-estate office, where he learned typing, accounting, and mathematics. When he was seventeen he was accepted to Stanford University, based only on his math test scores. He enrolled in mechanical engineering but switched to geology in his first year. Although Hoover was a mediocre student and spent much of his time at part-time jobs and campus activities, he was successful because of his high EQ.

After graduating as a mining engineer, he ended up operating a mine in Australia. He was very competent in this role and was regularly promoted. He was sent to China to run the company's operations there as a full partner. After some years he sold his shares and moved to London to become an independent mining consultant. His skill at improving mining operations throughout the world led to substantial wealth for Hoover. He became a lecturer at Stanford and Columbia on mining technology and was elected a member of the Board of Trustees at Stanford.

Hoover was still living in London when World War I broke out in 1914. Over a hundred thousand Americans were stranded in Europe. Working with others, Hoover organized support and food assistance for suffering and hungry civilians. In 1916 he was appointed by the president to head the US Food Administration and was responsible for shipping 23 million metric tons of food to the Allied Powers. Hoover gained a following in the United States because people saw him as an expert administrator and a symbol of efficiency. Herbert Hoover went on to many other great positions in government, including serving as the thirty-first president of the United States.

Herbert Hoover was not recognized as academically brilliant, yet his virtuous character and impressive administrative competence resulted in both personal success and saving millions of lives from wartime hunger and starvation. Hoover never saw himself as a humanitarian, but I see him as an Awesome Man.

10

The Awesome Man's Guide to Style and Dress

Style is the only thing you can't buy. It's not in a shopping bag, a label, or a price tag. It's something reflected from our soul to the outside world—an emotion.
—Alber Elbaz, fashion designer

Your Style and Dress Speak Volumes about You

At one time in North America, regardless of their socioeconomic class, most men made the effort to behave with civility and decorum. This approach to life certainly makes sense to the Awesome Man, who is consciously aware of his appearance and the importance of good manners as he interacts with all others. He knows that how he dresses and behaves has a great impact on how others see him as a person. The Awesome Man never allows his appearance or behavior to distract himself or others from the journey to happiness, joy, and contentment. The corollary to that is the Awesome Man knows that his appearance and behavior are a powerful nonverbal communication that speaks before he even opens his mouth.

During the great social revolution of the 1960s, for the first time in many years the standards for style, dress, and propriety were discarded by some as irrelevant and insignificant trappings of the past. Today, anything goes in terms of dress codes, fashion, relationships, and what used to be termed "civil behavior."

There seems to be an advantage to this attitude. It feels liberating to some men because by abdicating responsibility for dress and behavior, they as individuals gain a level of personal creativity and expression. Unfortunately, this "anything goes" attitude can lead to behaviors that are not always the most positive for the individual or those around him. If there are no guard rails on the road, it is easy to go over the edge.

Some young men say they are not responsible for other people's reaction to their appearance or behavior. But responsibility and freedom go hand in hand. By not taking responsibility for your impact on others through your appearance and behavior, you will suffer the consequences: a loss of freedom, exclusion and rejection by others, and being misunderstood and ineffective in getting your ideas or thoughts across to other people. Conversely, if you are appropriate in dress and behavior, more people will be open and welcoming to you and your ideas. And that is a very good thing.

In this chapter, I want to propose some ideas and concepts that provide for a level of personal creativity and expression and yet are seen by others as appropriate and correct. If you disagree with my idea that correct and appropriate behavior is a good thing, let me remind you that many organizations and sports teams now have codes of conduct and behavior for their members and that these rules extend to the members' personal lives.

Many people believe the word *freedom* means *no* responsibility, as in "I can do anything I want." But the more freedom you have, the more responsibility you have. In jail, a prisoner has no appreciable freedom. He also has almost no responsibility; in most cases he is not responsible for cleaning the jail, or cooking the meals, or paying taxes. The reverse is the Alaska homesteader, who is free to do whatever he wants on his property. He can dig a well, build a cabin, and stay up all night. However, he is responsible for his own well-being as he probably has no grocery store, no internet, no dentist or doctor nearby, no school for his kids. Your freedom is directly related to your responsibilities.

While we're on the subject of freedom, let me observe that just because you can freely do something, it does not make your action right or even a good idea. For example, except for eating and drinking items that are prohibited by law (endangered animals, certain liquids), you are pretty much free to eat and drink anything you want. But you are responsible to yourself and a great number of people, such as your family, who depend on you not damaging your body with poisons, obesity, or addictions.

The Book of Couth

My original working title for this book was *The Book of Couth*. The noun *couth* has fallen out of usage in the English language today and is not even in most dictionaries. Even though the word appears to have originated about a thousand years ago, by the 1800s it began rapidly declining in use. The derivative *uncouth*, which by definition is the opposite of couth, was still common in usage up to the mid-twentieth century. When I was a boy, it was a real insult if someone called you uncouth.

The thesaurus lists the adjectives for uncouth as: rude, uncivilized, bad-mannered, ill-mannered, foul-mouthed, coarse, vulgar, improper, impolite, and crude as synonyms for uncouth, and I think that just about covers it. Unfortunately, these adjectives describe too many of the inhabitants of Guyland and super adolescents today.

For those who say "It's my body, and I can do anything I want with it," I agree, but what will you have accomplished and how will the world benefit as a result of your existence? Nobody on their deathbed ever said, "I did too much good in the world," "I helped too many people," or "I took too good of care of myself and others." So if you want to die with no regrets, be responsible.

The Awesome Man knows he is one part of the universe, but a crucial part, and his effect on others is limitless.

When it comes to appropriate appearance, I have found that most of the individuals who dress outside normal societal constraints or wear outlandish clothes do not do it for themselves. In fact, the more radical, inappropriate, or contrarian their appearance is, the more likely they want to provoke a response from others. This behavior would indicate the need for recognition and attention from others that tells them they are unique and special. I believe the Awesome Man receives this recognition and attention through his actions, words, and behavior, not through his fashion statements. As shown in chapter 9, one of the best ways to be unique is to be competent.

For those who believe they have the freedom to do as they please in terms of appearance or behavior, they must again be reminded that with freedom comes great responsibility. This responsibility includes being aware of how you are affecting others. The Awesome Man knows that he has an obligation not to incite, provoke, instigate, or arouse inappropriate responses from others by his actions.

How Do You Want People to See You?

Be warned! I am now entering an area where I may get some serious objections from both caretakers and young men regarding appearance, grooming, and appropriate behavior. Just as young children use food choices to assert their individual personalities, young men often use dress and appearance styles to achieve the same goal. I've encountered many a young man who was ready for more responsibility and freedom and who was on his way to becoming an Awesome Man, yet he felt constrained by either an overly protective family or a cultural environment that was too insistent on conformity. Such men often try to assert their desire for freedom through their hair, style, and fashion choices. There's no problem with this, as long as they don't veer toward the inappropriate.

I truly believe that providing a little less restraint and little more freedom in other aspects of a young man's life will mitigate his obsessions with inappropriate fashion because he will be more engaged with other, more fulfilling aspects of life. A young man can find many excellent and positive ways to express his uniqueness and individuality without resorting to obsessions in fashion or style, or the lack thereof.

You may be thinking, "That all seems pretty obvious, so why the word of caution?" Here's why: It is my deeply held belief and contention that many styles and patterns of dress displayed by some young men today are simply inappropriate in many contexts. I know this sounds old-fashioned, and I'm certainly aware that society's norms on how formal one should dress have certainly loosened over the years—but I believe that for a young man to grow into being an Awesome Man, he needs to take his appearance and style seriously. He needs to be a cut above the rest.

Let's consider three very distinct types of apparel: a wet suit, a tank top and shorts, and a tuxedo. If you wanted to play some basketball with buddies, you would not wear the wet suit. On the other hand, if you were scuba diving off the coast of Maine, you likely would not wear the tank top and shorts. The tuxedo is as bad for basketball as the tank top is for attending the Academy Awards. I think you get my point—what is appropriate dress is based on the occasion.

To be clear, the Awesome Man is not overly focused on appearance, but he does understand that *appropriate* style and dress are important aspects of life and therefore deserve attention. Image is important. Think about it this way: If you met someone who displayed a significant absence of personal hygiene and appropriate dress and grooming, would you perhaps not wonder what other important areas of his life he is also neglecting?

One of the most common areas of family strife revolves around a young man's hair, especially its length. I recall how my mother had significant issues with my hair length, my sideburns, and later my trimmed beard. She preferred short hair. Remember, I grew up in the late sixties and early seventies, and my peers at the time considered my appearance very conservative—but not Mom.

With my own sons I took what I think was a more sensible approach to hairstyles and length. There are two factors I considered: Who was paying for the haircuts and styling? And how were my boys developing and maturing in other areas of their lives? I gave my sons a choice: "I pay, I decide" (but I did consider their input) or "You pay, you decide." It was amazing how this eliminated so many battles. In addition, my boys enjoyed a lot of age-appropriate freedom and responsibility in their lives, so they did not feel the need to use appearance as a symbol of their independence. If a son maintains good grades, stays out of trouble, and is on his way to becoming an Awesome Man, the hair should not be an issue of contention.

My oldest son, Matt, always had the wildest hairstyles, often with spikes, fluorescent colors, mohawks, and so on. And yes, that bugged me somewhat. I tried to be patient and coach him about the importance of personal grooming and appearance in life. Now at forty years of age he has a beard and a man bun (perfectly acceptable in the construction trade he works in), and he has a successful career and a wonderful family and home.

Despite his youthful exuberance when it came to his hair, Matt was introduced to the concepts of decorum, propriety, and etiquette at a young age—and that paid huge dividends as he grew into adulthood. He, like

The author's son Matt and family.

all young men who are striving to become Awesome Men, knew he was responsible to the people and the world around him. An Awesome Man will *never* say, 'If you don't like how I dress, don't look at me."

When speaking to young men regarding grooming, appearance, and behavior, I find that when they understand how these factors can affect their long-term goals and objectives, they tend to see what is in their best interest. I came across a quote by Ron Dennis from when he was the chairman and chief executive officer of McLaren Technology Group and the chairman of McLaren Automotive. McLaren is a very successful company in the technology and automotive industries, manufacturing some of the world's greatest race cars and super-exotic road cars. Mr. Dennis's employees range from mechanics and stock boys to millionaire Formula One drivers. What he said is:

> Everything is important. You have to start with the fundamental basics. When somebody walks into a room I notice straightaway such details as fingernails, whether they are cleaned and manicured, how the person is dressed, whether they are scruffy, or neat and tidy. If you don't have any respect for your own body, then I think you have a lack of personal discipline.

Mr. Dennis believes external appearance is a window into a person's character. Of course there are exceptions, but I do think there is validity to his attitude.

This belief implies how important it is for the caretakers of the world to start boys and young men off on the right foot, to set appropriate standards of behavior for those males who are under their guidance. They must be taught to use respectful language and to recognize and respect elders and people of authority. They must be trained to respect the environment and all of nature's creation. They must be educated about treating all people with respect and dignity.

If we as parents, teachers, coaches, and caretakers do not take on this task, we can destroy a man's soul. And as the Talmud states, "Whoever destroys a soul, it is considered as if he destroyed an entire world."

By the way, let me talk briefly about one very important attribute you should have when it comes to your personal style: flexibility. Nature has taught us that species that can adapt to changing environments have the best chance of surviving and flourishing. Believe it or not, this applies to the way you dress. By being flexible and open in your personal style, fashion sense, and general approach to life and to those around you, you increase your chances of happiness and success in your endeavors significantly. By having style options, you can move smoothly from situation to situation.

This ability was exemplified by Leonardo DiCaprio playing the character Jack Dawson in the motion picture *Titanic*. A drifter and artist, Jack, with a bath and proper clothes, is able to literally and figuratively rescue the heroine. By rescue I mean saving Rose (Kate Winslet) from a loveless marriage to the dastardly Cal (Billy Zane). Jack's ability to clean up and blend in with the first-class passengers was the key. If Jack had extreme facial hair, numerous piercings, and tattoos he would not have been successful in his quest.

As I've suggested above, the Awesome Man knows the world will positively react to his appropriate dress and behavior. This is why he strives always to maintain his appearance—to be fit, neat, clean, and groomed as is appropriate for his surroundings. You, too, by being flexible in your style and appearance, will become open to all the possibilities the world has to offer. Your appearance and behavior *do* have an impact on the people you come into contact with—at the very least they leave an impression. Inappropriate appearance and behavior won't do you any favors.

Rebel *with* a Cause

In American culture, the rebel has always been idolized. The whole history of America is based on rebellion and heroism, from the Boston Tea Party and the Declaration of Independence all the way to James Dean, Cesar Chavez, Muhammad Ali, and Clint Eastwood in his movie roles. Many fictional heroes are portrayed as having an "I don't give a damn about anything or anybody" attitude. We want to be like these rebels because they appear free and heroic.

However, if you look closely, rebels such as the fictional Dirty Harry and others, are competent and responsible in their vocations and are individuals of considerable character. Unconventional? Without a doubt. Heroic? Yes. But always ethical and caring. Han Solo in *Star Wars* was a rebel, and so were Oskar Schindler, Lt. Aldo Raine, and Ferris Bueller—all movie rebels and heroes. Paul Revere was heroic in the American Revolution, but when he wasn't being a rebel, he was a silversmith, industrialist, and foundry innovator.

So be a rebel if it suits you—but understand that being a rebel means you are competent, caring, and willing to fight injustice. Being a rebel is not about what you reject but about what you stand for. It is not how you dress and act but what you do. Just do not assume you can be heroic based on your fashion choices.

Being Appropriate

The Awesome Man knows that just as being appropriate in dress is not confining or restrictive, being appropriate in personal behavior is also not a restraint on personal freedom, individuality, or creativity. In fact, behaving in an appropriate manner is about maximizing your potential as an Awesome Man. It's about having the self-awareness and perceptual skills to see the world around you and to be in harmony with it and the people in it. Have you ever noticed how certain people always seem to do the right thing around other people? They do a good job being sensitive to and perceptive of others, and they know how to say the right thing to make those around them feel good. They try their utmost to avoid making other people upset or uncomfortable. It's this trait I'm referring to when I say "being appropriate."

Being appropriate ties in with the concept of EQ (emotional quotient) that we discussed in chapter 9. It's an approach to life based on treating everybody else with dignity and respect and being sensitive to their needs and comfort levels. It involves seeing the big picture of life and how you as an individual can make the world a better place.

It is the complete opposite of "I like doing my own thing," "I can't be responsible for others' feelings," or "Why should I behave to your standard?"

Inappropriateness, I believe, is the result of a selfish, self-centered, and myopic "me first" or "me only" attitude. It considers others in the world to be insignificant and of little value. Nobody with this attitude has ever achieved long-term happiness or made progress in becoming an Awesome Man.

Let me give an example. Many years ago, I was attending a seminar for the introduction of a new 13-speed transmission for heavy-duty trucks. A number of retail sales professionals attended, eager to learn all about the new transmission's features and benefits. It was an evening presentation, and some of my fellow salesmen had had more than a few drinks at dinner.

The presentation began and one fellow began to argue with the presenter about the superiority of old transmission technology in certain specific applications. Of course the boor was correct; in a very limited application

A Word about Swearing

In addition to being mindful of his behavior, the Awesome Man is always appropriate is in his speech and vocabulary. There are young men throughout the land who feel it is appropriate to use obscenities such as f*ck and variations thereof as universal substitutes for the correct language in their speech. They do not realize that most people forced to listen to their verbal diarrhea find it boring, boorish, and totally inappropriate. The use of obscenities should be used only when you are venting in private and alone.

the old transmission solution was superior. However, the new transmission being presented was superior in 99.5% of truck applications. Plus it was cheaper for the customer to buy, and easier and safer for the driver to operate. The presenter was gracious and patient with the blowhard. Eventually, people sitting around the loudmouth got him to sit down and shut up.

Let us look at the impact of this lout's inappropriate behavior:

- He did not learn anything about the new product.

- He made it difficult for others in the room to learn.

- In the eyes of the presenter and his company, he reinforced the stereotype that salesmen were a bunch of drunken idiots.

- He embarrassed and humiliated himself among his peers, and when his boss found out about the incident he was severely reprimanded and forced to apologize.

The excuse "I was drunk" is meaningless, as each of us determines our alcohol consumption, and each of us is fully responsible for the consequences. Forty years later I can clearly remember this fellow and his name. That night he dropped immeasurably in worth in my eyes. As I look back over my life, many of the worst examples of inappropriate behavior I witnessed often did involve alcohol or other emotional/chemical stimulus. So let caution be your guide.

You may recall somebody being stupidly inappropriate in your past. You and others might have found it hilarious, like the time a player on a high school football team mooned some coaches who were driving behind the team bus on the way to a road game. Some of the players laughed as they thought it was funny. As far as I was aware the coaches never said a word about the incident and never planned retribution. In the eyes of the coaches that player was a "loser," and they just ignored him for the rest of the year. After that season he never played football again. A few minutes of "fun," a lifetime of lost respect.

Let me give one final example of inappropriate behavior. Let us say I have been charged with a misdemeanor offense of disorderly conduct. I feel I am innocent, and my trial date has been set for two weeks from today. I have time to consider a number of alternatives regarding both appropriate behavior and dress in court:

A Deeper Look: Take Small Steps to Reprogram Your Brain

We have to accept that "being appropriate" can be a perplexing concept at times. What we believe is appropriate is often only based on our experiences with our peers. A typical reaction some of us have when someone questions our dress or behavior is to say, "What's wrong with it?" Then we tend to assert our right to do what we want without being responsible for how others feel about it.

Ask yourself if you believe your behavior and dress can affect others. If you answer yes but add the caveat that their reaction is not your problem or concern, let me ask you to consider this: If some stranger verbally harassed or upset a beloved person you cared a great deal about, how would you react? Would you accept the bully's contention that your beloved person should not be upset, because the bully cannot be responsible for his victim's feelings or reactions? I doubt it. Instead, you would hold the bully responsible for his behaviors when he causes pain and anxiety in people you care about. Do you see the linkage now? We do not like it when people create fear, anxiety, unease, or apprehension in us or in those we care about. That's why we must be careful not to cause similar unease and apprehension in others.

Tasha Rube, in her excellent web article posted on WikiHow, addresses how you can develop the skills to be more sensitive and empathetic to others.* Rube recommends that we do the following:

- Recognize the social cues of emotions. Learn to read expressions, body language, and nonverbal signs of emotions in others.

- Listen with empathy and understanding, acknowledging what people say without judgment.

- Communicate kindly, ask questions to ensure your understanding, and be positive and respectful in your responses.

- Recognize your own feelings, make sure you have adequate coping skills, and do not let your feelings cloud your views.

1. I can appear in court as scheduled, unshaven and with grimy hair, wearing flip-flops, and dressed in a dirty tank top with an obscenity written on it and baggy pants hanging below my ass.

2. I can appear neat and clean, dressed in slacks and a collared shirt. In other words, I can project myself as someone who is put together, takes life seriously, and respects the judge and the court system.

You might think, "Wait! Why does that matter? Isn't justice supposed to be blind?" Of course it is, and in theory I should get a fair hearing no matter how I look or dress. But the Awesome Man is playing the game at a higher level, and he understands that the people in the courtroom (judge, jury, and prosecutor) are subjective human beings who will form subjective opinions and first impressions about him. Will they feel comfortable? Will they feel receptive to my statements, explanations, and alibi? Will they be distracted by my appearance? Will they form a judgment about me based on my external appearance or demeanor? Will my appearance trigger negative experiences or memories? If I choose option 2 above, I'm maximizing the chances for making a positive impact during my court appearance because I am being, in a word, *appropriate*.

Tattoos, Piercings, and Body Art

In the last few decades, body art has grown exponentially in popularity. Nobody *needs* body art, but many want it. Why? Because it is a way to make a personal statement. It can be about fashion, it can be about image, it can be about a sense of belonging or confidence, or it can be a statement of repudiation.

The Awesome Man is not overly concerned with fashion and therefore is not concerned with body art in its numerous forms. To him, it is his character and his actions that are important, and he does not care to be noticed as a piece of art or a moving billboard. His actions and behavior toward others are what he relies on to make his "statement."

Specifically speaking of permanent tattoos and piercings, I suggest one caveat: You have only one body, and it has to last you a lifetime. Many of you will experience what is called the End of History Illusion. Almost

---

*Tasha Rube, "How to Be Sensitive to Other People's Feelings," February 24, 2020, https://www.wikihow.com/Be-Sensitive-to-Other-People's-Feelings.

every teenager and young adult knows that his tastes have changed regularly over the years. When you are nineteen years old you know that you are very different from the individual you were at age fourteen. Yet that same nineteen-year-old cannot envision what changes will take place by the time he is twenty-four. He assumes no changes will take place. As a nineteen-year-old, he believes that when he is twenty-four his tastes will be the same. Yet ask any twenty-four-year-old if his tastes and attitudes have changed in the last five years and you will see the fallacy of this belief.

So the illusion is that we believe our tastes will not continue to evolve and develop in the future. What results is that you make a permanent alteration to your body at a young age, assuming you will love it just as much in five or ten years. *Wrong!* The reality is that the only constant in life is change. As the years go by, many people who have made permanent alterations to their body become dissatisfied with what they thought a few years ago was just amazing.

So when you decide you want some piercing or a permanent tattoo, remember it is an excellent idea only if you do not plan to grow, develop, or evolve from that point forward. If, on the other hand, you think your tastes, attitudes, outlooks, perceptions, and feelings might change in the next five years as much as they have already changed in the past five years, don't do anything to your body that is lasting.

Let's take a brief look at the origins of certain male fashion items that are often worn inappropriately:

Earrings for men. The tradition of men wearing earrings originated in ancient sailing days. Sailors were aware they may drown at sea and were concerned that they would not receive a proper burial. They began to wear a single gold earring with the hope and belief that if their drowned body eventually washed up onshore, someone on land would discover the body, give it a proper burial, and keep the gold earring to cover the funeral cost. Since most young boys' exposure to pirates is in movies, which typically include some very macho sailors with earrings, it became a fashion statement over time. Of course the jewelry industry loves the growth market of this men's fashion.

Over the last number of years the practice of men wearing ear jewelry has become commonplace and accepted as appropriate in many social situations. As long as one is respectful and aware of the setting and the others in it, there should be no problem.

Baseball cap styles. For decades the purpose of a baseball cap was to shield the sun out of your eyes. Wearing the baseball cap reversed was likely first done by men moving faster than a jogging pace, because when you are running, bounding on a horse, or riding in a boat or open motorized vehicle, your hat will fly off unless it is on backwards. The sideways cap can have any number of different meanings to many different people. But in all cases, unless the cap is worn properly it will not do the job for which it was designed—to shield your eyes from the sun (which nicely illustrates the pointlessness of wearing the cap indoors).

One pundit once remarked that men wear their caps as an indication of where their life is heading. Think about it.

Sagging. Men who follow this style, primarily a male affectation, let the tops of their pants fall significantly below the waist. Two theories explain how this style of wearing of pants began in US prisons. One is that often prisoners were not allowed to wear belts and naturally their pants fell down. The other theory is that prisoners who were interested in attracting sexual partners in prison would advertise their interest by dropping their pants low.

Hair. At one time men had no practical or economical means of cutting the hair on their head and face, so they let it grow. Quite naturally it got dirty and sweaty. The invention of scissors and razors brought about a change in grooming habits, but initially only the rich benefited as these metal grooming tools were expensive. With the Industrial Revolution of the 1800s came better, lower-cost steels for knives and blades, so shaving and getting haircuts was now available to the population at large, particularly in the urban centers of the world. Now obviously there is nothing wrong with hair—I wish I had more myself—but it should be appropriate, neat, and clean.

Awesome Man Profile: Ralph Gilles

Photo courtesy Automotive Addicts

Ralph Gilles

One thing about Awesome Men is that they can appear to be like ordinary males. Above is a picture of Ralph Gilles, the head of design for Fiat Chrysler Automobiles, appearing appropriate at an outdoor car show. He is a man who appears confident and pleased, with no pretensions or need to project an image or persona of something he is not.

One day, during the early morning hours, Gilles was driving in Michigan with his wife, Doris, when he came across a two-car accident. Just before Gilles arrived, a 2013 Fiesta had collided head-on with a 2013 Edge SUV that had crossed the road's center line.

While his wife was calling 911, Gilles got out of his Jeep Wrangler to help the two occupants stuck inside the Fiesta—but he was unable to force open the jammed doors. As the vehicles remained on the road, a Buick sedan came along and struck the Fiesta, pushing it back into the SUV. This caused a fire to ignite in the SUV. The driver of the SUV escaped, but the driver and passenger of the Fiesta remained trapped as the flames rose from the adjacent vehicle. With the fire spreading, Gilles realized that if he was going to find a way out for the passengers, he would have to act quickly.

Gilles returned to his Jeep Wrangler, put it into four-wheel drive, and, heedless of the damage to his own vehicle, used it to push the burning SUV away from the Fiesta with the trapped passengers. With the risk of fire eliminated, Gilles waited for first responders to extricate the passengers.

This rescue was characteristic of Gilles's Awesome Man traits of effort and perseverance. After he was born to Haitian immigrants in the United States, his parents then moved to Montreal. He was drawing cars from the age of eight. When he finished high school, with the encouragement of his aunt (who coached and mentored him), he wrote a letter to Lee Iacocca, then head of Chrysler. He received a letter back from the director of Design at Chrysler, encouraging him to further his education and suggesting some specialized design schools. He quit his job as a grocery store clerk and returned to school. After graduation he was hired by Chrysler and is now the head of design.

Ralph Gilles is an Awesome Man because he takes action, follows his passions with discipline and enthusiasm, expends effort, and makes a difference in the lives of those around him.

Part Three:

Be the Awesome Man Instructional and Motivational Guide

A series of connected steps and exercises in sequence which over time will help you be the Awesome Man

Introduction to Part 3

Too often we wish the rules of life were like a recipe: add two large eggs to three cups of flour, then mix in butter and so on. Most times following the recipe produces the perfect result. Unfortunately, life is much more complex and variable than just mixing ingredients according to a set of instructions.

Parts 1 and 2 of *Be the Awesome Man* provided you, the young man who aspires to become so much more than he is now, with principles and concepts to help establish your basic understanding of what it means to be an Awesome Man. Part 3 introduces a step-by-step action plan that will enable you to develop a recipe for your life so you can become the Awesome Man.

Remember, the choices you make now will impact today, tomorrow, and the rest of your life. To make good choices, you need knowledge, so never stop learning. With knowledge (which includes awareness, understanding, and critical appreciation), you will make superior decisions which will lead you to your ultimate goal of being the Awesome Man. Most of our lives are spent making simple, mundane choices. Should I buy a case of Pepsi or Coke? Should we watch Netflix or HBO? Are the Clippers or the Lakers a better team? Sadly, many men spend more time thinking about choices like these rather than proactively making sound decisions about the truly important issues that will negatively or positively impact their lives.

In Part 1 of this book we discussed why the world needs Awesome Men, and why you should begin your journey to become an Awesome Man right now. We also discussed fear and other factors that prevent us from being the best version of ourselves.

In Part 2 the discussion focused on principles and concepts. We examined how attitude, effort, perseverance, and self-discipline are key to becoming an Awesome Man. On the subject of freedom, we stressed the importance of responsibility, which is the seed of freedom. You cannot be truly free unless you are responsible at all times. Having free will does not make all choices in life equally valid. Responsibility combined with knowledge allows you the freedom to make good choices.

Some of the concepts we examined were likely uncomfortable to some readers. Obedience, self-control, chastity, and appropriate dress are not typical topics of discussion in our society today. However, I hope you realize that they are as important as the other subjects explored in the first two parts of the book, and that all the concepts and principles we examined work together to provide you a better framework for understanding why an Awesome Man makes the choices he does in his life.

Part 3 moves from the conceptual to the practical. It provides a program of steps and exercises that will show you how to implement what you have learned. It is the motivational and instructional part of the book designed to help you strike out on your own path to being an Awesome Man. Part 3 contains the following sections:

1. How to Develop a Sense of Purpose

2. What Is Important in Your Life?

3. Setting Goals and Getting Things Done

4. Help with Setting Goals

5. Inertia and Procrastination

6. Quiz on Choices and Values

7. Frequently Asked Questions

Pablo Picasso stated that "Action is the foundational key to all success." Many of us have had great ideas, great thoughts, and great beliefs, but without action nothing is achieved. Even though reading the book to this point has hopefully been of value to you, you must take *action* or you will not move forward one inch on your journey to becoming an Awesome Man.

Part 3 is the hardest section. Why? Because most men are really good at nodding their heads in agreement with good ideas and concepts, and really poor at implementing them. Don't let that happen to you. This is the part where you individually need to step up and make changes in your life. Utilizing the guides and forms that follow will help you take action. The key words for you are **effort, action,** and **implementation.** *You* have to do it. If you do not, nobody else will and nothing will be accomplished. The onus is on you. You are responsible. I and others will be here to help and aid you, but from here on it is all about you and your ability and desire to get it done.

Read Part 3 with a mental and physical commitment to action. I have spoken about my confidence in you and your ability to become an Awesome Man. I have provided you with as much background information and wisdom as I can. Now you have to do your part. You may be afraid, but you now know how to deal with fear, so go boldly and begin your journey with vigor and confidence.

Section 1

How to Develop a Sense of Purpose

Making Great Decisions in Life Requires Knowledge

You're at a stage in life where you're likely grappling with two big questions: How do I figure out my purpose in life? How do I figure out who I really am?

When asked, "What do you want to be when you grow up?", the most common response young men give is "I do not know." Parents, aunts, uncles, and other caretakers seem constantly to be asking this and similar questions. As you grow older, the questions change: what school, what courses, what career, what sport? And most young men just do not have an answer. Chances are you do not have an answer either.

But why should this be the case? Why don't you know the answer? I can think of two main reasons for this. One reason is that the answer is simply unknowable because knowing it would require you to predict the future, and nobody can do that, even poorly. The other reason is that the answer requires investigation of the choices and options that are available, and you have not yet conducted this investigation.

We humans can't do much about the first reason, but we certainly can address the second one. Let me give you an example. Let us say you had never tasted ice cream, and somebody came up and asked you what your favorite flavor of ice cream was—you could not give him an answer that would sound very intelligible. Your ignorance about ice cream precludes making an effective choice or decision.

What you are lacking is *knowledge*. You cannot make effective choices about things you know nothing about. It is a lack of knowledge that makes you say, "I don't know."

Knowledge once acquired is never lost, and it will serve you the rest of your life. The Awesome Man is no dummy, because he is constantly learning and acquiring knowledge. And he uses the knowledge he acquires to make effective choices, to show responsibility, and to lead a more joyful and happy life.

How Do You Acquire Knowledge?

We've established that acquiring knowledge, whatever its form—learning, exploring, experiencing—is the best way to learn about yourself and to discover what your purpose in life may be. But how exactly do you go about this? Although it's true that everybody is different—unique, in fact—when it comes to acquiring knowledge, most of us learn using the same learning basic tools.

Most learning styles are first used during our childhoods. As infants and young children, most of us *observe* the world around us and repeat the behavior of our parents or caregivers. We hear a sound, then we repeat the sound—that is how we learn language. Usually with encouragement we *practice* and *repeat* the sounds until we are communicating.

As we get a little older, we may *ask questions* of our parents about what something is or what a word means and then *listen* to the explanation and for the proper pronunciation.

We may *experiment* with different sounds and even try to create new words. We may listen to people we are not familiar with and *study* their speech.

We will have picture books *read* to us. We will *observe* the pictures and begin to see the connection between the words and the pictures. We are now using *reason* to connect words and pictures.

As we observe, question, and ponder life around us, we will see that actions have a cause and effect and there are reasons things are the way they are. We have acquired knowledge.

Some of us prefer to acquire knowledge with a hands-on approach, others by reading or observing. Some of us like demonstrations and videos; some like to read and contemplate what is presented. There is no right or wrong way to learn. Some ways are just better for different people. But all of us should have the ability to use a variety of learning methods as the changing situations in life require. If we really want to solidify our knowledge, we can share with others by *teaching* or *writing*, because the very act of sharing our knowledge with others helps us further understand it ourselves.

The important thing is that you are constantly acquiring knowledge. You cannot learn too much. You cannot have too much understanding. The beauty about our brain is that it has no limit to its capacity; therefore, everything you learn is of value. It will cease to be available to you only if you do not use it. But before we go into how to use the knowledge you have gained, let us go into further detail on how to learn.

Observe

When some incident happens and the eyewitnesses are interviewed, I am always amazed by how different their descriptions of the event can be. Some people will give great detailed descriptions of what they saw, while others did not see or notice much of anything. Why is this? As we go through our daily lives, we concentrate or focus on different stimulus or details in our visual world. By being too narrow in our focus, we can miss important details and fail to grasp or understand the whole situation.

Jaguar MENA

For example, a nineteen-year-old male may see the lovely young lady in the photo looking toward him. He might tend to notice and focus on her. Quite possibly he does not notice the car (yes, there is a car in the photo, a Jaguar F-Type).

What can you tell about the possible location shown in this photo? Where in the world might the photo have been taken? What time of day? Did you notice the small pile of white behind the woman's left shoulder? Could that be snow? After you concentrate on the photo and study the whole scene, you can gain a great deal of information about what is taking place. You have gained knowledge by observing.

Watching and paying attention to what is going on around you is an excellent way to learn. As you go through your day today, make an effort to observe the world around you. To give you a commonplace example, as a pedestrian, I observe the cars driving around me; that way if somebody is driving erratically or dangerously, I will be ready to avoid being a victim. I'm sure you do the same thing.

Since one of the Awesome Man's goals is to grow and develop over the long term, being observant is a necessary way to learn and acquire knowledge. We as individuals are daily being bombarded with information, some valuable, most superfluous. Much of this superfluous information can be described as "noise." We have two ways to deal with noise: ignore everything or have active filters to stop information that is not of value to us so we intake only quality information.

Such filters are absolutely necessary to navigate today's busy world, but we must remind ourselves to be open-minded with our observations. Sometimes when we put in place filters, we can narrow our perceptions, often to reinforce already in-place biases. As expressed in the old Yiddish saying, "To a worm in horseradish, the whole world is horseradish." We all are very good at assuming that what *we* believe is true for all of creation and humanity. Rarely do we understand what is actually going on.

It is so important to expand your boundaries, to go outside your own jar of "horseradish" and really observe the world and its variations and complexities. If you believe you know the answers to a good many complex problems, consider the possibility that you may be living in a jar. Only when you expand your world of observation—while continuing to filter out the noise—will you will truly grow and develop.

Read

Patrick Gillespie

The George Peabody Library, Baltimore

Here is something that may be shocking to you: All the existing knowledge in the world is available to you through reading. Think about it for a moment. You can access all the existing knowledge there is, by yourself, through books. Punk rock, mathematics, sexuality, physics, gambling, philosophy, art, medicine—you name it, it is in books and is easily and cheaply available to you. All you have to do is read. Fiction or nonfiction, it is all there. What a gift you have! Millions of people over thousands of years have taken the trouble to write down all this knowledge, and it's all there for you to acquire—or at least that small fraction of knowledge that's of interest to you.

It amazes me when people say they do not like to read, because they are limiting their ability to access knowledge, and since you need knowledge to make good decisions, the nonreaders are dooming themselves to poor decision-making.

If you want to be a great decision-maker, just read. It is a tremendous way to learn and acquire knowledge. You can do it anytime and most anyplace. You will never be lonely, and it will take you places you never dreamed of. Read daily. You will be amazed at what you have been missing.

I have a personal policy to read every valid email I receive and respond to the sender within twenty-four hours. I find that when you bulk-screen correspondence you inadvertently discard a few important messages along with the junk.

One example: We once invited a friend, Ruth, to an event at our home, and she did not respond. Three weeks later, with the event just about to happen, she heard from a mutual acquaintance about the get-together and stated she would love to have been invited. The mutual acquaintance contacted us and said Ruth would like to attend. We explained that Ruth was one of our first invitees and did not respond. We called Ruth and re-invited her. She was embarrassed and explained she does not have time to read all her emails. I asked myself why would one set up a communication system like email and not use it properly.

As we become more and more connected with others through our tech devices, we must be diligent to read and retain important information while disregarding the clutter and noise. Most people look at their emails and texts and make a mental note to deal with the important ones later. It would be much wiser and more effective if they followed the old "handle once" rule, which for emails amounts to: If it is not important now, delete it. If it is important, respond now. Your objective it to filter out the junk and only read and deal with the valuable information, letting nothing important slip through the cracks.

Listen

The Greek philosopher Epictetus wrote, "We have two ears and one mouth so that we can listen twice as much as we speak." This two-thousand-year-old maxim is valid today. The next time you are at a seminar, public address, speech, presentation, or lecture, look around you and see how many people are genuinely focused and listening for content and meaning so they can gain knowledge. You will be amazed how many are only giving partial attention, if that, to the presentation.

It's always worth paying attention. Even if the speaker is a blithering idiot (which I seriously doubt), you will learn something. Otherwise, why are people attending? We as humans too often want to let other people know what we have to say, but rarely do we listen intently to others. Yet listening

Antenna

Who is really listening in this audience?

to others is key to discovering ourselves. We learn very little by voicing our own opinions, attitudes, and beliefs—we already know them! But listening to others, especially those who have expertise in topics we know little of, is one of the best ways to learn.

Remember, listening is not only important in formal settings. It is important to listen at home, at school, at work, and with your friends. If you find that your mind is busy formulating what to say before the other person has finished speaking, you are not listening. If you find your mind wandering, you are not listening. Even when you are walking by yourself, listen, with real commitment. You'll be happily surprised with the results.

Ask

Judge a man by his questions rather than his answers.

—Voltaire

Many young men are reluctant to ask questions in learning situations. This has been proved, based on the high incidence of workplace accidents involving young males. Hours will be spent in training, and still a number of students will not understand a crucial instruction. Rather than asking the instructor for clarification, they go along and act as though they fully

Dmitry Kalinovsky

Make sure you are fully familiar with all safety protocols before operating machinery.

understand the process they have been taught. Their lack of knowledge and understanding can result in injury to themselves or a coworker. Sometimes not asking questions can be a life or death matter.

Let me share with you a true story of a horrific death that occurred at a residential construction site. An eighteen-year-old worker was cleaning a portable cement mixer at the end of his shift to prepare it for the following day. The poor fellow did not understand that he had to turn off and disengage the mixer before cleaning it (or any machine for that matter). He became entangled in the mixer. A painter working near the victim heard cries for help and saw the victim's arm stuck in the machine and his body being pulled into the rotating mixer paddles. He ran to the mixer and attempted to turn it off but could not disengage the gears, so he yelled for help. A coworker heard the commotion, ran to the machine, and shut it off. Emergency medical services was called and responded within minutes. Rescue workers dismantled the drive mechanism to reverse the mixing paddles and extricate the worker. He was pronounced dead at the scene.

This is an extreme but real-world example of how asking questions could have made all the difference. So next time you do not understand, comprehend, or grasp some idea or concept, just *ask*. Even if you think you "get it," it never hurts to seek clarification. Remember, there is no such thing as a dumb question. I have learned from my experience in group training that if one person asks a question, most of the other class members are grateful because they were wondering about the same thing.

I am not leveling any blame toward the young worker who lost his life. But all he had to do was ask this simple question: "Do you have to turn the mixer off to clean it?" It would have been a lifesaver.

Study

Junior Gomes

When we see the word *study*, most of us think of being in school, studying for tests and exams. For some of us, these were stressful experiences. This is especially true if we were poor readers and had to study from books and notes. Even if you have finished school and are working, you will be confronted with manuals, handbooks, instruction books, guide books, and other literature that you are required to read in order to do your job effectively and safely.

The good news is that some great aids in studying are available to you. The website HowToStudy.org is just one. Also, it sometimes can be helpful to have a study partner, if that's feasible for your situation.

But the most important factor in successful study is your attitude. First, make sure you do not allow any negative self-talk about studying to taint your mind. Second, accept that studying is just another way of acquiring knowledge that poses little risk to you. I would rather study the safe operation of a chain saw rather than just experiment with one with no prior knowledge—the risk to the machine and me is just too great.

Besides studying for knowledge to increase your competencies in life, you should study the lives of other Awesome Men. By seeing how others have handled life's challenges, you will gain insight into your own. Studying is also a great way to develop personal perseverance, that key characteristic of all Awesome Men.

Practice and Repeat

y0s1a

It is useful to have knowledge, be it a skill or ability. However, you will lose that skill or ability if you do not practice and repeat it until it is "locked" in your brain. You may have been taught how to determine the area of a circle, but if you do not practice and repeatedly use that knowledge (the mathematical formula), you will soon lose that ability. It is amazing how many people will learn something today and by tomorrow will have completely forgotten what they learned.

Let us take card shuffling. If you watch a video that teaches you how to shuffle a deck of cards using the riffle shuffle, and if you practice the technique, you will soon know how to shuffle. But you will not be able to do it well unless you practice and repeat what you have been taught.

After showing a new skill to someone, I am always amazed how often they say, "I watched you. I know how to do that." I then say, "Okay, do it," and most of the time they fail. The process of being able to do something well requires repeated practice. Of course *knowing* how something is done is still valuable knowledge. I may know how a magic trick is done, but unless I practice and repeat the trick I will not have the ability to perform it myself. So always be careful to understand the difference between understanding and ability: Real knowledge involves ability. Golf professionals often hit ten thousand balls a season *after* they become professionals. As with most serious endeavors, repeated practice is the key to sustained success and excellence and a surefire way to expand your experience and knowledge.

Experiment and Try

We often have questions about the way things work and will spend many hours trying to figure these things out. Quite frequently just experimenting or trying is often the best and quickest way to gain the knowledge we require. For example, we can read many books about bicycles, but the best way to learn to ride a bicycle for most people is to sit on one, get comfortable, then start pealing. (Having assistance from someone who already knows how to ride a bike is also helpful!)

When you experiment or try things, always check that you have minimized dangers and risks (you do not want to end up on a "fail" video!). But you can acquire many skills just by practicing them without formal study. Now this does require some effort (remember, practice and repeat), but that is not a problem for you anymore. One key is to understand that the experiment may fail initially, but that is okay because failure is also a great way to learn. If Edison's first attempt at making a light bulb worked, he would have not learned much about electrical current, how it behaves, and how it affects various materials. Do not be afraid to experiment and try new ideas.

Reason

Douglas O'Brien

The Thinker by Auguste Rodin

Reasoning, figuring it out, working it out in your head, pondering, and contemplating are similar concepts in that you use your knowledge to establish connections and relationships in your brain, and to understand or face a new challenge. Speaking personally, I have spent many hours working solutions out in my mind. In fact, one such solution even led to an invention that I patented.

If you observe Auguste Rodin's statue *The Thinker*, pictured above, you will notice a couple of salient points that will help you in your thinking and reasoning process. Notice he is alone. Notice also that he has no tech devices or distractions. That allows a singular focus on the challenge at hand.

You should emulate him when you have your own hard thinking to do. I would suggest a pad of paper and a pencil so you can write down ideas as

194

they come to you. It is amazing what insights you can gain by just figuring things out. I am a little concerned that because of the plethora of internet-connected devices we all have and depend on, many people will just search the web for the answers they seek rather than reason things out on their own. Without a doubt, oftentimes googling knowledge is the right way to proceed, but just remember: The parts of the brain you do not use, you lose, so if you do not use your brain to reason, your ability to think will diminish.

To prove my point, when teaching people some new skill (imparting knowledge), I will ask them a question, usually starting with "Why do you think this is so?" Their first response almost always is "I don't know." I then say, "Think about it for a moment." Almost invariably, they still respond with some variation of "I cannot think why." Yet I know that if they use the knowledge they have and make some reasonable inferences from what I have been saying, they could figure out the answer. Why don't they? Because chances are they have done so little reasoning in their recent lives that their brain's reasoning ability has atrophied and needs to be reactivated.

Here is a little test of reasoning ability. See how you do:

Q. If the name of a game is formed by rearranging the letters of the word MODBANTIN, then what will be the first and the last letter of the name?

1. A, T   2. N, D

3. B, N   4. B, T

To solve this test, you have to rearrange the letters to form the name of the game. If you know the game (prior knowledge) and use some simple reasoning (spelling and counting), you will get the right answer. If you do not know the game, and if you cannot spell or count, you will not get it. (See the footnote below if you haven't figured it out and are curious.)*

---

* The game is badminton.

An hour of effective, precise, hard, disciplined and integrated thinking can be worth a month of hard work. Thinking is the very essence of, and the most difficult thing to do, in business and life. Empire builders spend hour-after-hour on mental work . . . while others party. If you're not consciously aware of putting forth the effort to exert self-guided integrated thinking, if you don't act beyond your feelings and you take the path of least resistance, then you're giving in to laziness and no longer control your life

—David Kekich, founder of the Maximum Life Foundation

Using your reasoning powers has great benefits to you. In your journey to becoming an Awesome Man, you are aware that you have priorities in your life, things to achieve and accomplish. By not using your thinking and reasoning abilities, you will waste a lot of your time doing the "month of hard work" Kekich speaks about. Often the difference between Awesome Men and others is the time Awesome Men spend on important things in their lives.

Teach and Write

My wife is a retired teacher, and one of the many lessons she has taught me is "If you really want to know something well, teach it."

As trite as this may sound to some, it is so true. I always was a football fan and believed I was quite knowledgeable about the game. However, when I started coaching the sport to young men, I quickly realized how much I had to learn. And learn I did, by reading, observing, listening, studying, asking questions of experienced coaches, and so on. Even after I had acquired the knowledge to coach my players, the act of teaching skills to the players caused my understanding to increase and solidify from what some people call "book learning" to a real understanding of the knowledge I had acquired. It was almost as if some sort of magical transformation of understanding took place. Ask any teachers you know if they have experienced the same transformation, and I bet they'll say yes.

So what that does mean for you? Simply this: If you really want to acquire knowledge and understanding, teach what you already know to others, either formally or informally. I guarantee that you and your student(s) will benefit.

A senior manager teaching a courier how to optimize his delivery route.

If for some reason there are no teaching opportunities available to you, then write. Yes, *write*. It well help you organize the knowledge in your mind by consolidating your understanding of it, and will also help you refresh your memory of what you know. In my case, I wrote a short manual on coaching youth football. I never tried to get it published or sell it. I did it for myself. Why not do something similar for yourself and your own benefit?

Next Steps . . .

In summary, you now have the tools to acquire knowledge and discover the world around you. To repeat, these tools are

- observe
- read
- listen
- ask
- study
- practice and repeat
- experiment and try

- reason
- teach and write

You want to acquire knowledge for three main reasons:

- to learn who you are and how you are a key part of the world
- to discover your purpose in life and to fulfill that purpose
- to be a great decision-maker and make great choices

Having these tools and abilities will make you unique and place you well on the road to becoming an Awesome Man. And, as a reminder, you need to use them properly and regularly (as you do with any tools and abilities) and keep them in tip-top condition for your ever-ready use.

The tools I have listed above are some that I use. I am sure there are others, and I encourage you to discover them. Initially, these techniques may take a little effort, but soon they will become second nature.

Here is your first task. Make a copy of, or type out for yourself, the two questions below. Then post the questions where you will see them daily to remind yourself of the different ways to acquire knowledge, to reflect on what you learned, and to plan to learn more, in some fashion or another, each and every day.

How did I increase my knowledge level today?

And how can I tomorrow?

A Note about Mentors

I have mentioned mentors several times in this book because I believe very strongly we all need others to help and assist us on our life's journey. I have been extremely fortunate to have had a number of mentors in my life. Let me share with you some common characteristics I have noticed about them.

In almost every case, there was no formal acknowledgment by either of us of a mentor–student relationship—and there does not have to be. Most of the time the relationship was based on knowledge and experience, where I was the learner and the mentor was a quality individual who had expertise he was willing to share. If, say, an acquaintance who I respected had a better tennis serve, I would ask how he did it and if he could teach me how to serve better.

Most importantly, I listened, paid attention, and asked questions at appropriate times, which proved to the person doing the mentoring that I was deserving of his time and effort. In areas that we disagreed on, I was never argumentative. I was always open to changing my viewpoint after consideration because I was truly motivated to learn and improve.

Mentoring is a two-way street. I always tried to be of assistance to the person mentoring me, as I realized the time and effort he was dedicating to me had value and I had to give value back. Finally, it was important for me not to exploit the relationship for any financial gain or similar benefit. My goal was to acquire knowledge, wisdom, and perspective—to become a better man.

When I was a child and a youth, my parents were my mentors—especially my father, who had a rich and varied set of life experiences and was able to maintain a patient and grounded attitude toward life. Later, I called on other family members for guidance and counsel. In school, there were a few teachers and professors whom I admired and respected and developed very positive and worthwhile relationships with. In the workforce, several of my mentors were my direct supervisors, especially in my early working career, which is always a good thing.

So where do you find a mentor? I recommend you start at home with your family and extended family. Is there someone whom you respect, who has character and integrity and is available to talk to you?

At school there are always special teachers who are willing to listen, advise, and support students like you. Of course you have to display a willingness to listen and learn in the classroom before you can expect extra help outside the classroom.

Oftentimes mentors can be found in various organizations such as Boys Clubs and other groups that are supporting young men to reach their goals. In various cultural or religious groups often you will recognize people of specific quality and character. Talk to them informally and try to assist them in their objectives, and they will surely reciprocate by sharing their wisdom and knowledge.

In my own experience, I doubt that most of the people who had mentored me realized they were my mentors. Most of them probably thought I was just a kid who was eager to learn and who was coachable. As I look back, my willingness to simply listen to what other wiser and more knowledgeable individuals had to say on all kinds of topics was the key to my benefiting from them—and they certainly appreciated that willingness to listen.

I think I should repeat a point: Always be coachable in every endeavor. That especially means you have to be prepared to accept negative feedback, even tough criticism. Good mentors tend not to be always sweet and gentle, especially when you do not meet expectations.

You will also have to be open-minded and accepting of diverse opinions, some of which may be contrary to your own. This does not mean you have to reject your existing values and principles for those of your mentors. It means that you have to consider possibly conflicting ideas and opinions and after deliberation make the choice that is right for you. In my own experience, some of my mentors had political outlooks that were different from mine. I listened, evaluated, and usually kept my political opinions to myself.

Section 2

What Is Important in Your Life?

I know how to snort cocaine (at least I do in theory), but that is not necessarily a valuable skill to have. Knowing how to steal, murder, cheat, and do evil to oneself and others are not esteemed skills either. Now some misguided individuals do these things so they can achieve their goals, these goals usually being wealth and power. I also know of criminals who justify their malevolent actions by saying they are doing these things for their family. We all know this is not true, and a delusional belief, because if they end up dead or in jail, they cannot take care of the family.

The key difference between the unwise individual and the Awesome Man is the values each establishes for himself. The Awesome Man bases all his goals and aspirations on the following foundations:

- family
- financial security
- spirituality
- physical and mental health
- personal values

You have to ask yourself what really motivates you today and going forward?

- Are you just trying to get by with not too much effort, going through the motions, not really involved in life?

- Are you looking for that quick hit of pleasure or satisfaction that will not last long and likely lead to more trouble?

- Do you want that quick score that will give you the money you need now, and you will worry about tomorrow later?

- Are you looking forward to some future event, while ignoring what is going on in the present?

- Do you want to be left alone, to do your own thing, without involvement in the world (which, by the way, is an impossible goal)?

- Are you acquiring skills and relationships that are dead-ended and have almost no potential for positive outcomes?

What values do you subscribe to and what significance do you assign to them? Do these values keep you motivated? Are they principles and tenets of your life that will keep you working and striving to achieve greater things?

Remember that others (usually mentors) can provide the opportunity for self-motivation, but only you can motivate yourself. It is you who will reap the rewards.

Here are the things that the Awesome Man believes are important in his life.

Family

Family is an encompassing term from the Awesome Man's perspective, extending from your ancestors to your immediate family to future generations. Your parents, siblings, and close relatives are of course the most important, but having respect and consideration for those who came long before you and those yet to be born are also part of the Awesome Man's thoughts and plans.

Let me expand on that idea to help clarify. The way you live and the freedoms you have did not just happen. The many people who came before you provided either DNA or a cultural and societal environment for you, or both. If the Awesome Man has an infection that is treated with antibiotics and he regains his health, he knows that many individuals were involved in the development of those antibiotics. Likewise, if by your actions and behavior you degrade the soil, air, or water, many generations of people from now will have to suffer from your selfishness. Your existence today is based on a continuum of life, that which has preceded you and that which is yet to come.

Related to this concept is the reality that we are connected to all those around us. When a viral outbreak occurs somewhere in the world, it is only a matter of days if not hours before it potentially has an impact on many of us. The Awesome Man considers family as a much broader and encompassing view than just immediate blood relatives. Consider all those who love you, and all those you should love, as your family.

Unfortunately, the family unit has become disordered in our society. We have absentee fathers, men who accept only minimal or even zero responsibility for being present daily in the raising of their children. We have jealous and self-centered parents and siblings shunning other family members because somebody did not do what they wanted or expected. And in the worst cases, we have adults committing horrific acts on children of the family.

The Awesome Man knows that family is important, that he has a responsibility to keep it strong and whole. This responsibility lies with the adult males as well as with children at an appropriate age level. Why? Because over the centuries it has been proved that the family is the building block of society. It is where values, character, and ethics are usually introduced. We know from real-world experience that if nurturing, love, and care do not exist in the family unit, not much good can follow from it.

Even at a young age the Awesome Man knew to be respectful, loving, and caring to all members of his family. He did not mock, ridicule, ignore, hurt, or defame anybody.

No doubt a number of Awesome Men were not nice and respectful as children. However, these males learned that they have the ability to grow and evolve into much better people as time goes by. Remember that your past does not dictate your future. You do.

Here are some actions you can take right now that will help you place your family as a high priority in your life:

- Never lie to your family and, just as importantly, never do anything you would have to lie about. Lying breaks down family trust, which breaks down family relationships.

- Listen to what your family has to say. You may not want to hear it, you may not agree with what is being said, but by listening to family members you validate them as being part of the family.

- When you are with family members, always be aware of their importance in your life. They are more important than tech devices and electronic media. Even hobbies and activities such as car restoration and sailing, which in themselves are benign, can turn into obsessions and preoccupations that can isolate you from family.

- Understand that family can be and is much more than just blood relatives; family can include whoever wants to be part of a family. And that is good.

- Realize and accept that your family is made up of human beings with all the weaknesses and frailties we all have. If your mother is an alcoholic, accept that reality and try to understand and help her fight the addiction. Whenever a family member does not meet expectations, do not cover up or hide the reality from yourself but rather forgive and support them.

- Be aware that evil people may use the pressure of family relationships to do wrong. Unfortunately, some of us may have an extended-family member who operates outside the bounds of good sense and character. We must use ethical judgment at all times, even when dealing with family. The annals of crime are filled with cases of individuals committing offenses by "just following" their siblings. If you think I am exaggerating, in the book *In My Father's House*, Pulitzer Prize–winning journalist Fox Butterfield writes that criminologists in the United States and other countries have found that 5 percent of families account for half of all crime.

- Remember that "taking care of the family" should never be an excuse or justification for immoral or illegal activities.

How did I strengthen my family relationships today?
And how can I tomorrow?

Financial Security

Most male adolescents want to be rich and famous, and if they cannot be famous, they will settle for being rich.

I am certainly not going to tell you that money is evil, because having adequate financial resources can definitely help reduce many of the stresses we feel in everyday life. Having enough money means that you can have a good home, eat well, and be healthy. You can have access to education and health care. You can afford to travel and to be charitable and kind with your time and resources.

Being financially secure is important in life, but I believe the Awesome Man would define "financially secure" as the ability to earn a living in order to meet his financial needs and those of his family in an ethical and honorable way—nothing illegal, unfair, unjust, immoral, or spurious. Nothing that takes advantage of others' weaknesses or is exploitative.

You do not want to earn financial rewards from any activity that is questionable or is contrary to society's highest and best standards, and yours. Being financially secure also means you will not be a financial burden on your family or society. Being locked up in jail means you are a burden.

Remember, it is not always about how much you earn but how much you spend that determines your financial security.

A Six-Step Starter Plan for Achieving Financial Security

There are many excellent books and videos on finances and money management, and I recommend that you take advantage of them. However, I want to provide you with a broader approach for achieving financial security. Consider these steps as a starter program for financial security, a program you should start today, even if you do not earn a nickel.

Step 1. Get an Education or Learn a Trade

The Awesome Man knows he has to work to provide for his family and himself. At a young age, he knows the two paths to successful employment are either obtaining an education or becoming a tradesman (by getting involved in either a formal or informal apprenticeship program). Both paths require the acquisition of knowledge and skills. The better he applies himself in either academic studies or on-the-job training, the better work opportunities he will have in the job market and the better chance he will have of achieving financial security.

Pause for a moment and understand this simple but important concept: The better you are at any job skill, the more money you will earn. Education and apprenticeship prepare you for jobs. So every time you do not do well in school, every time you skip a lecture, every time you goof off in class, you are costing yourself money—likely many thousands of dollars and perhaps hundreds of thousands over the course of a working career.

- So the first step is getting good education or learning a trade. When learning in school or in the trades, strive to be the best you can be.

- If you are in school, ask yourself daily, "Did I cost myself money because I did less than my best in every class today?"

- If you are working, are you trying to be the best employee possible? History has proved that the best employees make the most money and enjoy the best prospects for advancement.

- Last but not least, consider being an entrepreneur, being self-employed and having your own business. Many Awesome Men find being their own boss allows for more personal creativity and satisfaction as well as for more financial rewards. Many men have started careers as sidelines to their existing employment and saw them grow into great new occupations. Always be open for these sorts of opportunities.

Step 2. Build Your Financial Vocabulary and Knowledge: They May Be Your Greatest Asset

Know the difference between an asset, an expense, and memories. Acquire assets, minimize expenses, and be selective with memories.

- An asset in the simplest terms is something that has value over time. Some assets increase in value, like real estate in some communities. Other assets lose value (depreciate) quickly, like automobiles. Some assets maintain their usefulness (value to the owner) for years and years, like a good set of kitchen knives.

- Depending on your location, owning real estate has shown to be an excellent appreciating asset. You have to live somewhere, and owning your residence offers many advantages as the first asset to acquire. You can even start saving for your first home as a teen.

- Cash is always useful as an asset. It is the best asset for both opportunities and emergencies that will arise in your life. Many people keep of six months' worth of expenses in cash or cash equivalents in the bank for emergencies. Regardless of what happens, you have some breathing space to handle most contingencies that may arise with this reserve.

- An expense is something you expend or consume almost immediately, and it has no value in the future. When you buy a lunch, regardless how much you pay, chances are you will be hungry again at dinnertime. Going to a bar and buying a round of drinks for yourself and your buddies will likely be forgotten the next morning. Getting a parking ticket is a poor expense, and gambling is one of the worst expenses.

- Memories (for the purposes of this discussion) are things you acquire by spending money. Good memories will last a lifetime. Spending money to take your children camping or fishing is a great way to acquire positive memories for you and your family. Taking your wife out regularly to show her how important she is to you is a wonderful way to spend money. Of course you have to be sensible and selective about how you spend your money to collect memories. Every hoarder and binge collector started out small and then lost all semblance of self-control.

- Being prudent with how you use money will ensure your financial security.

Step 3. Save first

- The smartest thing you can do with every dollar you earn is to put at least 10 to 20 percent aside in savings. Always have at least one month's pay set aside for emergencies, and build up your savings to acquire assets that will grow over time.

- If you receive a windfall, an unexpected sum of money, save at least 50 percent.

- Always give some money to legitimate charities that need your support.

Step 4. Make your money work

- Once you have your basic living expenses covered, you can either begin acquiring assets that will grow over time or buying items that will help you generate money. Even putting a dollar a day into an interest-bearing savings account will grow significantly in one year. If you are a tradesman, you can buy a new tool that will make you more productive.

Step 5. Be prudent

- Avoid buying things you "want" or "have to have." Avoid so-called last-chance deals.

- Resist impulse purchases. Make sure that you really need the item and that it will genuinely improve your life.

- Wait a day before buying. If you can postpone the urge to buy by just one day, you'll be amazed at how often the desire to spend your hard-earned money simply disappears.

- Consider lower-priced alternatives.

Step 6. Avoid money pits

- **Fashion.** The fashion industry is a multibillion-dollar industry based on the simple concept that by buying products you will become a better person. Wearing a $150 team jersey, $250 endorsed sneakers, or $100 designer sunglasses only means you are spending money to make rich celebrities and companies richer. Is that really how you want to spend your money?

- **Prepared food.** The fast-food industry has convinced most of us that we are too busy to cook wholesome, healthy food at home. It is easy to forget how expensive fast food is, and the industry is constantly promoting "deals" to give us the illusion of savings and economy. Count the number of times you purchase "ready to eat" food and beverages in a week, and compare the cost to preparing that food at home—you will be amazed. Fast food tastes great because the industry puts in all the fat, carbs, sugars, and salt that we enjoy and sometimes are not healthy for us. Don't know how to cook? Take a course. It will be worth it.

- **Technology.** Internet, data, cell phones and devices, video game software and hardware. For many young men, expenditures for these items make up a major portion of their spending. Not that long ago nobody even had mobile phones! The point is you do not need the latest and greatest technology to lead an awesome life. Cut back, reduce, eliminate, and save the money you and your family are not spending on these items—not to mention the time you are sinking into them.

- **ATMs, credit cards, and buying on time.** Some of us are addicted to debt. We do not seem to be able to live and purchase the items we need and want by paying cash. We use credit to save 10% on the purchase price of something we really do not need, then pay 20% interest for months on that purchase. Rather than going to the bank once a week or once a month and withdrawing the cash we need, some of us use costly ATMs and pay a fee for each withdrawal.

  An example is going to the ATM and withdrawing $20 to buy some fast food for you and your date. The bank may charge you a $1 fee. And if you do not have the money in the bank, the bank provides an overdraft for a fee of $1. Your bank instantly begins to charge you interest on your overdraft until you pay it off.

  Now that $20 fast-food bill, which includes taxes on prepared food, costs you over $22. To pay for that meal, quite likely you will have to work at least an hour to earn that $22 after taxes and withholdings. Was that food worth one hour of your labor? How much cheaper and better would that meal be if you had prepared it at home?

  No matter how much the vendor encourages you to use some sort of deferred payment plan, you should pay cash. And if you cannot pay cash, make sure you really need the item. Finance charges on many purchases can double the cost of the purchase before the item is paid off.

  If you find you are carrying a credit card balance or other type of loan to cover your normal expenses, you are not budgeting properly and likely living beyond your means. Make the changes needed now.

- **Late and missed payments.** Many people believe if they do not have the money, they can defer monthly payments with little or no consequence. That is absolutely wrong. The service provider will charge you interest—usually at a very high rate—and your credit rating will be negatively affected so that your future borrowing for major items will become much more expensive. Make sure your monthly bills and installments are always paid on time and in full. Carrying a balance costs and costs.

How did I strengthen my financial security today?

And how can I tomorrow?

Spirituality

This section is not about your religion or about faith. Even people who are agnostic or atheists or do not believe in a higher power or God often accept there is some spiritual aspect to human existence.

It is very easy to deny the existence of things we cannot see. However, when you think about it, much of what we experience in life is not visible. For example, you cannot see gravity, or the wind, or even heat. But you can experience the effects of these things, so you know they are real. And if you are open to experiencing the spiritual side of your existence, chances are you will see all the proof you require.

Many young men do not think about the spiritual aspects of their lives. I believe it's possible to be an Awesome Man without being aware of the spiritual aspect of life, but I believe that it is easier to achieve awesomeness by recognizing and nurturing your spiritual awareness.

- Nurture yourself through contemplation of spiritual values and prayer. Either you can be involved with a formal religion or you can just spend a few minutes every day in quiet thought or meditation. Or both.

- Understand your spiritual self is not about material things. Praying for winning the lottery rarely works. Praying for courage in facing challenges always works.

- Other good things to pray for are wisdom, understanding, knowledge, fortitude, and patience.

- You do not need to become a monk, spend any money, join a cult, wear a sack cloth and spread ashes on your body, or have candles everywhere in your home to build and strengthen the spiritual aspects of your life. Getting to know your spiritual side is very much an internal journey.

- Inquiring and learning more about your spiritual self is positive, caring, and gentle. It's a way of taking care of yourself.

- Be grateful every day, and acknowledge all that you have received.

- Starting today, spend five minutes in a quiet space and think about what you have read here.

In 2017, Pope Francis, the head of the Roman Catholic Church stated:

Rivers do not drink their own water; trees do not eat their own fruit; the sun does not shine on itself; and flowers do not spread their fragrance for themselves. Living for others is a rule of nature. We are born to help each other. No matter how difficult it is. Life is good when you are happy, but much better when others are happy because of you.

This is a powerful statement that the Awesome Man readily concurs with. It shows how your life, the world, and your spiritual values are connected.

How did I strengthen my spiritual self today?

And how can I tomorrow?

Physical and Mental Health

In this section we are talking about what things are important to the Awesome Man and, I hope, to you as you pursue your goal of becoming an Awesome Man. So far we have focused on family, financial security (very different from wealth), and spirituality. Now we look at physical and mental health, two aspects of life that provide the foundation for all your other efforts.

Physical health and mental health are closely related. To be truly healthy and be all that one can be, both aspects must be maintained and optimized. To maintain and optimize good health, you should be aware of some basic concepts:

- Keep active, have hobbies, play sports, have fun, move, build something, hike, walk, run.

- Some things you do to your body and mind can be very dangerous in the short term and/or the long term. Avoid these things.

- Prevention is the best way to minimize injury and damage to the mind and body.

- Think and use your knowledge to make good choices about what you do with your mind and body.

- When you are tired, hungry, under the influence of alcohol, drugs, or emotional stress and pressure, it is very easy to make bad choices about your well-being. Avoid making decisions until you are calm, controlled, and clear-headed.

- To put it in another perspective, between 2008 and 2016 more US servicemen died as a result of accidents (mostly motor vehicle) and self-inflicted injuries in noncombat areas than died in Iraq and Afghanistan due to combat.*

- Be aware of the risk factors you face as a young man. The list on the opposite page was compiled by the Centers of Disease Control and Prevention in the United States for 2017 and applied to young white males in the United States. If you die in the United States between the ages of 20 and 24, there is almost a 62% chance it will be from an accident (unintentional injuries, but mainly motor vehicles), suicide, or homicide. Think about it for a moment: The three leading causes of death below are largely avoidable and preventable!

---

* Congressional Research Service, "Trends in Active-Duty Military Deaths Since 2006," July 1, 2020, https://fas.org/sgp/crs/natsec/IF10899.pdf.

Leading Causes of Death, 2017

All races and origins, male, by age group, USA[*]

	Age Group		
Rank	1–19	20–44	45–64
1	Accidents 33.8%	Accidents 38.9%	Cancer 24.7%
2	Suicide 14.7%	Suicide 13.8%	Heart disease 23.7%
3	Homicide 14.7%	Heart disease 9.1%	Accidents 10.1%
4	Cancer 7.3%	Homicide 9.1%	Chronic liver disease 4.4%
5	Birth defects 3.9%	Cancer 6.4%	Diabetes 4.0%
6	Heart disease 2.8%	Chronic liver disease 2.2%	Suicide 3.8%
7	Influenza and pneumonia 1.1%	Diabetes 1.7%	Chronic lower respiratory diseases 3.4%
8	Chronic lower respiratory diseases 1.1%	Stroke 1.3%	Stroke 3.1%
9	Stroke 1.0%	HIV disease 0.9%	Kidney disease 1.4%
10	Septicemia 0.6%	Influenza and pneumonia 0.7%	Septicemia 1.4%

How did I optimize and maintain my physical and mental health today?

And how can I tomorrow?

---

[*] https://www.cdc.gov/healthequity/lcod/men/2017/all-races-origins/index.htm

Personal Values: An Integral Part of Healthy Living

Remember that "A man who stands for nothing will fall for anything." It is important to have values and principles. Without these cornerstones of character your life will become aimless and unfulfilling.

As I said before, you do not have to choose the values that I've presented in this book, but *until* you have chosen your own, I recommend these: family, financial security, spirituality, and physical and mental health.

I also want to take this opportunity to ensure that you are very careful not to distort these values. To help you understand what I mean, I will use some stereotypes of individuals you may be familiar with. Each of these gentlemen believes he is being the best person he can be, but I want you to score these men with a check mark in the category where they are doing their best. Do any of these men get four check marks?

	Family	Financial Security	Spiritual Values	Physical & Mental Health
Corrupt policeman				
Pimp				
Drug Dealer				
Mafia Don				
Salacious Movie Mogul				
Hells Angel Member				
Numbers Runner				
Unethical Politician				
Awesome Man				

The Awesome Man makes great choices because he makes decisions in the context and consciousness of his personal values and code of conduct. It is not possible to excessively gamble when you are aware of financial security. It is not possible to steal from your parents if family is one of the tenets you adhere to. The Awesome Man considers these values as guide rails in his life, they keep him on the right track and ensures he reaches his destination.

Crime, Justice, Ethics, and Right versus Wrong

In your path to being an Awesome Man, you will be confronted with choices that will be legal yet not right. Some people tend to believe that if a choice is not specifically against the law, it is okay.

The problem with that attitude is that laws change, and the law at times can be too loose. In Canada and a number of US states, the usage of cannabis products is generally legal. There are individuals who choose to hold themselves to a higher standard and do not consume cannabis. They have thought about it and felt that the known and unknown risks of cannabis usage far exceed the benefits. They may never consume these items or they may rarely consume cannabis, but the legality does not overrule their judgment.

Millions of people have died as a result of cigarette smoking, which is a fact. Millions more suffer from other smoking-related illnesses. Yet smoking is legal. I certainly would not encourage anybody to smoke cigarettes based on the fact that it is legal.

I personally think there are too many laws and restrictions in Western society, especially in areas where the exercise of individual good judgment would work better instead, if everybody agreed to do it. Too many individuals engage in white collar crime, extorting, cheating, scamming, conning other people, and trying to justify it by saying that they did not break the law.

If anybody challenges you about your behavior or actions and you justify them by stating you did not break any law, it usually means you are not on the path to becoming an Awesome Man.

Section 3

Setting Goals and Getting Things Done

There is a good chance some of you reading the last chapter thought, "This self-development stuff is too hard. I am too busy and I do not have the time for all that, even if I wanted to."

Let us address the "it's too hard" complaint. Walking is hard for a baby, but you mastered it. Reading and writing are hard in grade one, but right now you're deep into a fairly lengthy book. The fact is that most everything in life is "hard" for everybody at some point in their lives. Usually after you master the challenge and know how to do something, it ceases to be hard.

Becoming and being an Awesome Man are without doubt "hard" things to do. But the Awesome Man has developed systems in his life to make things less hard, to ensure that he is not "too busy" for the important things that make him a better man. He structures his life so he can do the things he wants to do and devote time to be with those he loves. He sets goals and uses systems to stay on course and achieve his goals.

Most males will eagerly state they set goals, but when questioned further on how many of their goals they have achieved, they sadly say, "Not too many." Eventually, when you've piled up enough failures, the feeling of "Why bother?" takes over your life.

When you set a goal, it's important to do your utmost to achieve it. So let us see how you can be more successful in setting and achieving your goals. Hand in hand, your time management will improve, and you will have more time for the important things in life.

SMART Goal-Setting

In 1981, George T. Doran, a consultant and former director of corporate planning for the Washington Water Power Company, published a paper called "There's a S.M.A.R.T. Way to Write Management's Goals and Objectives."1 In the document, he introduces SMART goals as a tool to create criteria to help improve the chances of success in accomplishing goals.

I believe this is a great system of goal-setting. There are many other methods, and you may find a system that suits you better, but until you do I recommend Mr. Doran's SMART system. So here's what SMART stands for:

S: Specific, Significant

M: Measurable

A: Achievable, Acceptable

R: Realistic, Relevant

T: Time-based, Track Progress

Let's explore each of these aspects of SMART goal-setting.

S: Specific, Significant

A major reason people often fail to achieve their objectives can be found at the get-go: The language they use to define their goal is too vague and unclear. "I am going to do better in school," "I will be a safe driver," and "I am going to cut back on my gambling" are all nice sentiments, but they lack the detail and clarity needed for goal-setting.

You want to set a *specific* goal. Specific in this case means free from ambiguity. The wording of your goal should be clear and concise—no wishy-washy promises or "I'll try to be better" pledges.

Here are two examples of well-articulated, specific goals: "I am going to limit my video game playing to two hours a night for the next week" and "I will eat one meal a day at home with the family."

Another important factor in setting goals is that they should be significant in your current life situation. For example, if you are struggling to pay your rent, taking two months off work to learn to surf might not be a practical goal to set. But cutting your expenses by 50% each month would be.

M: Measurable

When it comes to goals, what do words like "better" mean? Goals that are not measurable are useless. Your goals must set a measurable start point and a measurable target. Let's say you weigh 245 pounds right now and want to lose 15 pounds. Your target weight is 230 pounds, which is a clear objective to achieve. If you fail to set measurable goals, how can you possibly know when you have achieved them?

A: Achievable, Acceptable

Amazingly, many people set goals that are worthwhile, specific, and measurable yet not achievable. They are not achievable because the goal-setter does not have the capacity or the ability to reach the goal. For example, a fifty-year-old male whose goal is to be an NFL quarterback by the time he is fifty-one years old is doomed to fail. To lose fifty pounds in two weeks at any age is not achievable for a healthy individual. There are many things in life that we cannot accomplish due to various limitations beyond our control. That fifty-year-old NFL wannabe would be wiser to aim for playing in a local men's flag football league, a much more achievable goal.

One way to ensure that your goal is achievable is to break it down into a number of subgoals. For example, if your goal is to do fifty push-ups in four minutes or less, you're likely going to have to build up your strength over a period of weeks. So set an initial subgoal at a sensible five push-ups in four minutes for the first two weeks. Then ten, then fifteen, and so on until you can do fifty in four minutes. Achieving your subgoals moves you ever closer to achieving your end goal.

The idea that the goal you set is *acceptable* means that it fits into the ethical structure of your life and is something an Awesome Man would do. Learning how to hot-wire cars so you can steal them is really not an acceptable goal, as the consequence of using this new skill can be devastating.

R: Realistic, Relevant

Let us say you set a goal to build a custom chopper motorcycle, but you have no shop to work on the project, you have no money to buy parts or tools, and you live on an island off the Alaska coast as a subsistence fisherman. It's probably the case that setting a goal to build that chopper is not realistic or even relevant to your situation. You do not have the resources you will require, you do not have a place to ride the chopper if and when it is completed, and there are likely more suitable and relevant projects you can set as goals. Building a barn or a shed might be a realistic first-step goal. The barn will be of use, the trees on the island will provide most of the construction materials, and when fishing season closes you will have the time to work on projects inside the barn.

It is crucial that the goals you set are realistic and relevant in terms of the resources, time, and talent you have available. Otherwise, you are setting yourself up to experience failure and frustration.

T: Time-based, Track Progress

I believe that more goals are missed because not enough time is allocated. You've probably noticed how just about any task always seems to take longer than expected. Another factor hampering goal completion is that progress (or lack of progress) is not tracked against the time allocated for completion.

Let us say today is Sunday and your goal is to clean and organize your room by Friday. With every good intention, you are going to start on the cleaning Monday night. Monday night rolls around, and you realize a crucial football game with playoff implications is on TV that evening, and you *must* watch it. Plus, you have some money bet on the home team in the office football pool this week. You rationalize that you have the whole rest of the week to work on your room.

Tuesday you have a bad day at work, on top of not winning the football pool. After dinner you have a few beers and soon find yourself too tired to work on your room. Wednesday night for sure.

Wednesday night rolls around and cousin Jimmy calls you up. He needs your help picking up some firewood for the family cabin at the lake. Since you use the cabin for free, you are obligated to help Jimmy.

Thursday night Amber calls and wants you to come with her to the mall to go shopping for a new laptop. Since she knows little about computers, she needs your guidance.

Friday morning your room is still not cleaned and Amber asked you to go with her to the county fair tonight. What is a man to do? Maybe next week you will get to the room.

This is a typical example of how life gets in the way of accomplishing things. You set a goal and you just cannot seem to get it done. The goal even had a time deadline, Friday, but that didn't help. But what if you kept the deadline of Friday but had *daily* time targets to measure as the week went by—such as working on your room ten minutes each day? If you took this approach, your chances of reaching the goal would have been much higher.

Here's an example of an easy-to-devise time chart to manage this scenario. Let's assume it will take a total of two hours to clean your room. Set daily goals as needed to achieve your end goal of having your room cleaned by Friday.

Chart for Cleaning and Organizing Room, 2 hour job

	Allocated	Actual	Notes
SUNDAY	30 minutes	30 minutes	
MONDAY	30 minutes	20 minutes	Monday Football: cleanup during pregame and halftime
TUESDAY	30 minutes	60 minutes	Do not drink until one hour completed
WEDNESDAY	30 minutes	————	Cousin Jimmy needs help
THURSDAY	reserve time, if needed	10 minutes	JOB DONE!
FRIDAY	reserve time, if needed	JOB DONE!	JOB DONE!

As you can see from the chart, the key to success was starting immediately, on the first day, and then making steady progress throughout the week. Keeping track of daily progress and being flexible enough to adapt to changes made it possible to achieve the goal ahead of time.

Remember, achieving your goals is made up of many tiny victories and small achievements.

Below you'll find an easy-to-use goal tracking template, based on the SMART System, that can be adapted to help you manage just about any goal you have in mind. Feel free to copy it and give it a try. I recommend that the first time you use it on a relatively simple goal. But once you get the hang of the system, you'll be ready to use it to tackle your bigger goals, and move yourself further on your journey to becoming an Awesome Man.

Goal-Setting Template
Utilizing the SMART System

S: Specific, Significant

What is your goal? Be specific.

_____

_____

_____

Is this goal significant in your life? Will it further you on the path to being an Awesome Man? Will it help you maximize the things that are important in your life?

_____

_____

_____

M: Measurable

Is there a start date and a finish date? Is there a specific measurable goal? Can you define and measure your starting point? Do you have a method of tracking progress at measurable intervals? Do you have targets for those intervals?

_____

_____

_____

A: Achievable, Acceptable

Is the goal that you are setting achievable based on the abilities and resources you have available? Is it acceptable and consistent with what those around you are trying to achieve? It makes no sense to set a goal to help at a retirement home if you have no means of transportation to get to the home. It makes no sense to set a goal to paint the barn if your father plans to tear it down. Your goals need to be acceptable and compatible with others around you.

_____

_____

_____

R: Realistic, Relevant

Is the goal you are setting realistic in terms of resources, time, and the talent you have available? Too often when setting goals, people underestimate the complexity of what they are trying to do and the resources required. Are you relying on somebody to assist you in reaching your goal, and are they as committed as you?

_____

_____

_____

T: Time-based, Track Progress

Is the goal you're setting feasible in the time you have allowed? You are not going to complete all four years of college in three months. On the other hand, you don't want to allocate seven years to attend college full-time to get a four-year degree. To reach your goal, are you prepared and do you have the ability to track progress at regular intervals?

_____

_____

_____

Some Further Tips on Goal-Setting

1. Start small and simple. Start out by taking small steps and achieving subgoals. An easy goal achieved is better than a lofty goal missed.

2. Initially, keep your goal to yourself and share it only with the people who need to know. When you have reached your goal you can tell the world. Too often we set a good goal, and people around us will discourage us.

3. Write things down, starting with your goal. Make lists and charts to help you track progress and stay on top of things. These tools make a huge difference in completing tasks; with them, you will never have to say "I forgot."

4. Do not delay or defer. The longer you wait to start, the less likely you are to achieve your goal.

Goal-Killing Phrases

- I am going to get in shape.
- I'll try harder at school.
- I will get to it, just trust me.
- I am going to improve.
- I will start tomorrow / next week / next month / next year / never.
- It is too hard.
- It will not happen again.
- What's the rush?
- I'm busy.
- It's not my fault.

There are a number of reasons these are goal-killing phrases. To start with, they are vague and not specific in regard to the objective or time frame, which guarantees that measurement of achievement or lack thereof is impossible. Some of these phrases absolve the individual from the responsibility to do anything specific. Others are like promises or good intentions, and as you know, the road to hell is paved with good intentions.

Recap on Goals

It's not unfair to say that your progress in becoming an Awesome Man can be based on how well you set and achieve your goals. We know from nature that if we are not progressing, we are regressing.

Now go set a goal, using the tools you have learned.

Be Sure to Live in the Present

Goals are not dreams and wishes. Goals involve action, while dreams and wishes are just thoughts. One way to ensure that you are setting good goals is to live in the present.

Too often people spend much of their time thinking of the past and how things could have been better. You cannot change the past—it is gone. All you can do now is decide how you evaluate the past as a basis for going forward in your life.

On the other hand, the future is not known or "guaranteed" to anyone. People who think that the future will be better without action on their part are deceiving themselves. The future is the land of hope, but the present is the land of action, where you work to create the future you hope for.

The only time in your life that is relevant to you is right now, the present. This is the only time you can have any direct impact on your life, and what you do now will affect your future. Now is action time. Now is where you have power and control.

Only if you do things now will your life change. Living with the expectation that something wonderful will occur in the future is a fool's game. Why wait to have an impactful event? Why not create one right now? Enjoy the present, savor the present, and use the present as a building block for the rest of your life.

Ask yourself: If what you are doing right now is not the best thing you could be doing for yourself, why are you doing it?

Section 4

Help with Setting Goals

Setting goals and working to achieve them is not easy. That is probably why so few people set worthy goals, let alone accomplish them. Bearing this in mind, and knowing that I have needed much help to achieve my goals, I have put together some ideas and suggestions that will aid you in reaching your goals. The key thing is to believe in yourself (confidence) and do the work required (effort). That's how Awesome Men achieve their goals, and that's how you will do the same. If you have trouble with procrastination, just start a little bit right now, and you will see how easy it will go from there.

- Make sure your goal is compatible with your values, such as family, financial security, spirituality, and physical and mental health.
- Identify the things you do in your life that do not reinforce your values and that you want to change. For some men, it is fantasy sports, porn, alcohol, casual sex, recreational drugs, video games, aimlessness and laziness, overreliance on family, lack of willingness to acquire knowledge, and satisfaction with the status quo resulting in inertia.
- When you're new to the practice of setting goals, it is far better to set positive goals. An example of a positive goal is "I will eat dinner with the family three times a week." When starting out on your journey to become an Awesome Man, a positive goal is better than a negative goal phrased as your committing to *not* do something, such as "I will not get fast food." Similarly, go for a positive goal like "I will play basketball for one hour a week at the park" rather than a negatively expressed goal such as "I will cut back on video games."

- Write down how you are going to accomplish the goal. Be very specific. For example: "On Monday, Wednesday, and Friday each week, I will come straight home from school, help Mom cook, and eat with the family. I will not make other plans for those nights, unless I substitute another night to be with family." That goal is worded with great specificity, so you know just what you are trying to achieve. Here are two more examples: "Saturday mornings at 10:00 I will go take part in the pickup basketball game at the park" and "Every day I will spend five minutes clearing my head in quiet calmness."

- Once you are more experienced with goal setting, you may wish to try setting "negative" goals, which are designed to minimize negative aspects of your life. If, for example, you are currently partaking in behaviors that are not compatible with your previously stated values, you could set negative goals such as: "I will not watch porn on Wednesdays," or "I will not drink on Tuesdays," or "I will be in bed by 11:00 p.m. every work/school night."

- Keep records and charts to monitor how well you are doing. Just relying on your memory is dangerous.

- Be patient with yourself. On average it takes about six weeks to achieve a goal involving behavior change so that it becomes permanent.

- There are no small or insignificant steps as long as you are always focused and moving toward your goal. Make sure you celebrate your achievements, even the small ones.

Tools to Help Every Day

Here's a collection of tools that will greatly support your efforts to become an Awesome Man. Please feel free to copy them for your personal use. And, of course, adjust them as needed to suit your particular goals and circumstances.

1. What Is Important in My Life?

2. My Goal(s) for the Long Term

3. My Goal(s) for the Medium Term

4. My Goal(s) for the Short Term

5. To-Do List for Today

6. Daily Reflection or How Did I Do Today?

1. What is important my in life?

Name_____

Date_____

These are the values that are important in my life, and I will base my actions on bettering them.

- My Family Relationships

- My Financial Security

- My Spiritual Values

- My Physical and Mental Health

Everything I do every day will be focused to the betterment of these values.

I know that each of these values is equally important, and in combination they are key to my achieving happiness, joy, and contentment in my life and becoming an Awesome Man.

NOTES _____
_____
_____
_____
_____

2. My goals for the long term

Name_____

Date_____

Below are my goals for the long term. They are not dreams or wishes or hopes. These are the things I want to achieve, and all my actions each day will bring me one step closer to achieving them. These goals may be modified or changed due to circumstances.

I have set this goals using the SMART system, my goals are: S—Specific, Significant; M—Measurable; A—Achievable, Acceptable; R—Realistic, Relevant; T—Time-based.

These goals are compatible with my the Values that are important in my life, my family relationships, my financial security, my spiritual values and my physical and mental health.

Goal: _____

S_____

M_____

A_____

R_____

T_____

Goal: _____

S_____

M_____

A_____

R_____

T_____

Notes on Long-Term and Other Goals

Usually long-term goals are one year or longer or, for students, an academic year.

All goals, be they short-term, medium-term, or long-term, must be compatible and complimentary with each other. Let us say your long-term goal is to graduate in four years with a bachelor's degree from the state university and you are entering your freshman year this week. If your medium-term goal is to spend two years surfing in Australia, these two goals are incompatible.

Often it is good to have medium-term goals be the measurable parts of your long-term goal. If your long-term goal is to graduate, then your medium-term goals would be to successfully complete all your courses each semester.

A short-term goal that would be compatible with the above goals could be to have all your term papers completed, proofed, and handed in two days before the due date.

3. My Goal(s) for the Medium Term

Name_____

Date_____

Below are my goals for the medium term. They are not dreams or wishes or hopes. These are the things I want to achieve, and all my actions each day will bring me one step closer to achieving them. These goals may be modified or changed due to circumstances.

I have set this goals using the SMART system, my goals are: S—Specific, Significant; M—Measurable; A—Achievable, Acceptable; R—Realistic, Relevant; T—Time-based.

These goals are compatible with my the Values that are important in my life, my family relationships, my financial security, my spiritual values and my physical and mental health.

Goal: _____

S_____

M_____

A_____

R_____

T_____

Goal: _____

S_____

M_____

A_____

R_____

T_____

4. My Goal(s) for the Short Term

Name_____

Date_____

Below are my goals for the short term. They are not dreams or wishes or hopes. These are the things I want to achieve, and all my actions each day will bring me one step closer to achieving them. These goals may be modified or changed due to circumstances.

I have set this goals using the SMART system, my goals are: S—Specific, Significant; M—Measurable; A—Achievable, Acceptable; R—Realistic, Relevant; T—Time-based.

These goals are compatible with my the Values that are important in my life, my family relationships, my financial security, my spiritual values and my physical and mental health.

Goal: _____

S_____

M_____

A_____

R_____

T_____

Goal: _____

S_____

M_____

A_____

R_____

T_____

To-Do List for Today

Date_____

These are the things I will accomplish today.
They are compatible with my values and goals.

_____ ☐

_____ ☐

_____ ☐

_____ ☐

_____ ☐

_____ ☐

_____ ☐

_____ ☐

_____ ☐

_____ ☐

_____ ☐

_____ ☐

_____ ☐

_____ ☐

Daily Reflection or How Did I Do Today?

Each day we should pause and review what happened. We should ask ourselves and answer honestly these questions. (By the way, "I don't know" is not a helpful answer. Strive for more clarity if that's how you feel.)

How did I increase my knowledge level today?

_____

How can I increase it tomorrow?

_____

How did I strengthen my family relationships today?

_____

How can I increase them tomorrow?

_____

How did I strengthen my financial security today?

_____

How can I increase it tomorrow?

_____

How did I strengthen my spiritual self today?

_____

How can I increase it tomorrow?

_____

How did I optimize and maintain my physical and mental health today?

_____

How can I increase it tomorrow?

_____

Note on Daily Reflection Questions

Thanking someone and helping someone are great ways to strengthen your spiritual self.

Quiet Time

Mark Twain's wife had a study built next to their house so the great author could write or take refuge in a quiet space undisturbed by his family and visitors. (Plus he smoked cigars, which his wife would not allow him to do in the house.) This room provided Twain a safe haven from the stress of daily life. You may not have a separate room for yourself, but it is important for you to be able to quiet yourself, be still, and relax for a time each day. Find a place for yourself. It might be a special chair, or a park bench, or just a log in the backyard where you can go and be quiet for a few minutes. We all need to be alone from time to time just to think or be still.

Section 5

Inertia and Procrastination

The really happy people are those who have broken the chains of procrastination, those who find satisfaction in doing the job at hand. They're full of eagerness, zest, and productivity. You can be, too.

—Norman Vincent Peale

There have been many times in my life when I just did not want to do anything other than what I was currently doing. If my dad wanted me to cut the lawn, I wanted to finish the drawing I was working on. If my mom wanted me to help her paint my bedroom, I wanted to sleep instead. Whatever I was doing was more important than anything else in the world.

Of course I always promised to do it later, with every good intention to do it later—which I rarely did because I was then doing some other thing I wanted to do more.

I learned I was not the only young man who acted this way. Later in life, as a father to three teenage boys, I became curious why they behaved the same way. One day after spending twenty minutes arguing with my son about why he should cut the lawn, I went out and cut it in twelve minutes. Then it hit me. My son would rather spend twenty minutes of his time arguing with me than spend twelve minutes cutting the lawn. To me, this seemed like an inefficient use of his time. Why would he do this?

My son was making a decision, even though he did not know it. He decided it was better to argue for twenty minutes than to cut the lawn in twelve. Of course when you look in terms of time spent, you can see what a dumb choice this was on his part, what a waste of his time.

But from his point of view, it made perfect sense because:

- he did not know how much time he was spending arguing,

- he did not really understand how little time it took to cut the lawn,

- he mistakenly believed that cutting the lawn was a difficult task,

- he did not understand that not cutting the lawn meant that I would have to do it and that I would lose some of my appreciation of him,

- he falsely believed that I wanted him to cut the lawn because I was lazy and did not want to do it (that I did not want to do it is correct, but not because I was lazy but because I had a more important family task to attend to), and

- he was under the normal emotional effects of inertia* and procrastination.

When we were immature, irresponsible children, our nature was to do only what we wanted to do, the things that were fun or easy. We especially wanted to continue what we were doing already. As responsible and free adults we understand there are things that have to be done if we want to be Awesome Men and reach our goals and achieve happiness, joy, and contentment. Neuroscience has shown that a male's brain may not be fully developed before the age of twenty-five, or even later. Now the science of brain plasticity also has proved we can intentionally develop our brains sooner (see chapter 2).

The point I am making is that often young males make poor decisions because their brains haven't fully developed and immaturity results. The good news is that the acquisition of knowledge can counter this immaturity and that learning can occur at a very young age. We can train our brains, especially in the areas of emotional maturity and responsibility. Let me make it perfectly clear that I as a young male with an underdeveloped brain made a number of dumb decisions as well—not too many, fortunately, and none that had long-term negative impacts. (This was because my parents always held me responsible for my actions and their results from a very young age. They taught me to try to think and control my impulses because I would have to live with the consequences.)

---

* Think of inertia as being an indisposition to effort, motion, or change.

In the book *Teen 2.0: Saving Our Children and Families from the Torment of Adolescence* and in several of his other writings, Robert Epstein states that society and culture have created the artificial concept of adolescence, which precludes young people from maturing and accepting responsibility as soon as they might otherwise.* The result is that they become trapped for a number of years in an artificial state. Young men, particularly, have had freedoms taken away that their counterparts had a hundred years ago, and as they have fewer meaningful choices and responsibilities, they end up making poorer choices.

Now back to my son and inertia and procrastination. My son would have made a better and more mature decision about cutting the lawn:

- if he had recognized that family is a top priority in his life and that answering a family request is a good thing for him and the family,

- if he had understood that acting maturely and accepting responsibility aid in the development of the brain, which would have benefited him in many ways,

- if he accepted that we are biologically wired to suffer from inertia and procrastination and that overcoming these inclinations is a good and important thing to do for our happiness, and

- if he had done the right thing at that time, he would have been one step closer to becoming an Awesome Man.

I have a confession to make, even at my age (I was born in 1949) I still have to fight inertia and procrastination every day. Since I have become a full-time author and work from my home, it is so easy to delay and defer important things. I can sleep in, sit around, read and talk, drink, have long meals, watch TV, stay up late. All these things I have to fight in order to get my work done—probably just like you. It is very tough for all of us. But if we want to reach our goals, we have to persevere. Each day I still make to-do lists (a mini-goal-setting exercise) of the things I want to accomplish and cross them off as they are accomplished.

Second, I find that if I schedule time to goof off every day, with a start and finish time, it is easier to do the things that need to be done.

---

* Robert Epstein, *Teen 2.0: Saving Our Children and Families from the Torment of Adolescence* (Fresno, CA: Quill Driver Books, 2010).

Failure Does Not Exist:
You Only Succeed or Learn

When I was about twenty-four years old, I worked at a Fortune 500 company. Through a careless error on my part, I shipped railcar loads of product across the country that had to be unloaded, then reloaded and shipped back, costing the company many thousands of dollars.

A very senior manager whom I had never spoken to before called me on the phone and asked me what had happened. I explained truthfully and apologized. He stated that was fine, but then he spoke words that I have used the rest of my life: "Okay, Dennis, what are you going to do to make sure that this mistake does not happen again?"

I knew just saying that I would be more careful, or that I would try harder, or that it was someone else's fault would not cut it. I paused, pondering a solution, and then said I would put some "blocks or firewalls" in the system to prevent a repeat of the error. He agreed that was a good solution.

I made the changes immediately and that error never happened again.

The key point in the lesson I learned is that when I or anyone does not meet expectations or standards, I immediately make changes to prevent a recurrence of the problem. When something goes wrong for you, rectify the problem, but your next priority should be to ensure that it does not happen again. The Awesome Man makes it a habit to analyze the situation when things go wrong so he can learn and do better next time.

Section 6

Quiz on Choices and Values

In my life, I have often found it worthwhile to mentally role play social situations that I am likely to experience, so as to better understand ahead of time how my personal values might mesh or conflict with them. Several times this preparation has paid big dividends by providing me with a ready-to-go strategy for certain difficult situations.

I recommend you undertake the same role-playing exercises, so that you can explore your understanding of your values and characteristics as you develop into an Awesome Man. Here is a quiz that will get you started. Let us assume you have chosen the following items as your values:

- family relationships
- financial security
- spirituality
- physical and mental health

Your answers to the questions below will help you understand how even minor decisions can impact your life.

1. You are of legal age and in a drinking establishment. You are feeling mellow and probably are intoxicated. You had planned to stop drinking. A buddy buys you another shot of whiskey. What do you do?

    a. Say thank you and down it in one gulp. You are a good sport and a team player.

    b. Say thank you, but say you have had enough and do not drink it.

    c.   It depends. Are you driving, are you working tomorrow, will you be expected to buy a round for your buddy next? Will your buddy be mad if you refuse? Will you feel pressure to drink in excess? Do you have a problem with binge drinking? What other factors are involved?

I cannot tell you what the right answer is. All I can say is you have to make the choice based on your values, and if health is important to you, excessive drinking is a bad choice, so probably you should decline the drink. Now in some male groups there is tremendous social pressure to drink excessively. If that is an issue in your group of friends, you will want to consider whether your friends are supportive of your values. If not, consider some changes, either in your values or your choice of friends.

2.   You have been playing your favorite video game for about forty-five minutes. You made arrangements to meet your elderly aunt for lunch, but you want to get at least to the next level of the game. What do you do?

    a.   Put the game away and honor your commitment.

    b.   Call your aunt and tell her something came up and you cannot make it.

    c.   Call your aunt to tell her you are going to be late.

    d.   Continue playing and arrive at your aunt's when you get there. Explain you were late because of traffic congestion, car trouble, or getting lost.

Again, I am not saying what is right for you, but if you look at your core values, it appears family relationships is one of them. You also know you can always come back to the video game later. Lying or deceiving anybody is always a bad choice.

3.   Your friend has told you that he robbed a convenience store, and he shows you the money he got, over $300. What would you do?

    a.   Nothing. He is a good friend. You are not a snitch so you mind your own business.

    b.   He is a good friend, and this is the first time you are aware he has committed a crime. Tell him nothing good can come from being a criminal and to give the money back. In fact, you will go with him.

c. Do nothing, but call the crime stoppers "snitch" line and hope to get a reward.

d. Tell no one. If he finds out you ratted him out, he will kill you.

This is a complex dilemma. It takes a tremendous amount of courage to tell a friend who has done wrong he should admit responsibility and make restitution. It also takes a lot of courage to walk with him on this path and give him support. Some of you may say it is not part of your values. But if you have spiritual values, it is likely they include caring for others (your friend and the convenience store owner). If you care about your friend, ask yourself what is in his best long-term interests. Is being a thief going to benefit either of you in the long run?

4. Both smoking tobacco and cannabis are legal in your state. All your friends regularly get together and have a little pot party. You have attended previously and enjoyed yourself. You have been invited to one next weekend. What do you do?

   a. Attend, of course. It is legal, you're of legal age, and pot is safer than alcohol. No harm, no foul.

   b. Do not attend. If one of your values is mental and physical health, you do not see how partaking in either of these recreational activities can contribute to your well-being. You have researched and studied the literature and can see no long-term benefit to yourself.

   c. You attend. Even though you agree with answer b, your relationships with your friends and peers will be in jeopardy if you do not attend. They will likely not involve you in their future activities and you might become lonely.

   d. You suggest an alternative get-together that does not involve legal or illegal drugs. Some of the group may agree with you, and possibly everybody will agree with you. Everybody knows that consuming recreational drugs, even when legal, is expensive and counterproductive to achieving most people's goals. You will earn respect and admiration from your true friends by suggesting such a positive option.

Again it is your choice. Hopefully, you will carefully consider the options available to you, some of which may not even be listed here. In your life you will probably find that peer pressure has the strongest influence on the decisions you make. If your peer group supports your values, you'll be in great shape. However, if your peer group has values that are inconsistent with yours, you may want to seriously consider new friends and peers.

5. You see in the local paper a neighborhood association is looking for volunteers to help clean up an empty lot so kids can use it as a playground.

    a. You feel good about the people organizing the effort but do nothing else.

    b. You consider helping out but realize that you wanted to sleep in that morning because you have been working hard.

    c. You consider it but do not want to go and be among people you do not know. You decide to not take part.

    d. You know that the community building is good for everybody. Since you are tired, you decide to go to bed early the next few nights so you will be well rested. To help with your reluctance at meeting new people, you ask a friend to join you at the cleanup event.

    e. You cannot make it, but you donate money to help buy supplies for the cleanup team.

I am reminded of a couple of maxims on excuses: "It is so easy to find a justification to not do good things in life" and "Excuses are merely nails to build the house of failure."

Helping the community is beneficial on so many levels. You have an opportunity to meet new friends and benefit the community at the same time. The physical activity will be good for you, and you will get spiritual and mental health rewards for doing something good for yourself and others. It is such a win-win for everybody, and is the type of activity that suits an Awesome Man. And beside, making an excuse to justify not participating is so petty and meaningless.

Thoughts on Lying

One common characteristic you will find in males who are far away from becoming an Awesome Man is the amount of lying that they do. They lie constantly and automatically about all sorts of things. They even lie about things they do not have to lie about. They lie so much they do not even know they are lying. When confronted with their lies, they just slough it off.

The lies are often about not taking responsibility for their actions, trying to improve their image without effort, or gaining some advantage over others.

Every time you lie, you hurt two people at least, yourself and the person to whom you are lying. You hurt yourself because you are deceiving yourself when you lie. You are describing a false reality that you may eventually believe to your own detriment.

In war we consciously lie to our opponent, since we want to hurt him. Unless you want to hurt yourself and someone else, be honest all the time. In all situations it is better to remain silent than to lie.

One of the most common reasons we lie is to avoid getting in trouble for something we did or did not do.

Teacher says, "Johnny, did you do your assignment?" Johnny says yes, a lie because he does not want to get in trouble. What has Johnny gained by lying? Johnny made a decision not to do the assignment. It was his choice. He was free to do it or not, but he did not do it. He has to accept the responsibility for his choice. Lying about it will not in any way change the fact that Johnny did not do the assignment. In fact, lying will only make things worse.

Of course Johnny thinks that by lying he will avoid any consequences, because in the past lying has worked for him. But even if the teacher does not check to confirm that Johnny is lying, what has he gained?

Think about it. Johnny has not done the assignment, has avoided learning something, has not followed the instructions of the teacher, and now has lied to her. Has Johnny gained anything or has he lost his self-respect and integrity? He has lost a learning opportunity and will likely do poorer on the final grades. Had he told the truth and had the teacher punished him by making him do the assignment plus stay for detention, he would likely do better in learning, to his benefit.

Section 7

Frequently Asked Questions

Q. You imply that satisfaction with the status quo is a bad thing. I am happy and content where I am in my life. I enjoy video games, watching sports, and having beers with my buddies. What is wrong with that?

A. If the things you mention help you optimize the values you hold and if doing these things is important to you to achieve long-term happiness, then that is okay. But I do not believe things that give you short-term pleasure will always give you long-term happiness, and they are certainly not the path to becoming an Awesome Man.

Q. Why the obsession with the long term? I am here for a good time, not a long time. I could be hit by a truck tomorrow and be dead.

A. Yes, you could be, but the chances are that you will live a long time, and when you get to old age, do you want to be a grumpy old man who is bitter and full of regrets or do you want to be happy, joyful, and contented? And when you do die, will you have left the world a better place?

Q. You make it sound as if your suggestions are the only possible way I can become truly happy.

A. No doubt there are other ways, but I truly believe that by following the suggestions set out in *Be the Awesome Man*, the chances of achieving happiness for many males will be much greater than if they continue what they are doing now.

Q. You seem to be really focused on spiritual values. Isn't that just a euphemism for organized religion?

A. Not at all. First, some organized religions and some cults and sects can be quite contrary to optimizing your values. Second, I will support my defense of the importance of spiritual values by saying that through the many thousands of years of human existence and evolution, spiritual values have always been important to people. It would seem humans are biologically wired for religion or spiritual values, and many scientists believe they have seen proof of this.[*]

Now I am not suggesting any religion or any specific form of spiritual values is required, but research has shown contentment levels are higher in people who have an active spiritual life.

Q. You seem to imply that many enjoyable things I do in my life are not that good for me. Now all my friends are leading the same lifestyle as well. Are you saying we are all wrong?

A. Let us go back to the beginning of my premise. You do want happiness and joy and contentment in your life, correct? I am stating that each of us must have some core values that are important to us. I suggest for most people that family, financial security, spirituality, and physical and mental health are some great ones. (Vince Lombardi, the great leader and coach, stated the only things that count in life are God, Family, and Job.) If the things you are doing are optimizing these values, great! If not, stop doing them. I also state that to make good decisions you need knowledge, so you must always be learning. When you make good decisions, you show responsibility, which works hand in hand with freedom. We all want freedom, which allows us to be happy, joyful, and content.

I am not against anything that you do that will lead you to becoming an Awesome Man. Yet you and I know that many of the behaviors exhibited by young men lead them away from supporting their values and prevent them from becoming an Awesome Man.

---

[*] See, for example, Dean H. Hamer, *The God Gene: How Faith Is Hardwired into Our Genes* (New York: Doubleday, 2004).

Q. I do not think everybody has to be or can be a superstar or an Awesome Man. What is wrong with being average and okay?

A. Understand that average is a mathematical term and not a state of happiness or achievement. Being average means nothing, because in the real world we stand on our own merits. There is nothing wrong with being average, whatever that means to you, if your values are optimized and you are happy, joyful, and content. Unfortunately, many people who classify themselves as average use it as an excuse not to try very hard to improve their lives.

Q. Why would I want to optimize my life by trying to become an Awesome Man?

A. Why wouldn't you want to be happy, joyful, and content? Why wouldn't you want to be a force for good and happiness to the people you care about? Why would you settle for less than what is possible? Would you be happy to watch half a movie, or eat half of an ice cream cone, or go out on just one date with a lovely young lady? Would you be happy if the dentist fixing your teeth was doing a mediocre job, if your paycheck was close to but a bit below what you actually earned, or if your bed was slightly uncomfortable? How about being in an airplane flown by a pilot who almost got through flight school? You are not likely to accept mediocre effort from others, so why would you settle for less than the best from yourself? Nobody expects you to do more than you are capable of, but if you are honest with yourself, you will admit you can do a lot better in many aspects of your life.

Q. Where I live, poverty, drugs, crime, and violence are a fact of life. You cannot escape it. You either "get with the program" or you are done for. The only way I can survive is to do a little thieving, a little dealing, and enjoy myself. What do you say to that?

A. I understand in many communities what you say appears to be reality. But what I have learned from others in similar situations is that one person can make a difference. It is not easy, it is not fast, but it can be done. And one person can create the beginning of a transformation in their community. Remember, if a person accepts and falls under the spell of evil, he will have to deal with the consequences.

You have choices, and with knowledge you can make the right ones. It is very difficult, but the rewards are worth it. When you look at the consequences of crime and violence, you won't find any long-term upsides.

Q. I try to become an Awesome Man, but it seems when I take one step forward, life comes at me with a vengeance and knocks me back two steps. I am tired of trying and failing.

A. I know of what you speak, and sometimes it is not just life but other people who are the things knocking you back.

When I get knocked about, after I pick myself up and dust myself off, I remember a few phrases: "If it was easy, anybody could do it," "You never lose, you just learn more for next time," and "It's the disappointments that make the successes so sweet."

Perseverance is a key part of the makeup of the Awesome Man. He knows that most things worth achieving will not be easy, that there will be challenges constantly coming at him, and that luck often is a fickle friend.

However, when you are knocked down, pause, regroup, consider what you have learned, and go forward. These are signs of becoming an Awesome Man.

Q. You talk about financial security and its importance, but you make it sound like being wealthy is a bad thing.

A. Being wealthy in and of itself is not a bad thing; in fact, many Awesome Men are very wealthy. The problem comes when wealth and the pursuit of wealth lead to several behaviors that negatively affect the values of family, spirituality, and physical and mental health. Unfortunately, too many well-intentioned men have sacrificed important values in their lives for a single-minded pursuit of wealth. When wealth becomes a goal, most men sacrifice too much of what is important to achieve that goal. Literature and history are filled with stories of wealthy men who were not happy, joyful, or contented. The great Mahatma Gandhi said, "There is a sufficiency in the world for man's need but not for man's greed."

Remember, some wealthy men may tell you greed is good, as Gordon Gekko stated in the movie *Wall Street*, but in the end of the movie he was facing jail time. So it is extremely important to keep money and power in proper perspective in your life.

Q. You seem to say playing video games and doing other things on the internet are bad. Why is that?

A. You may not believe it at this point in life, but your time on this earth is limited. The choices you make in how to use your time will determine if and when you will become an Awesome Man. I believe that there are ways to make choices and use your time to ensure that you enjoy the happiness you deserve. I believe that there may be better ways to allocate your time than spending it on video games and other internet diversions.

Of course, you do need to have rest, relaxation, and recreation time, and video games and the internet can be a component of this. However, these things have to be in balance with your goals and values. Recreations and diversions should be both compatible and complimentary with your life values and goals.

Unfortunately, many young men make chilling, slacking, and loafing their primary goals, to the detriment of the important things in life.

Q. You sound antidrug too, but marijuana and cannabis are legal in a lot of places. Why are you against the use of legal products?

A. To me, something that is harmful to a person, something that prevents them from achieving their goal of becoming an Awesome Man, is not good. Food is good, we all need to eat, but becoming morbidly obese does not help one be a happy person. Just ask a morbidly obese person if he is happy with his condition. Cigarettes, drugs, alcohol, and excess food are just a few examples of legal items than can cause a great deal of damage.

If you can show me how the regular consumption of cannabis products will improve your family, financial security, spirituality, and physical and mental health, I will have no objection to its usage. But make very sure you have acquired the depth of knowledge to make the right choice before you do.

A word of caution: Many of the "amusements" that are offered to you as being innocent and harmless are addictive psychologically, mentally, socially, or physically. Most people who begin self-destructive actions and behaviors are usually told the following:

- It is harmless.

- It is thrilling and pleasurable.

- It is what everybody is doing. It's cool.

- It will help you grow up.

- You are not a real man unless you try it.

- One time can't hurt.

- You can quit anytime.

- Try it and judge for yourself.

Remember, if something has a cost to it in terms of money, the advantage to the seller is to make it habit-forming and/or addictive and offer an initial free trial.

Q. Aren't you just pushing a constricted lifestyle with heavy religious overtones, no sex, no parties, no freedom, and no fun?

A. Absolutely not! More than just having fun, I want you, the reader, to be happy, joyful, and content, which are more satisfying than what you are afraid of losing. I do not endorse any specific religion but rather spiritual values. It has been proved that people who have spiritual values and actively practice them tend to be happier.

I encourage sexual relations in committed, long-term, loving relationships, because people who are in these sorts of long-term committed loving relationships have more fun and are happier.

I love to socialize and party myself, but when these activities involve excessive alcohol or drugs or behaviors that are detrimental to achieving important goals, care and diligence must be exercised.

Freedom comes from responsibility. The greater responsibility you show through excellent choices and decision-making, the greater freedom you will have. Think of someone you know who has great freedom; he also has great responsibility. A criminal who is in prison has no freedom and no responsibility.

Fun is great, children live for fun, but as we grow and develop as adults we understand there are better things than fun alone.

Q. Whom can I trust to give me good guidance? The news is full of examples of people who have let others down. And, specifically, why should I trust what you say in this book?

A. Great question! I feel one of the keys to deciding whom you can trust is asking questions. Before I put my trust in anybody or anything, I ask these questions:

1. What is the person's or organization's past history? The best indication of what a person or an organization will do in the future is what they have done in the past. Track records do count in many instances.

2. Does the person display happiness, joy, and contentment in his everyday life, or does he measure his success by his bank balance, possessions, and properties?

3. Is the organization focused on others or itself? There is a huge difference between the goals of the Red Cross and a Wall Street bank. Is the organization trying to do "good" or enrich itself? What are the organization's real values, and do you respect them? Is the organization trying to be awesome or is it mediocre?

4. Can you trust me and what I say in this book? That is a decision you are going to have to make. I can assure you in writing this book that my goal was to help young men be happy and lead better lives.

Nothing I recommend in this book will harm you, and if you follow my recommendations and you do not feel you are becoming an Awesome Man, you can follow some other path to that goal, or always go back to the way you were.

Q. I am often confronted with opportunities to make a positive difference, but the reasons not to do so are very powerful and usually win out. It usually has to do with the time available. I am just too busy to do any more.

A. Each of us is extremely time limited. There are only 1,440 minutes in a day, and if you require ten hours of sleep, that leaves you only 840 minutes to live your life. That is why it is so important to use every minute wisely. By having a set of values and priorities, you are able to schedule your time so the important and valuable things take priority. I can only speak for myself, but I found that as I went through the various stages in my life, I had to abandon activities that I enjoyed and even cherished to pursue more important activities related to my values and goals.

I was a recreational off-road motorcyclist and was away many weekends. I soon realized that as my family grew, my being away on weekends, spending money on motorcycling, and risking my health, which could affect my ability to work and support my family, were not consistent with raising and providing financial security for my family. I chose my family over my pleasure and quit motorcycling. I am happy I did.

Q. I had sex with my "friend with benefits" a couple of weeks ago. She just called me to say she is pretty sure she is pregnant. What are my options?

A. Too often by not considering the choices and consequences before we act, we are forced into very challenging situations where there is no good solution. By choosing to have sexual relations, one always has to be aware of and prepared for the consequences.

Here are some of your choices:

a. Marry the woman and accept all the consequences of that decision.

b. Suggest an abortion, pay for it, and take the woman to the necessary medical appointments.

c. Encourage the woman to carry the child and accept full responsibility for the costs of raising the child.

d. Be a coward and leave the country.

e. When it comes to sex, passion and emotion often result in making poor choices. As a man you can never assume anything other than you are responsible for whatever happens.

Q. I met a hot chick in a bar last week and ended up having wild sex with her. I seem to have developed some sores on a couple of different places on my face and body. Should I go to the doctor?

A. As stated before, you are responsible for whatever happens. Two of your choices are:

a. Go to clinic or doctor now. Be totally honest with them and follow their instructions fully.

b. Die a slow agonizing death. (I am joking.)

Realize that sex is best in a committed long-term relationship involving two adults, two aware and responsible partners. We all make errors in judgment and hopefully this one will not have negative long-term consequences for you. The passion and thrill of the pleasurable experience you had has likely disappeared now that reality faces you. In the future, think carefully before you are seized by passion and your judgment is diminished.

Conclusion

You now realize that you become an Awesome Man because of the decisions, choices, and actions you take. To make the best and most correct decisions, you need knowledge and you need a set of core values and goals.

By having knowledge, you can consider alternatives and options and choose the best path that reinforces your values. By having a set of core values, you will have a standard or objective to base your choices on. By setting goals based on your core values and the knowledge you have acquired, you will have clear milestones before you as you progress on your journey to becoming an Awesome Man.

I hope you agree that the world needs more Awesome Men. Not macho idiots who try to measure their manliness by the number of sexual experiences they have had, the size of their truck's tires, how much they can drink, the number of guns they own, or how rude and demeaning they can be to others. Awesome Men care about others, they are open to and respect diverse and opposing points of views, they are gentlemen, and others are proud to consider them their friends. Women especially value Awesome Men because they recognize these men make the best partners, husbands, and fathers.

The important thing is to believe that no matter what place you are in your life today, you can start right now, at this moment, on the path to being an Awesome Man.

Some may feel that being an Awesome Man is an unachievable goal. Rather, think of being an Awesome Man as a journey of adventure and discovery. Each day you try to be more awesome than the day before. You may not be perfect, and likely you will have challenges and interruptions in becoming the Awesome Man. However, if each day you strive to be a better man as outlined in this book, you will be well on the path to happiness, joy, and contentment, and to achieving the worthy goals you set for yourself. The key is each day to be honest with yourself, avoid any delusions, and be patient. Understand that it is not easy to achieve awesomeness, so feel good about the effort you are making. Take pride that you are on a remarkable journey to being the man you are destined to be—an Awesome Man.

A Final Note to My Readers, and to the People Who Care About Them

Much of what I wrote in *Be the Awesome Man* is without a doubt very different from the way in which boys and men live in society today. With the cultural emphasis on fun, pleasure, and minimal effort, some of the concepts and ideas presented in this book may seem alien, scary, and impractical. Remember that small steps and small victories mark the way forward. If a boy or young man is consciously working on becoming an Awesome Man each day, even if only in some very small way, the cumulative effect of his efforts will one day make a huge difference in his life, the lives of his loved ones, and the world.

To all my readers, I fervently wish you all the happiness, joy, and contentment you deserve.

Sincerely,

Dennis Gazarek

Please visit my website: betheawesomeman.com

I appreciate your comments and questions, and would love to hear your stories. Please contact me at info@betheawesomeman.com.

Appendix

Coping with Life's Challenges

The Awesome Man, knowing how important his mental health is, has developed a keen awareness of his emotional state. He is conscious of the signs of excessive stress and frustration and takes steps to handle them in an appropriate manner. He has developed effective coping skills so he can remain strong and focused, ready to work on his own goals and ready to assist the people around him. Being open, aware, and understanding of the factors that create and maintain good mental health is the first step to sustaining a vigorous and meaningful life and becoming an Awesome Man.

In the real world, bad things happen to all of us, and to the people we care about. We feel grief, anxiety, sadness, and frustration. We are also sometimes faced with difficult personal choices—often stemming from our attempts to deal with the stresses of life—that involve obsessions, compulsions, addiction, and abuse. The Awesome Man knows we need more than strength alone to resist these blows to our body and mind. He knows we need to have the resiliency and the ability to accept our circumstances, and then bounce back and overcome adversity. He understands that knowing how to cope with life's challenges is one of the greatest skills a man can possess.

Coping with Stress

The Awesome Man understands that stress is a fact of life. He also appreciates there is good stress and bad, or negative, stress. Negative stress, if not dealt with, can literally become a killer. He has learned that the key to maintaining a mentally balanced life relatively free of negative stress is to have a selection of appropriate coping skills which he can draw on and utilize when required. If one does not have these skills developed and available, then we are very susceptible to using inappropriate methods to handle stress and crisis in life.[*]

What Is Stress?

Stress is simply our body's response to change. Since our environment is constantly changing, we are constantly under some level of stress. Our nervous system is equipped to handle a certain "normal" level of stress. This normal level of stress—meaning the amount of stress that a given person can experience without distress—varies from person to person. When a male has surpassed the normal level of stress that his body is equipped to handle, he will begin to experience the physical and emotional effects of the stress, and his behavior will change as well.

What causes negative stress also varies from person to person, and is sometimes caused by seemingly minor things. Some people feel stress doing everyday things like standing in lines or using an unfamiliar bathroom. Others find it stressful to talk to groups of people or to be photographed. I remember the first time I had to use a computer mouse. Initially I did not have the fine motor skills to manipulate it properly. I became very stressed and anxious. You may find this hilarious, but I certainly did not.

Since striving to become an Awesome Man involves change, stress will surely arise. Just the simple process of making to-do lists can create negative stress, especially if you cannot or did not accomplish all that you set out to do. So everything you do in regard to becoming the Awesome Man must be considered carefully, and in the context of what is sensible and achievable. Do not fall into the trap that everything is a top priority and must be completed immediately. Patience, pacing, and practicality will allow you to accomplish much more than pushing yourself to the point of burnout.

What Are Coping Skills (Strategies)?

Coping skills are ways in which we learn to deal with various stressors. Over time, we all construct coping strategies that seem "right" for us as thinking and feeling individuals. "Right" is in quotes because many people

---

[*] This material was written with contributions from the excellent material found at mindfuloccupation.org/coping-skills-in-times-of-stress

often do not realize that how they deal with life's stressors is not only unhelpful, but also destructive, negative, and painful for not only themselves but for those around them. Some common but very poor coping strategies are anger and revenge, inappropriate isolation and avoidance, as well as addictive behaviors designed to numb the stress, such as porn, sex, gambling, alcohol, and drugs.

Poor coping strategies can hurt your social relationships, make preexisting problems worse, and even result in new and worsening physical health problems. One example is where a young man, stressed out from the pain and lack of mobility resulting from a sports injury, abuses his prescribed opioids and develops an addiction. This is not an uncommon result with high performance athletes.

Many of us have known someone who reacted inappropriately to stress, which resulted in him or her losing touch with a friend or loved one. Maladaptive coping strategies put pressure on your relationships with friends, family, comrades, and coworkers. They can damage your body or create more emotional pain in the long term, even when they seem helpful in the short term. In extreme cases, maladaptive coping skills can ruin lives.

If You Do Not Deal with a Problem, Does It Go Away?

Some people believe that it is best not to think about a troublesome issue, thought, or feeling, as getting upset about it may only make the issue worse. In some instances, this will be true, depending on how you react to any given situation. However, we must never put a troubling issue to the back of our minds in hopes that time will make it all go away. Such behavior is harmful in the long run. Sure, you will not be bothered by such thoughts right at this moment, but while you're ignoring your problems they are still present, and in fact might be growing.

The more beneficial approach is to constructively deal with any stress, anxiety, or troubling issue as it arises. Waiting for time to take its course in solving your problems risks creating more stress in your life. Now there are times when what is stressing you out is not within your power to affect. In those cases the healthy solution is to stop thinking about it. You need to cultivate the ability to recognize what is in your power to control and what is not.

When we use maladaptive coping mechanisms, we do not allow ourselves to analyze our emotions. Instead, these coping strategies involve hiding, sedation, avoidance, or numbing ourselves so we do not feel the stress. None of these are effective tactics as they treat only the symptom and fail to address the underlying source of the stress.

You should always allow yourself to feel a whole range of emotions. That is the first step to a healthy, constructive coping strategy. Once you are aware of what you are experiencing, then you can choose to react appropriately.

You have to be truly honest with yourself and others. Men often get in a situation where they are conflicted and not sure how or what they feel. Often they then stop talking. What we should never do is stop thinking and trying to understand our feelings. We can also share our feelings and thoughts with people we trust, who will help to put things in perspective. An example of putting things in perspective is understanding that feelings are always real, but sometimes are not valid. How we feel about a given situation often has a lot to do with our past experiences.

As a teenager, there was period of time when I would become faint in church. The anxiety and worry about fainting, derived from previous fainting episodes, often made this feeling worse. I would become nauseous and hot and woozy. It became so I and some classmates often avoided attending services. Since I attended a church-based high school, this avoidance got us in trouble with the teachers.

I had to do something. I spoke to my friends and discovered they had similar experiences. We talked and decided it was okay to leave the service if we felt faint. God did not want anybody to feel unwell. We decided that sitting close to an exit, where leaving would not cause any disruption, was always a good idea. Secondly, we realized the more you thought about fainting the more likely you would faint, so it was important to keep your mind off fainting. Eventually I discovered that for me, the best way to do this was to take an active part in the service by singing and praying. After learning this strategy, I never fainted in church again.

There are always effective and positive solutions to any stressful situation. Sometimes you just have to think about why you are suffering. Take some time and really analyze why you feel the way you do. And think about strategies for how to effectively deal with that feeling.

At times in my life, certain people have really irritated me, and others have done unjust things to me. I'm sure the same has happened to you. In those situations I used to become angry, which I came to discover is a very bad emotion for me. Over time I developed a constructive coping mechanism to handle these incidents. Now, when there is nothing I can do to redress the situation, I still get angry; however, I decide to be very angry for a *specific* time period, like ten minutes. In a private space I will scream, yell, curse, and get all the anger and emotion out. Then I'm ready to go on with my life. It works for me, and is a healthy choice to alternative, possibly self-destructive, actions.

Remember that change—even good change, like personal development—can create stress so be aware of the changes that are currently happening in your life. Plan your activities and goals with the knowledge that stress will likely occur, and be prepared.

How to Handle Frustration

In most people's lives, frustration arises from two main areas. The first is things we have no or minimal control over, like the weather, which way a golf ball bounces when it hits a rock on the fairway, or what color eyes we are born with. It makes little sense to expect things beyond our control will always go our way and then to be frustrated when they do not. So when you are feeling frustration, ask yourself, did you really have any control in the first place? If you didn't, you have to let it go. Letting go of things that we have no control over can be very hard, but necessary.

The other source of frustration involves things we *do* have some control over (or at least we think we do). Many times we are frustrated with ourselves, perhaps with our own lack of effort or lack of competence. Within reason, this is a healthy frustration, so long as you channel this negative energy in a productive way, seeking to analyze why you didn't perform the way you hoped to and strategizing how to do better next time.

But frequently in life our frustration lies with other people—and with few exceptions, we have little control over the actions of others. Unless we have provided them with some significant positive motivation or benefit, other people will usually act and behave the way they want, not the way we want them too. In some situations we can use coercion, or place them under duress to get them to do what we want them to, but those tactics are not usually effective nor repeatable.

The most constructive thing to do is to think about why a person is causing you frustration. An honest examination will often lead you to realize that you may have unreasonable or unachievable expectations about what the person is going to do (for you). The Awesome Man understands that when he expects somebody to do something and it is not done the way he expected, frustration can result—and he is prepared for that. He has learned that people do not meet expectations for a number of reasons, such as:

- People do not know what is expected of them because the expectations were not clearly set out for them.

- They never agreed to fulfill those expectations you set out for them.

- They were never taught or they never learned *how* to fulfill the expectations.

- The expectations you may have set for other people were not practical, important, or relevant for them.

- The expectations are unachievable because they are beyond the realm of capability for them.

The Awesome Man realizes that to avoid personal frustration with other people, his expectations of them have to be both realistic and clearly communicated. A smart parent should know not to get frustrated with a baby who soils his diaper. The parent knows the baby has no control over his bowel movements. However, if the parent has a sixteen-year-old son who regularly fails to complete his household chores in a timely fashion, some degree of frustration might be understandable. However, what if the parent has not clearly explained what the chores are and why the son is expected to do them? Then the parent's frustration is not valid.

The Awesome Man knows that most sources of frustration can be reduced and minimized by talking about, understanding, and analyzing the situation. He knows that life will continually place obstacles in his path, and he accepts and expects this, knowing he will overcome them.

So whatever it is that is frustrating you, please keep in mind that:

It is not the end of the world.

Accept you do not have much control over other people or many events.

The action or event was not targeted specifically against you.

There is an explanation for what is going on

(though you might not like the explanation).

There are many medical, spiritual and scientific resources available to assist you.

You should be active in using all the resources available to you.

By being active and supportive you can minimize some negative impacts on you.

This is just another bump in the path of life. This too shall pass.

If you have not communicated your expectations and received agreement from the other person, you have no right to expect compliance, and no reason to be frustrated.

Good Skills for Coping with Stress and Frustration

Meditation and relaxation techniques: Practicing deep breathing techniques, the relaxation response, or progressive muscle relaxation are ways to help reduce stress and induce relaxation.

Time to yourself: It is important to set aside time every day to allow yourself to relax and escape the stress of life. Give yourself a private mini-vacation from everything going on around you.

Physical activity: Moving around and getting the heart rate up causes the body to release endorphins (the body's feel-good hormones). Exercising provides stress relief.

Reading: Escape from reality completely by reading. Reading can help you to de-stress by taking your mind off everyday life.

Friendship: Having friends who are willing to listen and support you through good and bad times is essential.

Humor: Adding humor to a stressful situation can help to lighten the mood.

Hobbies: Having creative outlets such as listening to music, drawing, or gardening are great ways to relax and relieve everyday stress.

Spirituality: Actively believing in a higher power or divine being can have many health benefits. In recent studies, it has been found that people who pray have better mental health than those who do not.

Pets: Taking care of a pet helps distract the mind from stressful thoughts. Studies show that pets are a calming influence in people's lives.

Sleeping: The human body needs a chance to rest and repair itself after a long and stressful day. Sleeping gives the body this chance so that it is ready to perform another day. Avoid shortchanging your sleep.

Nutrition: Eating foods that are good for you not only improves your physical health, but plays a major role in your mental health. When your body gets the proper nutrients, it is better able to function in every capacity.

There are, of course, also negative coping skills, which are harmful to both mental and physical health and should be avoided. These include:

- Drugs
- Excessive alcohol use
- Self-mutilation
- Ignoring or storing hurt feelings
- Sedatives
- Stimulants
- Excessive working
- Avoiding problems
- Abuse of the vulnerable
- Self-mutilation
- Denial

These actions offer only temporary relief, if that, from stress. Ignoring or covering up how you feel does not solve the problem, because the next time the situation arises, you will still have no way of dealing with it.

If you find yourself faced with a difficult or stressful circumstance, remember to practice your new coping skills. These skills lead to good mental health and a happier you.

The Ten Minute Rule

Even Awesome Men get frustrated, angry, disappointed, or upset from time to time. The Awesome Man knows he has to deal with those emotions effectively and then get on with life. In other words, he doesn't let life's setbacks keep him down for long.

As I mentioned earlier, I have found when something really upsets me, I decide specifically how long I am going to allow myself to be bothered before I move on. In many cases, ten minutes of anger, venting, and being upset usually works. (I do this in private, or in the presence of an agreeable confidant.) Sometimes I need twenty or even thirty minutes in a place that is appropriate to express and deal with my feelings. The point is I give myself a limited amount of time to stay in "negative mode," and then I move on, knowing that dwelling in frustration won't solve anything.

Of course some things may take much longer to work out, like the death of someone close. The crucial thing is you allow yourself to experience and express the feelings you are facing in an appropriate manner. Your feelings are real and have to be addressed in a timely, positive, and healthy way. The Awesome Man knows that getting drunk, emotionally hiding, or throwing a temper tantrum are not good ways to deal with those feelings. If you do not deal appropriately with your emotions, they can and will gnaw at you to the detriment of your physical and mental health.

Where to Get Help if You Need It

If you are still in distress and your coping skills are not working, do not despair. It is time to seek help from your doctor or a trained mental health professional. Medical science has developed effective treatments for stress, emotional, and mental health issues. Nobody has to suffer alone or in ignorance.

In the US, if you or someone you know is in crisis, call **1-800-273-TALK (8255)** to reach the National Suicide Prevention Lifeline, a 24/7 crisis center. Or you can text **HOME** to 741741 to reach the Crisis Text Line.

Another 24/7 resource is the SAMHSA Disaster Distress Helpline. They can be reached at **1-800-985-5990** or by texting **TalkWithUs** to 66746.

Trained crisis workers will listen to you and direct you to the resources you need.

Further Reading

The Biology of Desire: Why Addiction Is Not a Disease, Marc Lewis, PublicAffairs (2016)

Guyland: The Perilous World Where Boys Become Men, Michael Kimmel, Harper Perennial (2009)

Man Disconnected: How Technology Has Sabotaged What It Means to Be Male, Philip Zimbardo and Nikita D. Coulombe, Rider (2015)

The New Hide or Seek: Building Self-Esteem in Your Child, Dr. James C. Dobson, Fleming H. Revell Company (199)

The Power of Now: A Guide to Spiritual Enlightenment, Eckhart Tolle, New World Library (2004)

Teen 2.0: Saving Our Children and Families from the Torment of Adolescence, Robert Epstein, Quill Driver Books (2010)

The Wonder of Boys: What Parents, Mentors and Educators Can Do to Shape Boys into Exceptional Men, Michael Gurian, TarcherPerigee, 2006

Acknowledgments

This book would not be possible if not for the support and encouragement of literally dozens of people, and I thank them all. Two people especially stand out, and I want to acknowledge them specifically.

The first is Kent Sorsky, my publisher and editor. Out of over two hundred agents and publishers I contacted, Kent was the only one who was willing to back my dream with his personal time, effort, and money. It takes courage to be in the publishing business, and when approached by an unknown writer from Canada with an unusual book pitch, Kent listened and said "Yes!" As we began working on the book, I realized Kent had become very passionate about the topic and was in fact totally committed. A writer cannot ask for more than that from his publisher. His enthusiasm drove me to work harder and do a better job as an author. Thank you, Kent.

Secondly, I want to thank my wife, Janet, who has had my back over the five years that I have been working on this book. Even though I would disappear for hours on end in my basement office, she never complained, never grumbled, and only ever expressed confidence and encouragement. Thank you, dear. I love you.

—Dennis Gazarek

Index

ABOUT THE AUTHOR

Born in a working-class neighborhood of Windsor, Ontario, **Dennis Gazarek** paid for college by working on farms, in factories, and in horse-racing tracks. His early work experience taught him the reality of heavy manual labor and an appreciation for the challenges faced by working people in everyday life. After receiving an honors degree in business administration from the University of Windsor, Gazarek worked in sales for Procter & Gamble and General Motors, as well as working in real estate and as a business consultant. He is the author of *Whacked! How GM Careened into Bankruptcy and Took the Innocent with Them*. Gazarek lives with his wife in the Toronto area, where he plays saxophone with the Markham Concert Band.